Capital Markets and Institutions

PRENTICE-HALL FOUNDATIONS OF FINANCE SERIES

PRENTICE-HALL FOUNDATIONS OF FINANCE SERIES

Ezra Solomon, *Editor*

Capital Markets and Institutions

Third Edition

Herbert E. Dougall

C. O. G. Miller Professor of Finance, Emeritus
Stanford University

Jack E. Gaumnitz

Associate Professor of Finance
University of Kansas

PRENTICE-HALL, INC., Englewood Cliffs, New Jersey

Library of Congress Cataloging in Publication Data

DOUGALL, HERBERT EDWARD.
  Capital markets and institutions.

  (Prentice-Hall foundations of finance series)
  Bibliography: p.
  Includes index.
  1. Capital—United States. 2. Finance—United States.
3. Financial institutions—United States.
I. Gaumnitz, Jack E., joint author. II. Title.
HG181.D59 1975   332.6'0973   75-2245
ISBN 0-13-113662-3
ISBN 0-13-113654-2 pbk.

Printed in the United States of America

10 9 8 7 6 5 4 3 2 1

PRENTICE-HALL INTERNATIONAL, INC., London
PRENTICE-HALL OF AUSTRALIA, PTY. LTD., Sydney
PRENTICE-HALL OF CANADA, LTD., Toronto
PRENTICE-HALL OF INDIA PRIVATE LIMITED, New Delhi
PRENTICE-HALL OF JAPAN, INC., Tokyo

Contents

Editor's Note

The subject matter of financial management is in the process of rapid change. A growing analytical content, virtually nonexistent ten years ago, has displaced the earlier descriptive treatment as the center of emphasis in the field.

These developments have created problems for both teachers and students. On the one hand, recent and current thinking, which is addressed to basic questions that cut across traditional divisions of the subject matter, do not fit neatly into the older structure of academic courses and texts in corporate finance. On the other hand, the new developments have not yet stabilized and as a result have not yet reached the degree of certainty, lucidity, and freedom from controversy that would permit all of them to be captured within a single, straightforward treatment at the textbook level. Indeed, given the present rate of change, it will be years before such a development can be expected.

One solution to the problem, which the present Foundations of Finance Series tries to provide, is to cover the major components of the subject through short independent studies. These individual essays provide a vehicle through which the writer can concentrate on a single sequence of ideas and thus communicate some of the excitement of current thinking and controversy. For the teacher and student, the separate self-contained books provide a flexible up-to-date survey of current thinking on each subarea covered and at the same time permit maximum flexibility in course and curriculum design.

EZRA SOLOMON

Preface

The aim of the third edition is to present a careful but uncompli-cated study of the institutions that funnel long-term funds into the capital markets and to assess the demand for funds in these markets so that the resulting yields can be noted and analyzed. We have tried to keep distinct the more recent developments in our ever-changing capital markets and institutions.

No attempt has been made to unify the theories pertaining to financial institutions and the long-term capital markets. Our effort has been directed toward helping the reader view the operation and growth of these markets and institutions as a logical process, with the hope that those who are not familiar with financial institutions will gain a better understanding and appreciation of why they are so im-portant in the development of our industralized society. Accordingly, a chapter has been added on the nature of the capital formation process, with particular emphasis on the need for financial institutions and how they should determine their assets and liabilities.

The dramatic changes in the capital markets and the investment policies of major financial institutions since the late 1960s again have required a substantial revision of the book. The forces lying behind the "credit crunches" of 1969 and 1973–74, the rise in yields on fixed-income instruments to unprecedented heights in 1974, the fading market for equities, the dramatic shifts in holdings of various security holders, and the growth of newer institutions, such as real estate in-vestment trusts and specialized investment companies, are described and analyzed. All tables, where possible, have been updated through 1973 and the data are again aggregated in a master table for the capital market as a whole. Developments in 1974 have been noted in the text.

The data have been drawn from a wide variety of sources. Primary sources are used wherever possible. The task of developing flow-of-funds figures has again been eased by use of information compiled by

Bankers Trust Company in its *Credit and Capital Markets*. Permission of the Company to cite this source is gratefully acknowledged. Other references in the book include a number of recent works.

The authors are indebted for many ideas and much information to a number of persons and organizations, and for data in advance of publication from the National Association of Mutual Savings Banks, the Federal Deposit Insurance Corporation, the United States League of Savings Associations, the Institute of Life Insurance, and the Securities and Exchange Commission.

The authors are grateful to Professor Eugene Lerner of Northwestern University for a thoughtful review of the manuscript.

H.E.D.
J.E.G.

Figures

Tables

Capital Markets and Institutions

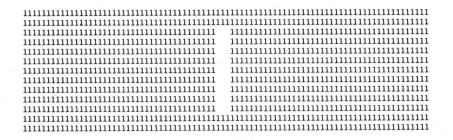

Nature and Scope
of the Capital Markets

Economic Capital

THE economic strength of a nation may be measured, in part, by the value of its accumulated wealth and by the rate at which this wealth grows through the savings and investment process. National wealth includes all structures, equipment, inventories, land, monetary metals, and net foreign assets. At the end of 1968, national wealth was estimated at $3,079 billion.[1]

Economic capital, in a narrower sense, pertains only to the stock of assets used in production: buildings (but not the land on which they're situated), equipment, and inventories. It does not include the claims to these assets, but instead consists of the assets themselves. Consumer durable goods such as automobiles and appliances are not considered economic capital because they yield immediate satisfaction. Residential housing is included, however, because housing can be thought to produce a service. Thus economic capital owned by individuals consists mainly of residential housing; by business, fixed assets and inventories; and by government, publicly owned facilities.

---

[1] U.S. Congress, *Institutional Investor Study Report of the Securities and Exchange Commission*, House Document 92–64, Part 6, Supplementary Volume I (Washington, D.C.: Government Printing Office, 1971).

Capital Formation

Capital formation is the growth in the stock of economic capital goods and is generally measured in dollar amounts or as a percentage of Gross National Product (GNP). Private domestic capital formation is the addition to the stock of capital goods less depreciation of those goods already on hand. The substantial increase in the stock of private domestic capital, both gross and net, for selected years since 1955, is shown in Table 1–1, together with Gross National Product and the rate of gross capital formation in terms of GNP. As it is the gross investment that must be financed mainly in the capital markets our main

TABLE 1–1.   Private Domestic Capital Formation in the United States, 1955–1973 (billions of dollars)

	1955	1960	1965	1970	1973
Producers' durable equipment	$ 23.8	$ 30.3	$ 45.8	$ 64.4	$ 89.8
New construction (other than residential structures)	14.3	18.1	25.5	36.1	47.0
Business inventories	6.0	3.6	9.6	4.5	15.4
Residential structures	23.3	22.8	27.2	31.2	57.2
Total gross capital formation	$ 67.4	$ 74.8	$108.1	$136.2	209.4
Capital consumption allowances	31.5	43.4	59.8	87.3	110.8
Total net capital formation	$ 35.9	$ 31.4	$ 48.3	$ 48.9	$ 98.6
Gross National Product	$398.0	$503.8	$684.9	$977.1	$1294.9
Rate of gross capital formation (percentage)	16.9%	14.8%	15.8%	13.9%	16.2%

Sources: U.S. Department of Commerce, *Survey of Current Business; Federal Reserve Bulletin.*

interest lies in that figure. Table 1–1 shows that since 1955 the rate of gross capital formation has ranged from a low of 13.6 percent of GNP in 1970 to a high of 17.0 percent in 1955 with an average of about 15 percent.

The low gross capital formation rate in 1970 was caused to a large extent by the comparatively tight money situation prevailing at the time, which resulted in only moderate increases in business and residential construction over previous years. In addition, the suspension of the investment tax credit on new equipment during this period (reinstated in 1971), and the unsettled domestic and international situation were also contributing factors. The rate of gross capital formation returned to about average in 1972 and 1973 as declining interest rates, available mortgage money, and government housing programs encouraged a sharp rise in residential construction.

In measuring present and estimated future capital growth, attention often centers on business plant and equipment expenditures. These costs, shown in the first two rows of Table 1–1, amounted to $136.8 billion or 10.6 percent of GNP in 1973. The Council of Economic Advisers has suggested that achieving a growth in output of 5 percent per year requires "private investment" to be between 10 and 11 percent of GNP.[2]

Another widely used measure of business plant and equipment expenditures is reported by the Securities and Exchange Commission and the Office of Business Economics of the Department of Commerce, and published in the *Survey of Current Business*. It is less comprehensive than the gross capital formation definition because it excludes investment by farmers, professionals, institutions, real estate firms, and insurance companies. This figure was projected at an annual rate of $97 billion for 1974. Regardless of the figures used, however, the need for financing economic goods and services has fostered the growth of the capital markets as well as the institutions serving this important segment of our economy. The financing of economic goods, and the institutions and individuals involved in the process—are the major factors in the capital markets and the primary focus of this book.

The Capital Markets: General Character and Definition

There is no such thing as a market for capital, that is, the economic capital goods themselves. But there is a market, or rather a group of markets, for the dollar instruments that represent either title to or claims to capital and to the other resources owned by government, business, and individuals. Just as economic capital represents assets of a more or less permanent nature, *capital* can be used to mean the money value of the instruments of ownership and of long-term claims to assets, and *capital markets* to mean the markets in which these instruments are exchanged.

Capital markets are the complex of institutions and mechanisms through which intermediate-term funds (loans of up to ten years maturity for example) and long-term funds (longer-maturity loans and corporate stocks) are pooled and made available to business, governments, and individuals, and instruments already outstanding are transferred. As in the case of the money market, the capital markets are local, regional, and national in scope.

---

[2] *Economic Report of the President* (Washington, D.C.: U.S. Government Printing Office, 1963), p. 62. Actually, GNP increased about 8.5 percent per year in the period 1963 through 1973, though private nonresidential investment averaged 10 percent of GNP.

Because they deal with instruments representing longer-term funds, the capital markets involve capital in the economic sense. Funds raised through debt instruments by business and individuals are invested in fixed assets and inventories. Admittedly, the proceeds of government bonds and corporate shares are used to finance a variety of expeditures and types of assets. This usage of terms in turn suggests a distinction between the capital markets, or markets for longer-term funds, and the money market for short-term funds (obligations with a year or less to maturity).[3]

The Money Market

The money market provides facilities for the quick and dependable transfer of short-term debt instruments used to finance the needs of business, government, agriculture, and consumer. A distinction may be made between the direct, negotiated, or customers' money market and the impersonal, or open, market. The former is found wherever banks and other financial firms supply funds to local customers. It also includes the bank correspondents who funnel funds into larger centers such as New York for direct lending. The open money market is mainly the complex of facilities in New York where idle funds, drawn from all over the country, are transferred through intermediaries. Federal Reserve banks, commercial banks (especially the big "money market" banks), business corporations with idle funds, insurance companies, foreign suppliers (including foreign banks), finance companies, state and local governments, and individuals all make short-term funds available to other similar institutions, to the United States Treasury, and to securities brokers and dealers for "street" loans. The intermediaries are chiefly Federal Reserve banks, big commercial banks, and government securities dealers. The instruments representing the short-term funds are chiefly Federal funds (excess member bank reserves), short-term government securities, bankers' acceptances, and commercial paper.[4]

The Investment Market

The investment market is similar to the capital market except that it encompasses security instruments of all maturities traded in all types

---

[3] Traditionally, the money market has been described as the market for short-term debt, with a year or less to maturity, and the capital market as dealing in long-term funds, both debt and equity. These designations leave a category of intermediate-term money represented by debt with from one to five or ten years to maturity. Transactions involving such debt are included in our concept of capital-market activity.

[4] For a more general description of the money market and money market instruments see R. I. Robinson and D. Wrightsman, *Financial Markets: The Accumulation and Allocation of Wealth* (New York: McGraw-Hill Book Company, 1974), pp. 127–222.

of markets. In this book we shall use the term *investors* to mean those who *supply* funds to business, government, and individuals by acquiring debt and equity instruments with their savings. The term *investment market* or *financial market* means the entire market for funds including the stock market, the bond market, the mortgage market, and so on.

Alternatively, the investment market can also be defined to include the market for *primary* and *secondary* securities. The *primary market* involves the sale of new securities for the first time by those needing funds (deficit units) to those with excess funds (surplus units). Hence, a sale of Treasury Bills by the U.S. Government, a new mortgage by an individual on a home, or new stock issued by a company to institutions and the public are examples of transactions occurring in the primary market. Transactions occurring in the *secondary market* are sales or exchanges involving securities that are already outstanding and held by investors. A sale of existing Treasury Bills from one bank to another constitutes a transaction in the secondary market as do sales of outstanding securities listed on the New York Stock Exchange.

Interrelations of the Money and Capital Markets

Although this book focuses on the capital market, the money and capital markets (or group of markets) are independent, for the following reasons:

(1) Suppliers of funds may choose to direct them to either or both markets, depending on their investment policies and on the available rates of return.

(2) Users of funds may obtain them from either market. For example, a corporation needing funds for additional inventory may borrow short term by selling commercial paper or by negotiating a bank loan. It may also float a bond issue or sell stock for working capital purposes. And, if long-term rates are high, as they were in 1974, the firm temporarily might borrow short-term funds with the expectation of securing lower long-term rates in the future.

(3) Funds flow back and forth between the two markets, as when the Treasury refinances maturing bills with Treasury bonds or when a bank lends the proceeds of a maturing mortgage to a business firm on short terms.

(4) Some institutions and facilities serve both markets; for example, dealers in short-term Federal securities also buy and sell long-term bonds, and commercial banks make both intermediate- and short-term loans.

(5) Yields in the long- and short-term markets are interrelated. A rise in short-term interest rates reflecting a condition of credit stringency is likely to be accompanied or followed by a rise in long-

term rates. Professional investors maintain the normal relationships in the maturity schedule by arbitrage. We should note, however, that money-market rates are more sensitive than longer-term rates and that geographical differences in short-term yields are less pronounced.

Perhaps the chief distinguishing characteristic of the two types of markets is that in the short-term market, as the word "money" suggests, the instruments traded are money or "near money." Federal funds (excess legal reserves of banks) are money. "Near money" instruments are exemplified by short-term government and commercial paper, the value of which is subject to slight price risk. It should be noted, however, that a capital market security held to maturity will function as a money market instrument in the last year of maturity. Notwithstanding, longer-term instruments issued in or traded in the capital markets, especially the stock market, show considerable price variation.

The Capital Markets: Classification of Characteristics

It is useful to classify the characteristics of the capital markets in several ways.

Major Users: Variety of Types

When funds are made available to those seeking capital, the latter deliver some kind of contract or instrument representing their relationship with the investors. The demand for funds comes from five general categories of users: individuals, corporations, the Federal government, state and local governments, and foreign borrowers. Individuals rely on the long-term markets for financing real estate and business transactions.

All longer-term business debts of individuals and unincorporated concerns, together with the equity in farms and smaller firms, should, in a broad sense of the concept, be included as capital-market contracts. Such components, with the exception of mortgage debt and bank term loans, are omitted from our discussion. This somewhat arbitrary treatment seems valid because measurement is difficult and, for the most part, such funds are raised locally and in relatively small amounts. Consumer installment debt, for example, for financing durable goods, is also omitted. This omission is consistent with the exclusion of the durable goods themselves from the economic concept of capital. We are, therefore, left with the mortgage market, both primary and secondary, as the chief type of capital market insofar as individuals are concerned.

Transactions that involve demand for new funds by business corporations, as well as transfers of outstanding corporate instruments, are carried out in two main markets—the corporate note and bond market, and the stock market. These two are mainly open markets and include both primary and secondary transactions. A market for corporate intermediate-term loans may also be said to exist, but it has no separate identity, being primarily a segment of bank and insurance company loan activity.

As for government securities, our interest lies mainly in the intermediate- and long-term Treasury securities, issued in primary and traded in secondary open markets, and the obligations of state and local jurisdictions, whose market is mainly local and over the counter.

The volume of foreign financing in the American capital markets has become very substantial in the postwar period. The markets for foreign securities are comingled with the domestic corporate bond and stock markets.

Each of these markets has distinctive characteristics of supply and of demand that result in different interest rates and yields. The various segments, however, are interrelated in that they all compete for the supply of funds, and many of the groups seeking funds may choose among the various capital markets to satisfy their financial needs.

Type of Instrument or Contract: Debt or Equity

The instruments that represent funds supplied to and obtained from the capital markets are either debt instruments—personal and corporate notes, corporate bonds, mortgages, and obligations of governments—or equity instruments such as corporate stocks that are sold to raise new funds.

Maturity of Instruments

Somewhat arbitrarily, transactions represented by debt instruments with maturity of a year or less are said to take place in the money or short-term market. This leaves intermediate-term funds (up to five to ten years maturity) and long-term funds for the capital markets. As we have seen, the two markets cannot be completely distinguished.

Degree of Centralization

In the broadest sense, the scope of the capital markets is very wide. A market exists wherever a bank or an insurance company makes a term loan, a corporate bond or stock is transferred, a government sells a new bond issue, or a householder borrows money on a mortgage. Capital markets are primarily local and regional, except for Federal government securities and the bond and stock markets. Centralization exists insofar as intermediate-term money is concerned, through the concentration of great banking facilities in very large cities. We shall see, however, that geographical barriers are breaking down and that both the supply of and the demand for long-term and even intermediate-term funds tend increasingly to flow on a national basis. Nevertheless, much geographical stratification does persist. Regional and local markets are particularly important for both issuing and trading in obligations of smaller users of funds—local governments, local businesses, and individuals—and in the stocks of smaller corporations.

Direct Versus Open-Market Transactions

When a savings and loan association makes a mortgage loan to a local customer, it is allocating the funds of a number of savers directly to the financing of real estate. The relation between the financial intermediary and the borrower is direct and personal. This is also the case for direct borrowing by governments and corporations and for the private sale of corporate shares by the issuer. Many thousands of direct transactions occur daily between all types of users and suppliers of funds; these transactions are not centrally reported and are competitive only in a very general way. They take place in a vast and segmented market. By contrast, open-market transactions in bonds, stocks, and some mortgages are competitive and immediately influence the market price of funds, as in the case of a national offering of corporate bonds at a known price and yield, or an issue of Treasury securities.

The line of demarcation between direct (personal) and open-market (impersonal) transactions is not entirely distinct. In general, the latter are characterized by the use of marketing intermediaries— dealers or brokers who bring together the demand and supply of funds, provide transfer facilities, and "make a market" for various instruments. The known yields prevailing in the organized open markets do, however, influence those determined by direct bargaining.

Primary Versus Secondary Transactions

Most transactions in the capital markets represent transfers of existing instruments among investors rather than the raising of new funds. For example, the volume of trading in outstanding securities vastly exceeds the value of new issues. Such mere trading does not represent capital formation. However, the prices and yields at which existing instruments are transferred determine the prices of new issues. Thus, when a corporation offers new bonds for money, their after-tax yield must equal or exceed the after-tax yield on outstanding bonds of the same quality and maturity.

The terms *stock market* and *bond market* usually refer to secondary markets for securities. The term *mortgage market* has, until recently, implied mainly a primary market. Our later discussion includes both the primary and secondary markets for various instruments.

Magnitude of the Markets

Later chapters include discussion of the size of capital markets in terms of the assets and obligations of the institutions involved, the magnitude of various sources and uses of funds, and the flows of funds that influence yields. At this point certain selected data (Table 1–2) are presented to indicate the size of the markets in terms of the outstanding instruments that represent longer-term funds. Individual and noncorporate debt other than mortgage debt is omitted.

United States government debt includes the guaranteed obligations of the Federal Housing Administration. Marketable debt excludes Savings Bonds and other nontransferable instruments. Net long-term

TABLE 1–2. Selected Media in the Capital Markets, at Year End, 1955–1973 (billions of dollars)

	1955	1960	1965	1970	1973
U.S. government debt:					
Total	$281	$290	$321	$389	$470
Marketable	163	189	215	248	270
Due in over one year	97	105	121	124	142
Federally-sponsored agency debt (nonguaranteed)	3	8	14	39	59
State and local government debt:					
Total	48	75	107	156	202
Long-term securities	44	67	95	131	173
Corporate long-term debt:					
Net long-term	90	139	209	360	492
Bonds outstanding (domestic)	59	85	116	193	247
Corporate stock (domestic, at market value):					
Listed	239	335	573	681	764
Traded over the counter a	37 b	53 b	181	205	196
Mortgage debt:					
Total	130	207	326	452	635
Residential (1–4 family)	88	141	213	280	386

a Includes investment company shares.
b Estimated.
Sources: *Federal Reserve Bulletin* (including flow-of-funds tables); *Treasury Bulletin; Survey of Current Business;* Securities and Exchange Commission, *Annual Reports;* U.S. Department of Commerce, Bureau of the Census, *Governmental Finances* (annual).

debt of state and local governments excludes sinking funds and inter-governmental duplications. Corporate net long-term debt also ex-cludes intercompany holdings. It includes debt over one year to original maturity: mortgages, term loans, and net long-term trade credit.[5] The figure for bonds outstanding is most important for our purposes. It excludes bonds held outside of the United States.

The corporate stock figures are crude in that they include inter-company ownership of shares. They exclude the value of stock of closely held companies. The corporate stock figures are important for two reasons. First of all, corporate stock represents, by far, the largest single category. Second, corporate stock prices are the most volatile, and, as a result, it is not uncommon to see substantial drops (or rises) in stock values from year to year. As will be seen later, it is the sharp reduction or little appreciation in equity values in recent years that has caused considerable problems for the capital market as a whole.

Net Suppliers and Users of Funds

Table 1–3 shows the total financial assets and liabilities of various sectors including households, businesses, state and local governments, U.S. government, and financial institutions at the end of 1973. It is readily seen that households have been large net suppliers (surplus units) of funds to the financial markets, and businesses and govern-ments have been large borrowers (deficit units) of funds.

Financial institutions are substantial participants in the financial markets as evidenced by their holding $2,042 billion in assets and $1,927 billion in liabilities outstanding at the end of 1973. The insti-tutions included as financial institutions in the table are basically the same as those discussed in this book and, in addition, include sales finance companies, credit unions and one or two other minor ones. It is interesting to note that financial institutions are net sup-pliers of funds to the financial market but that they essentially "net out" their assets and liabilities in performing their intermediation function. They generally have received funds from individuals and others and issued their own securities or other obligations. These institutions have then taken these funds so received and lent them to government and business. At the end of 1973, of the total assets of $2,042 billion held by financial institutions, net credit market in-struments issued by deficit units—business, governments, and others —amounted to $1,590 billion. On the other hand, of the $1,927 billion in total liabilities, approximately $1,429 billion represented claims due surplus units (primarily households) with asset holdings in the

---

[5] For an explanation of the derivation of net debt, see *Survey of Current Business* (October, 1950), p. 13.

TABLE 1–3. Financial Assets and Liabilities of Various Sectors, December 31, 1973 (amounts outstanding in billions of dollars)

Sector	Total Assets	Total Liabilities	Surplus	Deficit
Households	$2,302	$ 592	$1,710	
Nonfinancial business	528	925		$397
State and local governments	98	202		104
U.S. government	102	469		306
Financial institutions	2,042	1,927	115	
Rest of world	201	194	7	
Total	$5,274 a	$4,309		

a Excess of total assets over liabilities consists of gold and corporate shares other than investment company shares less minor discrepancies that are not included in sector assets.

Source: *Federal Reserve Bulletin*, flow-of-funds tables.

form of demand deposits, time, and savings deposits, and insurance reserves.

The total liabilities for business, listed as $925 billion, do not include corporate shares, which represent ownership accounts. When analyzing corporate accountability at the aggregate level, however, it is occasionally useful to include corporate shares in the totals to determine the total amount "owed" to investors. If the $960 billion in outstanding corporate shares from all sources at the end of 1973 were added to the listed liabilities, the total for nonfinancial business would amount to $1,895 billion or a net deficit of *financial* liabilities exceeding *financial* assets by $1,367 billion.

Financial Institutions and Financial Intermediaries: Distinction

The terms "financial institutions" and "financial intermediaries," although often used interchangeably, technically are not the same. "Financial institutions," the broader of the two terms, encompasses not only those institutions involved in the intermediation function described above, but also those that function primarily as brokers or agents in the financial markets by bringing buyers and sellers together through the use of their facilities. Brokerage houses that buy and sell securities for customer accounts are financial institutions, but not financial intermediaries. Insurance companies that sell only term insurance with no savings feature are not functioning as financial intermediaries in the strict sense even though the insurance premiums might be invested in stocks, bonds, or mortgages. A life insurance company that sells policies with a savings feature, such as an ordinary-life policy, is performing an intermediation function when it invests the savings in securities or mortgages. Property and liability insurance companies are not intermediaries in the strict sense because they do not issue liabilities in their insurance commitments. Conversely, it could be contended that the substantial surplus and reserve funds that are temporarily invested in capital market securities would theoretically be returned to policyholders or shareholders after all claims and expenses were paid. In this respect, excess funds over and above expected losses and expenses are technically entrusted to them and they might be considered an intermediary. While perhaps somewhat arbitrarily, we have included property and liability insurance companies in our discussion of intermediaries.

The important distinction between the two terms is that financial intermediaries intersperse themselves between surplus units—those units with excess funds—and deficit units that need funds. They supply funds at one level of interest rates to the deficit units (users) and receive funds from surplus units, paying them a lower interest rate on securities issued to them. Thus, they relieve the market of primary securities such as mortgages, bonds, and so forth, issued by the deficit users of capital and substitute their own—indirect securities or financial assets such as savings certificates, deposit accounts, and others—whose safety and liquidity warrant a higher price and lower interest rate. The spread between the yields paid on primary securities compared with those paid on indirect securities is the intermediaries' compensation for the special services they perform.

As with most financial intermediaries they are not always performing a pure intermediation function. Yet it is difficult to separate the nonintermediation and intermediation functions of most institutions and, hence, we tend to classify an institution as an intermediary if (1) its primary function is one of intermediation, or (2) the institution is a large factor in terms of total resources committed to the intermediation process.

The more important financial institutions that fit these specifications are savings and loan associations, life insurance companies, mutual savings banks, pension funds, and government lending agencies, among others. In addition, we include commercial banks who, although they perform numerous other functions, are a major factor in the intermediation process and act as financial intermediaries by accepting deposits (indirect securities) and purchasing primary securities such as state and local bonds, federal government securities, and mortgages.

Classification of Institutions

The instruments or contracts that represent claims to or ownership of assets are issued and traded through a complex of institutions. These institutions serve as channels through which those needing longer-term funds draw on the savings of others. Some savings are invested directly by the savers themselves, and some flow to other users without an intermediary. But for the most part, the savings of millions of saving units flow to other users through a host of institutions. To quote Kuznets, "Financial intermediaries obviate the need for each group of savers to seek out and choose among the wide variety of capital users and, conversely, for each group of capital users to seek out and choose among the wide variety of savers.[6] We may expand this concept to include the transfer of already outstanding marketable instruments. The development of institutions has provided a vastly more effective use of savings and greater liquidity of capital issues.

The American financial system includes a remarkable variety of institutions. In this short book we must confine our attention to those institutions that form a major part of or serve the various capital markets. These may be classified as follows:

Deposit institutions:
    Commercial banks; Federal Reserve banks
    Mutual savings banks
    Savings and loan associations
Insurance and pension institutions:
    Legal reserve life insurance companies
    Property and liability insurance companies
    Noninsured private pension funds
    State and local government retirement funds
    Federal retirement and insurance funds
Investment institutions:
    Investment companies
    Real estate investment trusts

The common characteristic of these institutions is that their assets consist primarily of financial instruments, a substantial portion of which represents intermediate- or long-term debt or equity. The first two groups—deposit and insurance institutions—are further characterized by the fact that their liabilities represent contractual obligations to savers.[7] They are real financial intermediaries, receivings funds from individuals, business, and government, and channeling these funds to users on intermediate or long terms. A net increase in their liabilities (and assets), other than from transfers and market revaluation, reflects a net increase in productive capital and an expansion of economic activity.

Investment companies buy securities of various types and issue

---

[6] Simon Kuznets, *Capital in the American Economy: Its Formation and Financing* (Princeton, N.J.: Princeton University Press, 1961), p. 31.

[7] The exception is the property insurance group whose obligations are not dollar contracts with savers but services owed to customers.

bonds or shares against their own portfolios. Although they too hold financial assets, any increase in their portfolios (other than one reflecting a change in market value) represents mainly a transfer to them of debt and equity instruments from other owners.

Real estate investment trusts place most of their funds in direct ownership of real estate properties, in short-term construction loans, and in long-term mortgages.

Certain omissions from the list should be noted. Credit unions are also deposit institutions, but they deal almost exclusively in consumer credit. Fraternal life insurance organizations and the insurance departments of mutual savings banks are relatively small in relation to the "legal reserve" companies, and complete historical data are not available. Bank trustees manage a vast aggregate of assets, but they do not own these assets (in the strict sense) and issue no obligations against them. Investment development companies and small-business investment companies are too specialized to be included in a short book. Sales finance companies obtain some funds in the capital markets, but their activities are confined largely to financing consumer durables.

Federal credit agencies could be classed as a separate institution specializing mainly in mortgage investment. They are discussed in Chapter 8, along with the financing of the Federal government proper.

Two main groups of marketing institutions play a prominent role in the capital markets by serving as middlemen. The first consists of investment bankers and mortgage companies, who merchandise new debt and equity instruments. The second includes securities brokers and dealers, securities exchanges, and mortgage brokers, who aid in the transfer of already outstanding instruments. The work of these marketing types is discussed in Chapters 8 through 12.

```
2222222222222222222222222222222222222222222222222222222222222222222222222222222
2222222222222222222222222222222222222222222222222222222222222222222222222222222
22222222222222222222222222222222222222   222   2222222222222222222222222222222222
22222222222222222222222222222222222222   222   2222222222222222222222222222222222
22222222222222222222222222222222222222   222   2222222222222222222222222222222222
22222222222222222222222222222222222222   222   2222222222222222222222222222222222
22222222222222222222222222222222222222   222   2222222222222222222222222222222222
22222222222222222222222222222222222222   222   2222222222222222222222222222222222
22222222222222222222222222222222222222   222   2222222222222222222222222222222222
22222222222222222222222222222222222222   222   2222222222222222222222222222222222
22222222222222222222222222222222222222   222   2222222222222222222222222222222222
2222222222222222222222222222222222222222222222222222222222222222222222222222222
2222222222222222222222222222222222222222222222222222222222222222222222222222222
```

Nature of the Capital
Formation Process

THE growing institutionalization of the savings and investment process has attracted much attention and, in some respects, has caused a great deal of concern over the last decade. The rapid growth of insurance companies, pension funds, commercial banks, savings and loan associations, and other financial institutions since World War II makes it appear that this phenomenon has occurred only rather recently. Although the rate of growth has varied in the past, the institutionalization of the savings and investment process has been evident at least since the Civil War and, in fact, has paralleled the growth of our industrialized society. This result is not surprising if one assumes that an orderly and complex society necessarily requires a well-developed financial market system. Thus the growth of financial institutions, in whatever form, should be viewed as a logical and rational step in the economic expansion, development, and capital formation process of a highly industrialized society.

This chapter discusses some basic concepts that are helpful in understanding the role of financial intermediaries and individuals in the savings and investment process. The type of industrial environment that is conducive to a favorable growth in financial intermediaries is also discussed. Finally, brief mention is made of the theoretical process that financial intermediaries and individuals undertake in determining what assets to hold or liabilities to assume.

The Capital Formation Process and
the Rise of Capital Markets

Although some goods might be exchanged through barter, in most primitive societies the savers and users of capital were the same. The amount saved by a family or productive unit was generally invested back in the property and, consequently, there was no need for an intervening third party to hold assets or funds for one unit and lend these funds to another unit. Similarly, it is possible to imagine a modern economy where there is a high level of savings and investment yet where no need for financial intermediaries exists. In this situation each of the economy's spending units—individual, business, or government—would have a balanced budget on income and total spending, and (1) each unit's current income would equal the sum of current expenses plus expenditures for fixed assets, and (2) each unit's saving would exactly match its investment in physical assets. In this economy of balanced budgets no securities would be issued by spending units, no financial assets would be accumulated, and (to repeat) the savings and investment process would function without the need for financial intermediaries.[1]

On the other hand, it is possible to visualize an economy that is highly conducive to financial intermediaries. In such an economy all current and capital expenditures could be made by units that had no current income, and all current income could be received by units that spend nothing. One group of spending units would have a deficit equal to the amount of its expenditures while the other group would have a surplus equal to its current income. The spending units would tend to issue securities equal in total to the amount of their deficit and the surplus units would tend to accumulate financial securities equal to their surpluses. As a result, security issues and financial-asset accumulations would tend to approximate total GNP or the aggregate expenditures and a very favorable environment would exist for financial intermediaries.

In our own economy we have been considerably closer to the first case than the latter. That is, with few exceptions, the amount of primary security issues by spending units in a year has been historically averaging only about 10 percent of GNP. *Primary securities,* viewed in their broadest context, are those issues that represent direct obligations of the spending units and include (1) corporate and foreign bonds, (2) common and preferred stocks, (3) farm and non-farm mortgages, (4) consumer debt, (5) U.S. government and agency

---

[1] This discussion follows much of the reasoning contained in John G. Gurley and Edward S. Shaw, *Money in a Theory of Finance* (Washington, D.C.: The Brookings Institution, 1960).

debt, (6) state and local debt, and (7) other miscellaneous debt, such as commercial paper, from other sources.[2]

Overall, the percentage of primary securities to GNP throughout the period 1960–1973 was slightly more than the historical level of 10 percent. Table 2–1 shows that in recent years the ratio of primary securities to GNP has risen from 6.6 percent in 1960 to 13.7 percent in 1971 but dropped back to 11.8 percent in 1973.[3] A contributing factor to this increase has been the rapid growth in farm and non-farm mortgages. The growth in mortgages in recent years can be attributed, in part, to the high demands for housing, government housing programs, and the rapid increase in the cost of construction. Although the ratio of primary securities to GNP is considerably closer to zero than 100 percent, it is still sufficient to generate substantial growth for financial intermediaries.

TABLE 2–1. Net Yearly Primary Security Issues of Spending Units and the Total Issues as a Percentage of Yearly Gross National Product (billions of dollars)

Net Issues	1960	1965	1970	1971	1972	1973
Corporate bonds	$ 5.0	$ 8.1	$ 22.8	$ 23.7	$ 19.7	$ 14.6
Common and preferred stocks	1.7	—	6.8	13.3	13.5	7.8
Farm and nonfarm mortgages	15.7	25.7	26.4	48.2	65.5	69.9
Consumer debt	4.6	9.6	6.1	11.2	19.2	22.9
U.S. government debt	−2.1	1.7	12.8	26.9	19.0	7.9
State and local debt	5.2	6.8	11.4	17.0	12.2	10.5
Other debt [a]	3.4	5.3	8.6	4.5	6.8	19.1
Total primary securities	$ 33.5	$ 57.2	$ 95.0	$ 144.8	$ 155.9	$ 152.7
Gross national product (current dollars)	$503.8	$684.9	$977.1	$1054.9	$1158.0	$1294.9
Percentage primary securities to GNP	6.6%	8.3%	9.7%	13.7%	13.5%	11.8%

[a] Excluding bank loans and open-market paper.

Source: *Federal Reserve Bulletin:* flow-of-funds. (Totals may not add due to rounding.)

---

[2] As this book focuses on capital market instruments and capital market financial institutions, consumer debt will be excluded from further discussion in subsequent chapters. We include it here to give an overall view of total primary securities including those issued by individuals, as well as corporations and governments. In addition, certain corporate debts, such as commercial paper and short-term loans, are primary securities but are short-term in nature and, consequently, not capital market instruments. Discussion of these latter instruments likewise is not included in later chapters.

[3] In general, the figures in Table 2–1 correspond to the data in other chapters of the book. On occasion slight differences may exist between the figures based on the Federal Reserve's flow of funds data and data based on trade associations or from other sources.

Direct and Indirect Securities

As noted previously, in a world of balanced budgets where each spending unit's current and capital expenditures were financed entirely from its current income, aggregate expenditures in the economy would be internally financed and would approximate GNP. In a world where deficits and surpluses exist among spending units, some expenditures would be financed externally. The extent of such financing would be measured by the sum of the deficits (or surpluses) undertaken (generated) by the spending units. If GNP is $1,300 billion and the sum of all spending units' deficits is $130 billion, then 10 percent of GNP is financed *externally* and 90 percent is financed *internally.*

External finance may be direct (primary) or indirect. The distinction between the two forms depends on the nature of the assets held by the surplus units. The financing is called *indirect* if the surplus units acquire claims on financial intermediaries, for example, savings deposits and pension balances. It is *direct* if surplus units acquire claims issued by the deficit users such as common stocks, bonds, mortgages, and so on, which are not supplied by financial intermediaries.

The proportion of GNP that is financed externally has not changed much over the past half-century; however, the relative proportion of direct and indirect securities representing the total amount of externally financed funds has changed significantly. Indirectly financed securities—those issued by financial intermediaries—have risen sharply while the proportion that is directly financed—those issued by deficit units to surplus units—has dropped substantially. Thus, a growing share of primary issues has been sold to financial intermediaries rather than directly to the surplus units. The implication is that either surplus spending units—mostly individuals—have expressed a preference for the financial intermediary issues over the direct issues of deficit units or else they have been inhibited in their efforts to acquire direct issue securities. In general, it appears that the former holds, although the size of certain direct securities such as mortgages and the minimum order size for some U.S. Government debt securities have been inhibiting factors to direct participation by surplus units. In any event, it appears that surplus units by holding indirect securities have opted for lower returns and lower risk than they might receive on holding a larger proportion of direct securities.

Table 2–2 shows the relative amounts of primary securities (broad definition) acquired by individuals and by financial institutions. The amount of primary securities purchased by individuals and others declined sharply in 1973. In fact, financial institutions added more primary securities to their accounts than the net increase in amounts issued in 1972 and 1973. The large decline was attributable to purchases of consumer credit accounts by banks and sales of securities by individuals and others.

TABLE 2–2. Purchases of Primary Security Issues by Individuals and Financial Intermediaries (Representative Years 1960–1973)

	1960	1965	1970	1971	1972	1973
Total primary securities issued in year	$ 33.5	$ 57.2	$ 95.0	$144.8	$156.2	$152.7
Purchased by financial institutions	$ 26.2	$ 56.4	$ 87.2	$130.6	$158.6	$185.9
Net purchases by individuals and others	$ 7.3	$ .8	$ 7.8	$ 14.2	—$2.4	—$33.2

Source: *Federal Reserve Bulletin*, flow-of-funds.

In summary, surplus units have accumulated financial assets in total amounts that, over long periods, have been fairly steady as a percentage of GNP. These accumulations over time, however, have been more and more in the form of indirect financial assets—issues of major financial intermediaries—and relatively less in the form of primary securities such as corporate bonds, stocks, and mortgages.

Financial Intermediaries—
Asset and Liability Structure

This section briefly analyzes the theoretical asset and liability structure of a typical financial intermediary. A changing intermediary structure should be viewed as a logical response by a financial institution in meeting the needs of investors in a competitive environment.[4] Such a structure, however, must necessarily be modified according to the constraints imposed by governing authorities.

Financial Institution Asset and Liability Structure

The formation, growth and the evolving asset and liability structure of financial institutions has been shaped by three major factors: (1) the need to fulfill the demands for funds by users as well as serving as a depository of funds for surplus units, (2) the legal constraints on the various aspects of financial intermediary operations in order

---

[4] In the discussion that follows and especially when the meaning is clear, the term "investor" will be used interchangeably and to mean both surplus and deficit spending units. Although technically the term "investor" has generally been applied to those who take an active part in the investment process while "savers" have been considered those who adopt a passive role, the distinction is becoming more obscure and is not of importance to the discussion in this chapter.

to insure safety of principal, and (3) the nature of the markets serving the demand and supply for funds that are amenable to the intermediation function. Financial intermediaries have grown to fill a basic need in a developing economy. But this growth has been substantially influenced and restricted by regulatory agencies established by state and federal governments who have formed legal and implied constraints on various aspects of financial intermediary operations. In succeeding chapters the most important of these constraints will be indicated.

Dual Objectives of Regulatory Constraints

Historically, legal constraints have been imposed on financial intermediaries in order to (1) foster competition in the demand and supply of funds, on the one hand, and (2) to ensure the profitability and financial stability of the institutions on the other. In most respects, these dual objectives are inherently incompatible and public policy has dictated that the two goals should be balanced.

Encouraging too much competition results in marginal firms leaving the industry which, in a purely competitive environment, is normally viewed as a favorable consequence. Public policy, however, especially since the great depression, has deemed this to be too great a burden to bear for those who have entrusted their funds to an institution primarily for safekeeping rather than for profit. As a result of these dual, yet contradictory, objectives, financial intermediaries find themselves in a more regulated market than that experienced by the average industrial firm. The consequence of such regulation is that local monopolies may be fostered, inefficiencies may arise, and marginal firms may remain in business for a much longer time than would normally be the case. The benefit, and hope, is that, through regulation, the stability and safety of one's principal funds are better assured.

The legal constraints customarily imposed on the institutions in varying degrees pertain to the (1) types of deposits, payments and contributions they can accept from surplus units, (2) the rate paid on these funds, (3) the services they can offer or operate, (4) the type of assets or claims issued by deficit units that they can hold, and (5) the rates they pay on their deposits or charge to their customers.

More recently, there has been a relaxing of these restrictions and financial institutions have been allowed to compete on a broader scale. One of the major reasons for this change has been the growing strength of financial institutions, which diminishes the need for the safety of principal objective. This relaxation of restrictions has taken the form of (1) increased competition for time and savings deposits, (2) expanded areas of investment, particularly for banks, insurance companies of all types, and savings associations, (3) increased maximum percentages invested in any particular type of asset, and (4) fewer filing requirements and easier entry into a financial area. Nevertheless, financial institutions are still constrained by numerous laws and traditions that have remained through the years. These constraints have restricted the assets and liabilities of at least some of the financial institutions to an asset and liability structure that they might not prefer. But to others it is a small price to pay for the overall stability that is desirable in our financial markets.

The Hedging Principle

Operating within the constraints mentioned above, the financial institutions are free to choose the asset and liability structure they want to pursue. It is often said that the asset structure of an institution is determined by the liabilities it accepts or that an institution determines as its assets, *given* its liabilities. We say that financial institutions are open-ended on their liability structure. That is, they stand willing to accept certain types of liabilities without restrictions on the amounts received. Banks, for instance, are generally willing to accept almost unlimited amounts of several types of savings and checking accounts. Insurance companies accept long-term liabilities in the form of insurance policies. And mutual funds are open-ended in the amount of fund shares they will issue. Presumably, this process should continue at least as long as the financial institution can relend or reinvest the funds at a rate of return greater than the cost of obtaining and placing the funds.

The basic rule applied by financial institutions in structuring their assets, given their liabilities, is the *principle of hedging*. If an institution accepts a liability, say, in the form of a deposit that is short-term in nature, it should offset or *hedge* the liability by lending on a short-term basis for the same length of time. In theory, as the asset matures it is used to pay off the debt that comes due at the same time. Presumably, the financial institution is content to make its profit on the spread between the interest rate paid on the liability to the surplus unit and the rate charged on the loan to the deficit unit.

Although the concept of hedging as applied to financial asset and liability management is an oversimplification, it nevertheless is helpful in analyzing the financial data in later chapters. This concept is illustrated in Figure 2–1 where panel A shows a perfectly hedged position with the asset holding period exactly offsetting the time to maturity (holding period) of the liability.

Even ignoring legal constraints, most institutions probably would maintain only an approximate hedged position in order to attain

FIGURE 2–1.   Comparison of Asset and Liability Holding Periods Showing
a Hedged, Refinancing and Reinvestment Position

Time in Years

	Asset Holding Period	0 ————————— 4
A. Perfectly Hedged Position	Liability Holding Period	0 ————————— 4

	Asset Holding Period	0 ——————————————— 6
B. Refinancing position	Liability Holding Period	0 ————————— 4

	Asset Holding Period	0 ————————— 4
C. Reinvestment Position	Liability Holding Period	0 ——————————————— 6

greater flexibility and possibly greater profitability. Lack of an overall
hedged position for the aggregate of assets and liabilities held by a
financial institution, however, forces the institution to face either a
reinvestment or a refinancing decision. For instance in panel B,
Figure 2–1, the institution accepts a liability for a shorter period of
time (four years) than the assets in which it places these funds (six
years). When the liability matures the institution faces a refinancing
decision if the funds are withdrawn by the original depositor and
not returned to the institution. (In actuality, of course, the institution
need only concern itself with the net position after aggregating the
maturities and amounts for all assets and liabilities.) Panel C shows
that the institution faces a reinvestment decision at the end of four
years if the asset matures before the loan is paid off. That is, it must
reinvest the funds for two more years until the liability is liquidated.
In either case, B or C, the institution is said to be speculating on the
differences in asset and liability holding periods and its profit margin
may be greater or smaller depending upon the refinancing or reinvestment rates paid, or received, respectively.

As the latter procedures (B or C) are not generally acceptable to
financial institutions and could cause cash management problems,
most firms will attempt to structure their assets and liabilities to
conform more or less to the hedged position (panel A). Unfortunately,
legal constraints have effectively limited some institutions to an unhedged position. Although, as noted previously, this relationship is
far from perfect, this concept is helpful in understanding a financial
institutions asset and liability structure; a preponderance of short-
term liabilities normally should be offset by short-term assets while
long-term liabilities should be offset with a substantial amount of
long term assets. This basic concept should also prove useful in
analyzing long run changes in financial intermediary asset and
liability accounts discussed in later chapters.

Table 2–3 shows the principal asset and liability structures of four representative financial institutions divided into maturities of *five years or less* and those *greater than five years*. The figures in the table are the estimated percentages of assets and liabilities held in each maturity range. The table shows that, as a group, commercial banks have a high percentage of their assets as well as liabilities in short-term instruments. At the end of 1973, it was estimated that better than 90 percent of both their assets and liabilities were of a short-term nature, hence, a substantially hedged position.[5] Similarly, life insurance companies with a preponderance of long-term liabilities in the form of insurance policies and retirement obligations likewise exhibited a substantially hedged position in that a large proportion of their assets (95 percent) were in long-term securities such as stocks, bonds, and mortgages.

TABLE 2–3. Estimated Maturity of Asset and Liability Holdings of Representative Financial Institutions (in percentages)

| | | | Maturity Structure Based on Initial Holding Period | |
Financial Institution	Total Assets/ Liabilities (in billions of dollars) 12/31/73		Less than Five Years (percentage)	Greater than Five Years (percentage)
Commercial banks	$835.4	Assets	92	8
		Liabilities	88	12
Life insurance companies	$252.4	Assets	5	95
		Liabilities	10	90
Savings and loan associations	$272.4	Assets	8	92
		Liabilities	92	8
Mutual savings banks	$106.7	Assets	5	95
		Liabilities	91	9

Sources: *Federal Reserve Bulletin* Tables 3–3, 4–3, 4–7, 5–1.

The data in the table for savings and loan associations and mutual savings banks, however, suggest a poorly hedged position. These institutions have relatively short-term liabilities (in savings deposits) and comparatively long-term holdings (in mortgages). More than 90 percent of their liabilities are in relatively short-term obligations

---

[5] Estimates based on Federal Reserve data including "Ownership of marketable securities" and flow-of-funds. Analysis of maturities based on initial maturity period of debt.

(less than five years) while, on the other hand, more than 90 percent of their assets are of a long-term nature (greater than five years). In rapidly changing markets, such as 1974, when savings and time deposits were transferred on short notice from one institution to another, savings and loan associations and mutual savings banks are likely to experience a cash flow problem, face a "refinancing" decision and be forced to seek funds from other sources. In the event of savings withdrawls, they will seek additional funds such as borrowings from Federal Home Loan Banks, or else sharply curtail their lending activities. In either case, the consequences tend to disrupt their operations and the effective functioning of the mortgage market.

The primary reason for the deviation from a hedged position by savings and loan associations and mutual savings banks can be traced to the legal restrictions placed on these institutions in the management of their asset holdings. Although there has been some relaxation, these constraints have generally restricted savings and loan and mutual savings banks to lending in the mortgage market, which is long term by nature, while their liabilities—savings shares and deposits—tend to be relatively short-term. Based on the hedging principle, analysis of probable future direction for these institutions would suggest an attempt by mutual savings banks and savings and loan associations to offer either longer-term liabilities or else hold shorter-term assets. This is discussed in greater detail in later chapters.

Preferences for Asset Holdings

Another influence on the functioning of our capital markets concerns the selection of assets to hold or liabilities to assume by individuals, firms, or financial institutions. Basically, the participants in the financial markets must choose among the assets to hold and the liabilities to assume as well as choosing whether to invest or consume the funds they have in their possession. It is the interest rate received or paid on the various security instruments and the corresponding rate changes among these instruments that effectively facilitates the process of balancing the demand for funds with the supply of funds consistent with a given level of gross national product.

The Function of Interest Rates
and the Market Clearing Process

Investment or savings as opposed to current consumption can be characterized as *present sacrifice* for *future benefit*. As the present is well known, and the future unpredictable, the *certain* present sacrifice is exchanged for an *uncertain* future benefit. In order for investors to hold assets yielding uncertain benefits, they must expect the value of the assets at the end of the holding period to exceed their initial value, assuming the absence of inflation and restrictive markets.

In a similar fashion, firms that borrow large sums either directly from investors or indirectly from financial intermediaries likewise are exchanging a certain present benefit, which could be received by spending the funds so obtained for current consumption, for some future uncertain stream in the expectation of receiving a return over and above the cost of the funds borrowed. The rate so received must be expected to exceed the cost of the borrowed funds.

Accordingly, based on the laws of supply and demand, interest rates will continually adjust so that the desired asset and liability balances for individuals, firms and financial intermediaries, along with the appropriate maturity structure for each asset and liability account, are brought into balance.

The interest rate received on each asset held, or paid on each liability assumed, is a function of the pure time value of money—called the riskless rate—and the degree of uncertainty or risk associated with the given security instrument. Risk includes such things as the risk of default, inflation, expropriation, and so forth.

Changes in the time value of money (riskless rate) occur as a result of changes in the consumption and investment preferences of investors. For example, if inflation is an important consideration, surplus spending units could be expected to consume more of their present income for fear of higher prices. Or, alternatively, they would demand a higher interest in order to be persuaded to postpone consumption. A good illustration of this last point was in 1973 and 1974 when the high rate of inflation caused interest rates to rise to unprecedented levels.

Two conclusions that are important for the analysis of financial intermediaries follow from this discussion: (1) the rate of inflation and the riskless rate of interest tend to move together because higher rates must be paid to encourage investors to postpone consumption when prices are rising, (2) the longer the prediction period the greater the uncertainty associated with that prediction and, therefore, the higher the risk premium demanded by investors.

Finally, the level of interest rates and the adjustment process is important to the effective functioning of financial markets and financial institutions. Any abrupt changes in interest rates are likely to result in more erratic market operations as investors, and others, substantially alter their consumption and/or investment patterns in light of the changes.

The Choice of Asset Holdings

The selection of assets or combination of assets to hold by investors is a function of the expected return of each asset and the associated risk. By associated risk we mean the inherent risk in the asset itself tempered by any mitigating factors that reduce the risk that results from combining the given asset with other assets already held in the portfolio, or that are under consideration. This latter aspect, frequently referred to as the portfolio problem, is that component of risk that can be diversified away by a judicious combination of asset holdings in a portfolio.

In any event, the risk among competing investments is by no means constant over the business cycle and investors will often adjust their portfolios to reflect this change. Federal government securities, being riskless instruments, are generally not affected by the business cycle though other securities often are affected. When the economy is booming, it is not surprising to see the yields on high-grade corporate bonds move closer (or the yield differential to decline) to federal bonds of the same maturity.

In general, investors are assumed to be trying to attain that mix of asset holdings such that the holdings give them the greatest benefit. This process more or less continues indefinitely as asset holdings are adjusted to reflect differences in market factors, interest rates and attitudes towards risk. One of the major areas of interest in subsequent chapters is to follow the new methods or procedures, and security instruments as well as the changes in holdings of investors and financial intermediaries in recent years as they adapt to changing market conditions. Many of the major shifts that have occurred in asset and liability holdings over the last few years can be traced to substantial changes in (1) the level of interest rates, (2) the number and types of new securities offered, and (3) the degree of competition among financial intermediaries particularly with regard to the competition for savings. Many of the concepts briefly discussed in this chapter will, one would hope, prove helpful in analyzing changes in these latter areas and aid in predicting future directions in the capital markets.

```
3333333333333333333333333333333333333333333333333333333333333333333333333333333333333333
3333333333333333333333333333333333333333333333333333333333333333333333333333333333333333
333333333333333333333333333333333333   333   333   333333333333333333333333333333333333
333333333333333333333333333333333333   333   333   333333333333333333333333333333333333
333333333333333333333333333333333333   333   333   333333333333333333333333333333333333
333333333333333333333333333333333333   333   333   333333333333333333333333333333333333
333333333333333333333333333333333333   333   333   333333333333333333333333333333333333
333333333333333333333333333333333333   333   333   333333333333333333333333333333333333
333333333333333333333333333333333333   333   333   333333333333333333333333333333333333
333333333333333333333333333333333333   333   333   333333333333333333333333333333333333
333333333333333333333333333333333333   333   333   333333333333333333333333333333333333
333333333333333333333333333333333333   333   333   333333333333333333333333333333333333
3333333333333333333333333333333333333333333333333333333333333333333333333333333333333333
3333333333333333333333333333333333333333333333333333333333333333333333333333333333333333
```

Commercial and Federal
Reserve Banks

WE shall first discuss the institutions that accept deposit funds. Their role in the capital markets is to serve as funnels through which savings are invested in intermediate- and long-term instruments. Be. cause of their fiduciary responsibility to depositors, their investment activity is heavily regulated. They are allowed only small holdings of corporate stock and are restricted to "investment grade" securities in their purchases of corporate and municipal bonds.

Three important deposit institutions are involved in the capital markets: commercial banks, mutual savings banks, and savings and loan associations. Commercial and Federal Reserve banks are discussed in this chapter. Federal Reserve banks are not deposit-type institutions, but their relations with commercial banks, their holdings of federal obligations, and their influence on yields require our attention.

Commercial Banks

As of June 30, 1974, there were 14,337 commercial banks in the United States, operating more than 41,674 offices including 27,336 branches and additional offices. As of June 30, 1974, there were 4,693 national banks, all members of the Federal Reserve System, with total assets of $517 billion; 1,068 state-chartered member banks with $176 billion in assets; and 8,347 state nonmember banks with $179 billion. The rate of growth in total assets in the last decade has been the greatest in *state nonmember banks*, which is also the largest single category in terms of number of banks. It should be noted, however, that members of the Federal Reserve System still control over 79 percent of all bank assets.

The traditional role of commercial banks has been to furnish short-term funds to individuals, business, agriculture, and government; however, through the years they have become veritable department stores of finance. Their multifunctional role includes substantial activity in the granting of intermediate--term credit through term loans, and long-term credit through the acquisition of government and corporate bonds, and mortgages. More recently they have expanded into such areas as computer processing for businesses, and insurance and mutual fund sales to individuals.

Sources of Funds for Capital-Market Assets

No exact relationship exists between specific sources and uses of bank funds. Funds are derived from demand deposits, savings and time deposits, stockholders' investments, and, recently, from the sale of debentures. Because the turnover of savings and time deposits is so much slower than that of demand deposits (one compared with about sixty times per annum), these, together with net worth, constitute the major source for investment in capital-market assets. Time deposits now constitute almost 60 percent of total deposits, and their growth has been largely responsible for the shift in bank activity from specialization in short-term financing toward general financing.

With few exceptions, time and savings deposits have expanded steadily since the 1950s, reflecting the general growth of savings in the economy, the rising level of interest rates, and the increasing flexibility banks have been allowed by regulatory agencies in competing for these deposits.

Bank growth has been greatly influenced by the limits imposed on time deposits by the regulatory authorities (Federal Reserve Board and Banks and Federal Deposit Insurance Corporation). In the past, such limits have at times encouraged, and at other times discouraged, the flow of savings to commercial banks, depending on the rates available at other types of savings institutions and in the open money and capital markets. More recently, interest rate ceilings imposed by the Federal Reserve have been allowed to increase such that there is no current maximum rate applicable on some deposit-type accounts.[1]

---

[1] In late October 1974, the annual rate on bank passbook deposits was limited to 5 percent; single-maturity time deposits (including certificates of deposit) could

Table 3–1 shows the growth of savings and time deposits for all commercial banks from 1955 through 1973. The rate of growth in these deposits has accelerated in the last few years due to the increased level of savings, higher interest rates and the intensified competition for savings dollars.

TABLE 3–1.   Savings and Time Deposits and Capital Accounts,
All Commercial Banks, at Year End, 1955–1973
(billions of dollars)

	1955	1960	1965	1970	1973
Savings and time deposits [a]	$48.4	$71.6	$146.7	$229.0	$358.2
Capital accounts	15.3	21.0	30.3	43.0	56.9
Total	$63.7	$92.6	$177.0	$272.0	$415.1

[a] Excluding interbank deposits.
Source: *Federal Reserve Bulletin.*

An analysis of the data by bank size and location reveals that time and savings deposits are relatively more important as a source of funds for small- and medium-sized banks than for large-city banks. At the end of 1973 time and savings deposits amounted to more than 60 percent of total deposits for medium and small banks but only 33 percent of the total for large commercial banks.

This figure for medium and small banks represents a jump of over 9 percentage points (51 to 60) since 1968. It is an important statistic because medium and small banks are the major competitors of savings and loan institutions for savings dollars and it underscores the intense competition occurring among all savings institutions.

Perhaps the biggest casualties, however, as a result of the competition for time and savings deposits and the corresponding rise in interest rates paid on deposits, have been the stock market and those institutions and other entities primarily investing in the stock market. This would include investment companies and individuals in particular. Individuals, especially, have avoided common stock purchases in favor of the higher current yield and lower risk type instrument afforded by bonds and by time and savings deposits.

Table 3–1 also shows the growth of capital funds (net worth and debentures) of commercial banks. It is generally desirable for banks

---

pay from 5½ percent on less than $100,000 principal with maturities of 90 days to 1 year up to 7½ percent for maturities of 4 years or more. There was no rate limit on single maturity certificates of deposit in denominations of $100,000 or more. The rate paid on some CD's was up to 12 percent. Savings and loan associations were offering up to 5¼ percent on passbook accounts and up to 7¾ percent on term accounts. In the open market, U.S. Treasury bills brought 7.2 percent and high-grade corporate bonds brought 8.8 percent.

to have an expanding capital base as the national economy grows in order to meet the demands of large borrowers. Maximum loan limits to one borrower as well as the total amount of assets held in buildings and equipment by a bank usually are related to the size of the capital account. Furthermore, the appeal of capital-market assets, with the greater price risk, as compared with money-market assets, is affected by the relative size of the equity cushion. Other factors influencing the equity base include the volatility of demand deposits, the types of loans on the books, the ratio of loans to deposits, the relative yields on short-, intermediate-, and long-term loans and investments, together with such influences as the attitudes of bank examiners, changes in bank legislation, and the general need for liquidity of individual banks and of the banking system as a whole.

Annual Sources of Funds

The annual changes (see Table 3–2) in adjusted savings and time deposits and capital help explain the variations in uses of funds indicated later in this chapter.

The very tight money and capital-market conditions in 1966 and 1969, which culminated in the "credit crunches" for those years, seriously impaired growth in savings deposits at commercial banks. This situation was particularly bad in 1969 when deposits actually declined by $9.7 billion (Table 3–2). The relative and absolute declines in deposit accumulations during these two years were caused by comparatively low maximum rates allowed on bank time and savings deposits, which were not competitive with open-market rates or the rates offered by savings and loan associations, and by the lower rate of savings by individuals. Increases in the allowed maximum rates of interest in late 1966 and again in early 1970 helped reverse these trends and commercial banks enjoyed unprecedented deposit growth in the early 1970s. In fact, the maximum rates allowed on commercial bank time and savings deposits in some categories (deposits over $100,000) matched or exceeded those allowed savings and loan institutions. The deposit growth in the 1970 to 1973 period, reflecting the higher rates and easier monetary policy, increased from $40 to $50 billion in these years.

As commercial banks invest in both money-market and capital-market assets and derive funds from demand deposits as well as from time deposits and capital, annual changes in the latter two sources cannot properly be called a flow of funds for investment solely in longer-term loans and securities. In some periods, after liquidity requirements have been satisfied, funds from demand deposits are invested in capital-market assets. At the same time, in most years a substantial portion of time deposits and even net worth is held in liquid

TABLE 3–2.   Annual Changes in Savings and Time Deposits and Capital, Commercial Banks, 1965–1973 (billions of dollars)

	1965	1966	1967	1968	1969	1970	1971	1972	1973
Savings and time deposits [a]	$20.0	$13.3	$23.7	$20.6	−$9.4	$37.3	$41.2	$42.6	$50.1
Capital accounts	2.5	1.8	2.3	2.6	3.0	3.0	4.3	5.4	5.5
Total	$22.5	$15.1	$26.0	$23.2	−$6.4	$40.3	$45.5	$48.0	$55.6

[a] Excluding inter-bank deposits.
Source: Federal Reserve Bulletin.

form. Shifts among assets also take place, even though their total may not change.

Because it is not feasible to associate specific sources and uses of bank funds, the actual flow of funds into capital-market instruments must serve as our data on such investments (see Table 3–5). For 1965–1973, flow of funds into capital market investments were as follows (in billions of dollars): [2]

1965	1966	1967	1968	1969	1970	1971	1972	1973
$12.7	$6.8	$26.5	$23:3	$0.9	$26.0	$32.7	$38.4	$32.2

By relating these figures to the previous figures of changes in adjusted time deposits and capital accounts (Table 3–2), we see that except for 1969 the growth in time deposits and capital accounts was greater than the increase in longer-term assets. The longer-term sources thus provided some funds for cash reserves and short-term assets. The very substantial changes in the annual data, especially in 1966 and 1969, as well as the subsequent rebounds, are discussed later in this chapter.

Uses of Bank Funds in the Capital Market: General

When the somewhat arbitrary definition capital-market financing (equity investments, intermediate-term debt, and long-term debt) is applied to commercial banking activity, the volume of bank operations in the capital markets is found to be very substantial. They include a variety of direct as well as open-market transactions and involve the whole range of users of funds—individuals, business, and government.

Table 3–3, showing the combined assets of all commercial banks since 1955, is a somewhat unrealistic indication of the role of banks in the capital markets as contrasted with their role in the money market.

---

[2] Derived from data in Federal Reserve Bulletin; Federal Deposit Insurance Corporation, Annual Reports; Sources in Table 3–5.

The data do not distinguish between short- and long-term assets. In addition, there is a constant flow of funds between assets with different maturities; the flow is influenced by the need of banks for liquidity, by the demand for different types of credit, and by the earnings rates on different credit instruments. Transfers from money-market to capital-market assets, and vice versa, are both deliberate and automatic. A bank may sell a long-term Federal bond and invest the proceeds in a short-term bond or make a short-term loan. Or an opposite transaction—from short- to long-term—may be chosen. An automatic shift from long- to short-term results from the maturing of loans and investments that, when first acquired, represented intermediate- or long-term credit but that move, with the passage of time, into the short-term maturity schedule. In any event, the basic hedging principle as discussed in Chapter 2 implies, namely, that as the average term to maturity increases for the bank's liabilities the bank's assets likewise should be invested in relatively longer-term securities.

TABLE 3–3.   Combined Assets of All Commercial Banks, at Year End, 1955–1973 (billions of dollars)

	1955	1960	1965	1970	1973
Cash assets	$ 46.8	$ 52.2	$ 61.0	$ 94.0	$119.2
Loans					
Commercial and industrial [a]	33.2	43.4	71.9	113.4	160.8
Farm (excluding real estate)	4.5	5.7	8.2	11.2	17.3
Real estate	20.8	28.8	49.7	73.3	119.1
Individuals	17.2	26.5	45.7	66.3	100.8
Securities	5.0	5.1	8.5	9.9	12.0
Financial institutions	0.6	7.7	15.5	18.6	40.9
Other	2.5	2.9	7.3	24.0	48.5
Total loans [b]	$ 82.6	$118.1	$202.8	$310.6	$492.2
Investments [c]					
U.S. Government securities	61.6	61.1	59.7	62.0	58.8
Bonds of federal agencies and corporations	1.9	1.8	4.6	13.5	29.3
State and local government bonds	12.7	17.6	38.7	69.8	95.1
Corporate bonds	1.6	0.9	0.9	2.6	5.8
Other securities	0.5	0.6	0.8	0.5	.8
Total investments	$ 78.3	$ 82.0	$108.7	$143.4	$189.8
Other assets	3.0	6.0	10.4	22.4	34.2
Total assets	$210.7	$258.4	$378.9	$575.4	$835.4

[a] Includes commercial paper.
[b] Total shows net of reserves.
[c] Includes trading account securities.
Sources: Federal Deposit Insurance Corporation, *Annual Reports; Federal Reserve Bulletin.*

The asset figures do, however, indicate the important banking functions. The two major categories of "earning assets"—loans and investments—represent, in part, capital-market financing. We shall discuss the significance of the intermediate- and long-term portion of each main type of loan and investment, omitting mention of consumer financing even though some of this (for example, housing improvement loans) may qualify as long term on a strict maturity basis. In general, the earning assets discussed fall outside the "secondary reserves" of the banks—money-market loans and short-term Federal obligations—held primarily for liquidity rather than for income.

Term Loans

The growth in bank term loans has been a most important postwar development. These loans have over one year to original maturity (seldom over ten) and are usually amortized on a regular basis. They form a major part of the commercial and industrial loan figure in Table 3–3 and, to a minor extent, the individuals category. Term loans are frequently used by businesses as alternatives to bond financing because (1) they offer more flexibility in that often they can be prepaid without penalty, (2) the term loan can be "closed" or approved quicker and can be cheaper over-all, (3) no time-consuming and costly registration procedures (which can take up to six months in bond financing) are required, (4) standard sinking fund requirements, refunding provisions, and other restrictions on firm operations, frequently contained in the bond indenture agreement, can be avoided or minimized, and (5) the term loan frequently can be renewed, extended, and otherwise tailored more closely to a firm's needs and current operations.

Term loans are also a desirable replacement for former short-term loans in that (1) they do not have to be continually renewed at maturity as often and (2) the interest rate is generally fixed rather than variable, which aids a firm's financial planning. In making term loans banks compete chiefly with life insurance companies.

Information on the volume and characteristics of bank term loans is irregular and incomplete. The proportion of term to total loans differs greatly among banks; for some large banks it is now over 50 percent. Very large banks (with deposits of $1 billion or more) held slightly over one-half of the total term loan volume in 1957.[3] But term credits are becoming increasingly important to small business. In 1957 they constituted 46 percent of all bank loans to borrowers with assets of less than $50,000. This is capital-market fiancing at the local level. At the end of July 1974, term loans held by large commercial banks

---

[3] The 1957 data were based on the original maturities. As principal is constantly reduced, the amount of outstanding term debt declines unless offset by new loans.

(which held 70 percent of all bank loans) totaled $45 billion, or 42 percent of their commercial and industrial loans.[4] At this rate the figure for all banks would be over $76 billion.

Term loans to business offer the advantage of flexibility in particular covenants and in type of security required; this flexibility helps to explain their use in financing working-capital and fixed-assets requirements, especially during periods of buoyant business activity and ample bank credit. But even during periods of credit stringency, the ratio of term to total business loans increases. In such periods, many borrowers, especially smaller firms, turn to these loans when unsecured short-term funds are hard to get.

Finally, large firms waiting for lower long-term rates or more favorable stock market conditions may finance for shorter periods through short-term loans.

Mortgage Financing by Commercial Banks

Table 3–4 shows the composition of bank holdings of mortgages from 1955 through 1973. Commercial banks are one of the major institutions in the mortgage market. They have not committed as many resources to mortgages, however, as their total asset size might suggest because mortgages are generally long-term instruments and carry fixed interest rates that at times are lower than rates in competing money-market instruments. Recently banks have committed about 14 percent of their total assets to mortgages.

The table also shows that commercial banks have been very selective in the type of real estate loans they finance. They have favored, especially, single family to four-unit buildings much more than multifamily structures. This contrasts with the real estate financing of insurance companies and savings and loan associations, which have much more balanced real estate portfolios. Banks have also preferred conventional private financing over government-guaranteed financing represented by the Federal Housing Administration (FHA) and Veterans Administration (VA) loan programs. Reasons generally attributed to this preference include the paperwork, time delays, and maximum allowed interest rates on FHA and VA loans, which are frequently below competing market rates.

Farm mortgage loans   As a group, banks are far less important in agricultural real estate than are insurance companies and government agencies specifically designed to aid rural housing. At the end

---

[4] *Federal Reserve Bulletin.* A new compilation of term loans of large banks has appeared monthly in the *Federal Reserve Bulletin* beginning with the May 1968 issue.

TABLE 3–4.   Mortgage Loans Held by Commercial Banks,
at Year End, 1955–1973 (billions of dollars)

	1955	1960	1965	1970	1973
Farm	$ .13	$ 1.7	$ 2.9	$ 4.4	$ 5.4
Residential:					
1–4 family	15.1	19.2	30.4	42.3	68.0
Multifamily	0.8	1.1	1.9	3.3	6.9
	$15.9	$20.3	$32.3	$45.6	$ 74.9
Commercial and industrial	3.8	6.8	14.5	23.3	38.7
Total	$21.0	$28.8	$49.7	$73.3	$119.1
Conventional and other	$12.7	$20.1	$39.3	$62.8	$107.6
FHA-insured	4.6	5.8	7.7	7.9	8.2
VA-guaranteed	3.7	2.9	2.7	2.6	3.3
Total	$21.0	$28.8	$49.7	$73.3	$119.1

Source: *Federal Reserve Bulletin.*

of 1973, the $5.4 billion in farm mortgages held by commercial banks represented less than 1 percent of all commercial bank assets.

Residential mortgage loans   Although experiencing a relative decline in mortgage financing compared to other institutions, in terms of both the number of loans and their dollar amount, bank financing of residential real estate has increased substantially in the postwar years reflecting the great expansion in housing activity. Residential one-to-four-family mortgage loans held by commercial banks totaled $68.0 billion at the end of 1973. This was approximately 17 percent of the $387 billion of one-to-four-family mortgages outstanding in the United States, down from 21 percent in 1950. The share of total FHA-insured, VA-guaranteed loans outstanding held by banks declined from 26 percent in 1950 to 8 percent in 1973.

As noted earlier, although the commercial bank position in the mortgage market relative to other institutions has declined in importance, banks are still major factors in certain mortgage market sectors. The postwar increase in single family residential mortgages held by banks reflects the general rise in demand for home financing, increased yields on this type of asset, the great growth in time deposits, and the expansion of federally underwritten loans. In 1968, national banks were permitted to lend on conventional home mortgages up to 60 percent of their time deposits or 100 percent of capital and surplus, whichever was greater. No such restrictions applied to FHA-insured and VA-guaranteed liens. Mortgages as bank investments had fallen into disrepute in the 1930s, but the availability of federally underwritten liens (with their safety and secondary market), together with the use of amortized payments and longer maturities, led to a substantial shift toward this type of credit. Another factor in this shift had been the increase in the maximum loan-to-value ratio of amortized conventional loans to 75 percent of appraised value, with a limit on maturity to twenty years. State banking regulations on mortgages vary from state to state. Some regulations are more strict, others less strict, than those applying to national banks.

Commercial bank holdings of multifamily mortgages has remained low, amounting to only $6.9 billion at the end of 1973. There has been some renewed interest in these loans, however, as the growth of highrise housing, the desire for higher yields, and the rapid growth in bank deposits have caused banks to search for additional loan placements.

In addition to direct lending on mortgages held to maturity, some banks originate loans that they pass along to others. To a certain degree, then, they help to make the mortgage market national in scope. Recently, banks have also engaged in interim construction financing with the eventual permanent mortgage being placed with a life insurance company, savings and loan association, mutual savings bank, or real estate investment trust. They also "warehouse" or carry mortgage loans originated by mortgage companies until the latter pass these along to permanent investors, and make short-term loans to real estate investment companies. Actually, given commercial banks' short-term liabilities, participation in the mortgage market by concentrating on shorter-term assets suits the banks' investment portfolios.

Commercial and industrial mortgage loans   Commercial mortgage loans have grown substantially in the last few years and totaled almost 39 billion at the end of 1973. This figure represents about 31 percent of the total of such mortgages outstanding in the United States. The growth in commercial mortgages held by banks is attributable in part to (1) the normally higher yields on commercial mortgages as opposed to residential and multifamily mortgages, (2) the need for additional investment outlets by commercial banks, (3) the heavy demand for loans by businesses that causes banks to "reach for security" in order to make the loans through mortgage loans secured by commercial properties, (4) the sharp increase in bank interim construction loans on commercial properties, and (5) fewer legal restrictions on corporate mortgages.

Securities Loans

Although securities loans are short term in nature, they play an important ancillary role in the securities market. They are made (1) to investment bankers to carry new issues through underwriting and distribution, (2) to dealers for the financing of customers' margin accounts, and (3) to individuals for their purchases of securities.

The volume of securities loans fluctuates with changes in margin requirements, securities prices, the dollar volume of securities trading, the volume of new securities, and interest rates. Margin regulation under the Securities and Exchange Act of 1934, the growth of private placements of securities, and the increased reliance by business on internal financing have all reduced the demand for securities credit. Table 3–3 shows that, at the end of 1973, outstanding securities loans of all commercial banks totaled $12.0 billion, or less than 2 percent of total commercial bank loans outstanding. This compared with $17 billion or almost 30 percent of outstanding loans in the autumn of 1929.

Banks also make loans secured by securities collateral—"nonpurpose" loans—for purposes other than purchasing or carrying securities. These are classified as either business or individual loans.

Bank Securities Investments

In addition to loans, investments in the form of bond and note issues held are the second major category of earning assets for commercial banks. Investment assets held by commercial banks amounted to less than 23 percent of total bank assets at the end of 1973 compared to over 55 percent for bank loans. This has not always been the case. As recently as 1950, investments constituted 44 percent of total bank assets but loans amounted to only 31 percent. The relative importance of the two main types of earning assets since 1955, shown in Table 3–3, reveals the continuing shift in emphasis from securities to loans by commercial banks for their earning assets.

Most of the investment assets held by commercial banks are comprised of U.S. government securities, federal agency securities, and state and local government bonds.

Bonds other than United States obligations, often with two years or less to maturity, constitute the bulk of the investment portfolio of banks. These bonds constitute a residual account that provides income from funds not needed for loans and serve to diversify the assets of the banks. The risk of changing market values is reduced by spacing maturities, although in years like 1973 and 1974, with bond prices at record lows, the potential losses on the sales of bonds contributed greatly to the credit strain and the high level of interest rates. The credit risk (in other than United States obligations) is minimized by applying high investment standards, as required by regulation, and by diversification.

The volume of bond investments is affected by seasonal, cyclical, and secular influences, especialy the demand for loans and the available yields on securities compared with interest rates on loans. Federal

Reserve policy also affects the ratio of investments to loans. In periods of credit restraint, as in 1974, investments are reduced in order to obtain funds for loan expansion.

United States government securities   Except from the standpoint of income taxation and yield, Treasury obligations are almost ideal bank investments. They involve no credit risk and the least price risk for a given maturity. They can be used as collateral at other banks or at the Federal Reserve banks without penalty rates, have perfect marketability, and are preferred by bank examiners. Shorter maturities provide liquidity as well as safe income, and banks can change the composition of their federal bond portfolios by shifting between short- and medium-term maturities. In periods of credit ease, banks take the initiative in acquiring medium-term securities for income. Primary reserves are ample and may be expanded by using Federal Reserve credit. In periods of credit strain and higher yields (as in 1959 and 1969 through 1974), securities may be sold to provide loan funds. Such contraction of the investment portfolio is, however, limited by the aversion of the banks to selling the longer maturities at a loss. This critical situation came to a peak in the early summer of 1974 and helped force the prime rate to 12 percent.

Commercial banks tend to buy short-term federal securities in periods of economic recession when the banks have idle funds, even though yields may be low relative to other government securities in order to preserve their liquidity (Figure 8–1). Conversely, they tend, when necessary, to sell bonds in prosperous years at higher yields and lower prices in order to increase loanable funds. This policy almost inevitably leads to losses on resale, which are, however, allowed as expenses for federal income tax purposes.

Commercial banks are the largest private institutional owners of direct United States government securities (see Chapter 8). At the end of 1973 their holdings totaled $59 billion, or 13 percent of gross Treasury debt. About 90 percent of these securities had maturities of five years or less. In recent years, the yields on federal short-term securities have often matched or exceeded the yields on longer maturities. Hence, there is little purpose in holding long maturities that have substantial price risk because of changing market yields. When declining interest rates are probable, some new funds may be placed in longer maturities to maximize income and allow banks a better asset/liability hedge position. But this situation has not prevailed during the 1960s or 1970s.

The total dollar amount of bank holdings of federal securities has been fairly stable since the 1950s—around $60 billion as noted earlier—although the percentage that this represents of total bank assets has dipped significantly from slightly over 35 percent in 1950 to less than 10 percent at the end of 1973.

Much of the relative decline of federal securities held by banks can be attributed to higher after-tax yields that banks can receive on business loans, federal agency securities, and state and local government issues; furthermore, when loan demand is heavy, federal securities, because of their low yield, are likely to be liquidated first to meet this demand and, consequently, banks' holdings of these securities tend to drop sharply. The process is essentially reversed when loan demand slackens. For example, from the end of 1972 through July, 1974, federal securities held by commercial banks declined from $67.7 billion to $53.0 billion or a drop of over 21 percent.

The bank procedure of buying federal securities when loan demand is slack and selling federal securities when loan demand quickens tends to be cyclical in nature and aggravate interest rate swings, causing rates on federal securities to go higher in high loan demand times and lower in slack periods. Nevertheless, it is probably more likely that bank investment policy has influenced the spreads between the prices and yields of different maturities of federal securities more than the yield structure as a whole.

Federally sponsored agency securities   At the end of 1973, commercial banks held $14.5 billion or about 9 percent of their total investments in federal agency securities. This represented about 24 percent of the outstanding notes and bonds (including participation certificates) of federally-sponsored agencies such as Federal Intermediate Credit Banks, Federal National Mortgage Association, Federal Land Banks, Banks for Cooperatives, and Federal Home Loan Banks. The yields on these bonds are slightly higher than those of Treasury obligations, but because of their moral support by the federal government, these obligations have little risk and good marketability. The growth in the amounts of these issues outstanding, together with their higher yields than straight federal securities, has undoubtedly contributed to the relative decline of federal securities in bank portfolios alluded to earlier. Changes in the credit financing arrangements instituted in 1974 (see Chapter 8) as well as greater emphasis on programs funded by federal credit agencies promise that these securities will most likely continue as important assets in bank portfolios.

State and local government obligations   "Municipal" bonds constitute the largest single holding in investment securities by banks. In contrast to the relative decline in federal bond investments, holdings of state and local government bonds have risen 60 percent since 1968 and at the end of 1973 totaled $95.1 billion, or 50 percent of total investments and 11 percent of total assets. This increase reflects a number of factors: (1) the great growth of state and local government borrowing since World War II (banks are the principal market for the bonds of smaller municipalities); (2) the attractive yields of "tax exempts" compared to the after-tax yield on other bonds; (3) the good investment record of these bonds; (4) the variety of serial maturities available; and (5) the increasing activity of the banks in the underwriting and distribution of municipals.[5] The chief disadvantage of municipals is their lack of a good secondary market. Most banks, however, hold such securities to maturity and in 1974 when yields on "munis" reached all-time highs and prices reached all-time lows, such a practice was virtually mandatory.

Banks are not limited in the amount of "investment merit" or qualified general obligatory bonds that they are permitted to own because such bonds are backed by the "full faith and credit" of the issuing governing body, which includes the power to tax. Member banks are restricted in investing in qualified state or local revenue bonds up to 10 percent of capital and surplus. This suggests that apparently the regulatory agencies feel that the additional yield does not offset the riskiness of the bonds as the funds for interest payments and principal amortization are based only on the revenues generated from the assets financed through sale of the revenue bonds.

In general, banks emphasize municipal bonds with maturities less than ten years. They do, however, adjust their purchases of tax exempt securities to meet loan demands and reserve requirements. Changing conditions in these two factors, together with the varying supply of state and local bonds resulting from bond elections, have a pronounced short-run effect on municipal bond yields (see Chapter 9). In the long run, the countercyclical tendency of banks to invest in municipal securities when their own liquidity is high (and interest rates are low) rather than when yields are high provides a supporting influence on this market.

Commercial banks are the largest institutional owners of municipal securities. At the end of 1973, their holdings of $95.1 billion constituted slightly more than 50 percent of total state and local debt (see Table 9–1).

Corporate bonds and other securities   At the end of 1973, commercial banks held $6.2 billion in corporate bonds and other securities, constituting about 3 percent of their investments and less than 1 percent of their total assets. This was almost double the amount held two years earlier, reflecting the appeal of the very high interest rates in these securities that have prevailed since 1969. The lack of bank activity in the corporate bond market is explained by the high standards of quality and marketability required by law and regulation for investment in these obligations, by the greater appeal of federal obligations for safety and liquidity, by the favorable after-tax yields

---

[5] Banks are permitted to act as principals in underwriting new municipal issues, excluding revenue bonds.

on state and local government bonds, and by the growth of term loans. The demand for corporate bonds by tax-exempt institutions (for example, pension funds) or by those enjoying light income-tax rates (such as life insurance companies) has driven down the yields on high-grade corporate bonds to a level where they are unattractive to the fully taxed banks (see p. 173). Larger issues of high-grade corporate bonds do offer good marketability; but the longer maturities involve more price risk than do alternative investments. Railway equipment obligations, with their serial maturities are, however, attractive to banks, their principal owners. Despite some recent relaxation of the rules, convertible bonds are not attractive; banks are not allowed to pay more than the "investment" or straight bond value for such securities and rates are often lower than those for competing instruments.

At the end of 1973, commercial banks held less than 3 percent of corporate bonds outstanding (see Chapter 10). Except for rare occasions, banks are not permitted to buy corporate stocks as investments.[6] They do, however, influence the prices and yields of stocks through the volume of loans used to purchase or to carry securities and through the discretionary power they have in managing personal trust accounts.

Annual Uses of Funds
in the Capital Market, 1965–1973

The annual net changes in bank holdings of capital-market investments are shown in Table 3–5. The data include all maturities of federal securities. The most pronounced increases are found in municipal bonds where during relatively slack periods, such as 1970 to 1971, banks seek investment outlets. In the 1970 to 1973 period, banks tended to place similar dollar amounts into home and other mortgages, term loans to business, and federally-sponsored agency securities even though the relaitve percentage additions in these corresponding securities differed substantially. Again the high dollar amounts invested by banks in other mortgages in the 1970s can be traced, in part, as noted earlier, to business firms needing funds and willing to mortgage their assets, if necessary, in order to secure the loans and to the growth in interim construction financing. In fact, during the period from 1969 to 1973, mortgages made to nonfinancial businesses increased by

---

[6] Exceptions are ownership of stock in Federal Reserve banks by member banks, stock in affiliates, and a few miscellaneous types. For instance, various statutory provisions explicitly authorize national banks to buy stock of particular organizations, such as safe deposit companies, bank premises subsidiaries, small business investment companies, and so on.

more than 44 percent and about matched in dollar amounts the total allocated to commercial and industrial loans.[7]

TABLE 3–5. Annual Changes in Capital-Market Assets, Commercial Banks, 1965–1973 (billions of dollars)

	1965	1966	1967	1968	1969	1970	1971	1972	1973
U.S. government securities [a]	$–3.0	$–3.4	$ 6.3	$ 2.0	$–9.8	$ 7.0	$ 3.2	$ 2.1	$–8.8
Federally-sponsored agency securities	0.6	0.3	2.9	1.2	–0.3	3.5	3.8	4.0	7.5
State and local government bonds	5.2	2.3	9.1	8.6	0.2	10.7	12.6	7.1	5.6
Term loans to business [b]	4.4	2.7	2.9	4.5	5.8	2.3	2.0	6.7	7.8
Corporate bonds	–0.1	0.1	0.8	0.3	–0.1	0.2	1.3	1.7	0.4
Home mortgages	3.1	2.4	2.4	3.5	3.0	0.7	5.6	9.0	11.0
Other mortgages	2.5	2.3	2.2	3.2	2.4	1.6	4.2	7.8	8.7
Total	$ 12.7	$ 6.8	$26.5	$23.3	$ 0.9	$26.0	$32.7	$38.4	$ 32.2

[a] Inter-bank items deducted.
[b] To nonfinancial corporations.
Sources: Federal Deposit Insurance Corporation, *Annual Reports; Federal Reserve Bulletin.* Term loans from Bankers Trust Company, *Credit and Capital Markets* (New York, annual). (Some columns do not add to totals because of rounding.)

As expected, the greatest variation is found in holdings of Treasury securities, which show substantial increases in recession years such as 1967 and substantial decreases in expansion periods such as 1966, 1969 and 1973 as banks moved to fund customer loan requests.

The variation in savings and time deposits materially influences the investment policies of banks. In such years as 1967, banks were able to supply rising demands for business, housing, and consumer credit without liquidating federal securities and were able at the same time to record increases in their holdings of state and local government bonds and mortgages. In 1969, however, liquidation of Treasury securities was necessary in order to (1) increase investment in higher-yielding assets in order to cover the higher interest costs on savings accounts, (2) accommodate the demand for loans, and (3) aid the liquidity management of banks that, in the aggregate endured net savings and time deposit withdrawals of over $9 billion in 1969 (Table 3–2).

The tight money conditions in 1966 and 1969, reflected in Table 3–5, show that only $6.8 billion and $0.9 billion of capital-market assets were added, respectively, in these periods. One of the reasons

---

[7] See "Recent Patterns of Corporate External Financing," *Federal Reserve Bulletin,* December 1973, pp. 837–46.

for the sharp drop in banks' savings deposits in 1969 was a result of the interest rate ceiling imposed by bank regulators. To correct this situation, the rates allowed on bank time and savings deposits were substantially liberalized in January 1970. The result of this rate relaxation was an unprecedented growth in bank time deposits in 1970 through 1974, much higher rates on time deposits among all competing institutions and ultimately, higher interest rates, in general, on bank loans of all types. For example, the "prime" rate reached a high of 12 percent (12¼ in a few instances) in July 1974.

Flexible Rate Notes

In order to compete more effectively for savings dollars, several major banks offered flexible-rate notes in 1974. Although receiving a less than enthusiastic reception from banking authorities and strong opposition from other financial institutions, about $1 billion of these notes were sold. The notes guaranteed the holder a specified return usually for a minimum of 6 months and then a variable return based on the general level of interest rates thereafter until maturity. The flexible-rate notes allowed the investor to hedge his investments against rapidly changing interest rates while at the same time committing his funds for longer periods of time of up to about two years.

Bank Holding Companies and
Implications for Banking

Historically, banking laws have prohibited banks from engaging in nonbanking activities. The justification was that the fiduciary responsibility of banks in protecting depositors' funds and the need for bank soundness was so overriding as to require laws confining the business of banking to banking only, and prohibiting banks from engaging in extraneous business such as owning and operating industrial firms. It was feared that, if this was not done, pressures might force banks to make loans to favor customers of subsidiary businesses or make unreasonable loans to businesses they own.

To avoid and otherwise obviate certain provisions of the laws, many banks formed holding companies that held the stock of the subsidiary bank. The holding company itself, then, was free to acquire other firms and engage in any other type of business. Only the bank, being a subsidiary engaged in banking, was within the banking laws.

This loophole was closed by the Bank Holding Company Act of 1956 that essentially reestablished the traditional separation of banking and nonbanking activities by prohibiting a bank holding company from acquiring any shares of any company that was not a bank. Recognizing, however, that a strict interpretation of the laws could be too damaging, the act allowed bank holding companies to engage in business activities that were *closely related to banking*. In general, this was interpreted to mean (1) investing in companies that furnish or perform services directly for the bank holding company, such as auditing or investment counseling firms, (2) acquiring companies or buying stock in firms such as safe deposit companies, or (3) acquiring shares of firms whose activities are solely of a financial, fiduciary, or insurance nature and are "closely related" to the banking business, such as firms writing credit life insurance for a bank's customers.

In the 1956 act and in an amendment in 1966, Congress specifically exempted one-bank holding companies, feeling that including them would conflict with the objective of fostering local ownership of unit banks, as local banks are frequently owned by people engaged in other forms of business. A problem with the one-bank holding company exemption that became acute in the late sixties during the surge of conglomeration and the merger wave was that several firms that acquired one large bank only were exempt from the law. The loophole grew to such magnitude that the assets of one-bank holding companies soon exceeded the assets of those covered by the Banking Holding Company Act.

A growing fear that the conglomerate firms were going to acquire many of the large banks provided the catalyst for an amendment to the act in 1970 that closed the loophole and placed one-bank holding companies under the act's control. As a result, one-bank holding companies can now engage only in banking and in activities closely related to abnking.

At the same time, however, the amendment (1970) considerably broadened the Federal Reserve Board's interpretive powers in determining which activities are closely allied with banking. So far the board's decisions have given banks considerable latitude in engaging in businesses such as insurance, investment counseling, courier services, and so on, such that in the future these activities could add significantly to the operating income of banks.

Traditionally, banks have relied on income from loans to individuals and businesses, and investment income to supply the bulk of operating revenues. In 1969, these two sources provided better than 88 percent of bank income (Table 3–6) while other income amounted to only 5.4 percent. In 1973, despite rapid growth in loans and investment securities held by banks, income from other sources rose to $3.4 billion or 6.5 percent of bank operating income.

The implication of these figures and the favorable interpretations by the Federal Reserve Board pertaining to "closely allied activities" under the Banking Holding Company Act is that banks are increasingly expanding their nonbanking functions, which means increasing competition for other financial intermediaries. This appears to be consistent with the general government policy of encouraging increased

TABLE 3–6. Sources of Income of Insured Commercial Banks 1960–1973 (billions of dollars)

	1960		1965		1970		1973	
	Amount	Percentage	Amount	Percentage	Amount	Percentage	Amount	Percentage
Interest on loans	$ 5.9	63.6	$11.2	66.7	$23.9	65.7	$37.7	71.4
Interest on securities	2.3	21.5	3.5	20.8	6.6	21.3	9.1	17.2
Service charges and fees	.8	7.5	1.2	7.0	2.0	6.1	2.6	4.9
Other income [a]	.7	6.5	.9	5.5	2.1	6.9	3.4	6.5
Total operating income	$10.7	100 %	$16.8	100 %	$34.6	100 %	$52.8	100 %

[a] Other income includes trust department income, income from trading accounts, and from other sources.
Source: *Federal Reserve Bulletin*. (Some figures may not add to totals due to rounding.)

competition among all financial intermediaries by removing traditional legal barriers or modifying existing policies.

Federal Reserve Banks

Capital-Market Functions

Although the Federal Reserve banks have their greatest direct influence in the short-term money market, some discussion of them is pertinent to our study, on several grounds: (1) these institutions invest some of the funds representing member bank and Treasury deposits in intermediate- and long-term credits and so may be classed as financial intermediaries; (2) the Reserve banks are the third largest institutional owners of United States government obligations; (3) their credit policy has an important impact on the prices and yields of long-term securities and mortgages; (4) their open-market operations in Treasury securities now involve longer-term obligations; and (5) as fiscal agents for the Treasury, they play an important role in the marketing of federal securities.

Sources of Federal Reserve Funds

Member bank deposits, Treasury deposits, Federal Reserve notes, and capital accounts provide the funds for the investments of the banks in securities and other assets. Member banks are required (1974) to hold reserves ranging from 8 to 18 percent of their demand deposits depending on asset size—8 percent for banks with less than $2 million in demand deposits up to 18 percent for reserve city banks.[8] They hold 3 percent of savings and from 3 to 5 percent of time deposits— again depending on size of total time deposits and time deposits at the Federal Reserve banks of their districts, less some vault cash counted as reserve. At the end of 1973, member bank reserve deposits totaled $28.4 billion, or nearly 28 percent of Federal Reserve assets. Their increase since 1945 (from $15.5 billion) reflects the growth of

---

[8] Effective Nov. 9, 1972, a new criterion was adopted to designate reserve cities, and on the same date requirements for reserves against net demand deposits of member banks were restructured to provide that each member bank will maintain reserves related to the size of its net demand deposits. The new reserve city designations are as follows: A bank having net demand deposits of more than $400 million is considered to have the character of business of a reserve city bank, and the presence of the head office of such a bank constitutes designation of that place as a reserve city. Cities in which there are F.R. banks or branches are also reserve cities. Any banks having net demand deposits of $400 million or less are considered to have the character of business of banks outside of reserve cities and are permitted to maintain reserves at ratios set for banks not in reserve cities. For details, see Regulation D and appropriate supplements and amendments. (See *Federal Reserve Bulletin.*)

bank deposit liabilities, offset by reductions in member bank reserve requirements. The size of reserve accounts is also influenced by the composition of the deposits of the member banks (demand versus time).

Federal Reserve notes outstanding totaled $64.3 billion, or 62 percent of assets at the end of 1973; capital stock and other capital accounts totaled $1.7 billion.

Two cautions should be indicated here: (1) It is appropriate to think of the liabilities of the central banks as the result of asset acquisition rather than vice versa. "Federal Reserve funds" are supplied by Federal Reserve bank credit outstanding (United States government securities held, discounts and advances, and float), gold stock, and Treasury currency outstanding, and are absorbed by currency in circulation (including Federal Reserve notes), deposits (including reserves of member banks), and minor accounts. (2) In any consolidation of banking system funds, that is, where funds of commercial and central banks are combined, the member bank reserve deposits at the Federal Reserve banks are eliminated to avoid double counting. Such deposits are not additions to the deposits of the member banks on which they are based. For this reason we omit any annual sources of funds data for Federal Reserve banks similar to the data presented for other institutions.

All liabilities of Federal Reserve banks should be considered as very short term, and so their assets must be highly liquid. For this reason, the chief impact of the Reserve banks on the capital markets is more indirect (through other financial intermediaries) than direct.

Uses of Funds: Ownership of
United States Government Obligations

The Federal Reserve banks play a direct role in the capital market through their holdings of federal and agency securities (the only securities they own). Federal securities held have increased from $52.9 billion in 1968 to more than $78.5 billion at the end of 1973. Annual changes in ownership of direct and guaranteed federal debt in the period 1965 through 1973 were as follows (in billions of dollars): [9]

	1965	1966	1976	1968	1969	1970	1971	1972	1973
U.S. Government obligations	$3.8	$3.5	$4.8	$3.8	$4.2	$5.0	$8.1	−$0.3	$8.6
Obligations of federally-sponsored agencies	—	—	—	—	—	—	0.4	0.6	0.7
	$3.8	$3.5	$4.8	$3.8	$4.2	$5.0	$8.5	$0.3	$9.3

All federal securities held are fully marketable, and maturities of five years or less constituted almost 90 percent of total holdings at the end

---

[9] *Federal Reserve Bulletin.*

of 1973. This is in contrast to December 1968 when 78 percent of total holdings were in maturities of five years or less. This indicated a shift towards shorter maturities and also implied little activity by the Federal Reserve officials in influencing rates on long-term debt.

Unlike private lending institutions, Federal Reserve banks do not seek the highest yields. Investment decisions are based on factors such as money supply, market stability etc. rather than the availability of profitable outlets for their funds.

Influence on Market Yields

The chief influence of the Reserve banks in the long-term capital markets is through the impact of their credit policy on the loan and investment activities of banks and other financial intermediaries. Changes in the reserve requirements of member banks (sporadic), in the discount rate (more frequent), and in the volume and direction of open-market operations (purchase or sale) of federal securities (almost continuous) all influence the size of member bank reserve deposits and thus encourage the contraction of expansion of member bank lending activity. The second and third of these types of credit control have a specific influence on bank loan rates and other short-term rates in the money market. They influence the volume and yields of intermediate-term loans and mortgages as a part of total bank loans.[10]

The immediate impact of changing Federal Reserve credit policy is felt on short-term interest rates. Thus the increases in the discount rate to 8 percent in August 1973 and to $8\frac{1}{2}$ percent in April, 1974, for member banks were designed to stiffen short-term market rates as part of the program for curbing credit expansion. The most sensitive short-term rates, those on Treasury bills, serve as bellwether rates for other short-term instruments.

The most continuous tool of credit control is open-market operations. From 1953 to early 1961, the purchases and sales of Treasury obligations directed by the Open Market Committee (OMC) were concentrated on "bills only." It was felt that any change in short-term interest rates would, through arbitrage and substitution, eventually make itself felt in yields on longer-term Treasury obligations and, by arbitration, on other bond yields. In 1961, the "bills only" policy was abandoned in favor of direct intervention in the long-term markets. But the extent of such intervention has been modest, and, in fact, since 1968 the actions of the OMC have been directed almost entirely to the short-term market.

Occasional attempts have been made by the OMC to adjust long-

---

[10] Changes in the Federal Reserve discount rate have an even more direct effect on the volume of and interest rates on term loans whose contractual rate is tied to the discount rate.

term rates while not appreciably affecting short-term rates or pushing short-term rates in the opposite direction. Thus, the OMC in conjunction with the Treasury undertook an "operation twist" in 1962 through 1964, where short-term rates were nudged upward (chiefly through the Treasury policy of emphasizing the sale of short maturities), and long-term rates were held firm, in keeping the Administration's desire to encourage domestic economic growth. During this period (1962–1964) the Federal Reserve banks increased their holdings of long-term federal bonds substantially to aid in this objective. In 1973 through 1974, the policy again shifted towards short-term securities as short-term rates were kept high to help combat inflation.

Changes in the general level of interest rates affect the prices of long-term instruments more than those of short-term assets and also lead to shifts among types of assets on the part of investing institutions.[11] A restrictive credit policy that eventually results in higher long-term yields encourages institutions to shift from Treasury issues to the more lucrative mortgages, corporate bonds, and municipal bonds. However, if the flow of savings funds is declining, such shifts are discouraged by the risk of price losses. The volume of forward commitments in mortgages also declines as institutions wait for higher yields in the future.

Marketing Federal Securities

The Federal Reserve banks participate directly in the marketing of federal securities. They receive the applications of banks, dealers, and others for new issues of federal securities, allot them in accordance with Treasury instructions, deliver them, receive payment, and credit the Treasury accounts (see Chapter 8). The banks redeem federal securities as they mature, pay interest coupons, and otherwise service the debt.

---

[11] A change from a 5 percent to a 6 percent yield would cause the price of a one-year obligation selling at par to drop to 99.04; a twenty-year 5 percent bond selling at par would decline to 88.44.

```
44444444444444444444444444444444444444444444444444444444444444444444444444444444
44444444444444444444444444444444444444444444444444444444444444444444444444444444
4444444444444444444444444444444    444    444444444444    44444444444444444444444444444444
44444444444444444444444444444444    4444    4444444444444    44444444444444444444444444444444
44444444444444444444444444444444    44444    444444444    44444444444444444444444444444444
44444444444444444444444444444444    444444    4444444    44444444444444444444444444444444
44444444444444444444444444444444    4444444    44444    44444444444444444444444444444444
44444444444444444444444444444444    4444444    444    44444444444444444444444444444444
44444444444444444444444444444444    444444444    4    44444444444444444444444444444444
44444444444444444444444444444444    444444444        44444444444444444444444444444444
44444444444444444444444444444444    4444444444    44444444444444444444444444444444444
44444444444444444444444444444444    44444444444    4444444444444444444444444444444444
44444444444444444444444444444444444444444444444444444444444444444444444444444444
44444444444444444444444444444444444444444444444444444444444444444444444444444444
```

Savings Banks
and Associations

THIS chapter discusses two types of savings institutions—mutual savings banks and savings and loan associations—whose emphasis on investment in mortgages, their similarities in structure, regulation, taxation, and savings plans frequently make them legal and political partners in the competitive struggle with other financial institutions. They differ from their chief rivals, commercial banks, in that their regulation is quite different, their turnover of deposits is less than that of commercial banks, and they focus primarily on mortgages.

Several recent studies have focused on the major problems confronting mutual savings banks (MSBs) and savings and loan associations (S&L's) in their competition for savings particularly with commercial banks. In recent years, commercial banks have been allowed to compete effectively with MSBs and S&L's for the savings of individuals. This has had a serious impact on these latter institutions in attracting deposits. MSBs and S&L's are not legally authorized to offer certain types of financial services, such as checking accounts, which penalizes them in seeking additional profitability. The problems facing MSB and S&L institutions in their quest for greater flexibility and profitability are discussed later in the chapter.

It is easy to get the impression that MSBs and S&L's are so similar that they can be discussed as one institution. Actually, there are con-

siderable differences regarding their respective asset size and investment policies that warrant a separate discussion of each institution.
We shall examine the general nature and functions, and sources and
uses of funds for each before turning to the joint problems faced by
them in competing with other financial institutions.

Mutual Savings Banks

General Nature and Functions

At the beginning of 1974, there were 482 mutual savings banks
chartered in seventeen states (mostly in the middle Atlantic states and
New England) and one in Puerto Rico, with total assets of $106.7
billion. Including 1,492 branches, 1,974 offices were operating, serving
nearly 28 million deposit accounts. Nearly three-quarters of the banks
were located in three states (New York, Massachusetts, and Connecticut) and held over four-fifths of the combined assets.

Though chartering of mutual savings banks is currently limited to
seventeen states, their investment operations have been national in
scope. In 1972, mutual savings banks held $18.6 billion, or 28 percent
of their total mortgage portfolio, in loans on properties located in the
thirty-three nonsavings bank states.[1]

Mutual savings banks are the only deposit institution functioning
solely under state charter. They are owned by depositors, who receive
all earnings after provision for adequate reserves. Management is in
the hands of boards of trustees.

Two basic functions of a mutual savings bank are to serve as a safe
depository for the thrift savings of individuals and to invest funds for
the maximum yield consistent with safety. Ancillary activities include
the sale of life insurance by banks in New York, Massachusetts, and
Connecticut.

Sources of Investment Funds

Savings deposits provide the funds for over 90 percent of the assets.
The balance, general reserve accounts, consists of retained earnings
reserved by law (such as the "Surplus Fund" in New York banks) or
restricted by management, plus contingency reserves and undivided
profits.[2] The ratio of general reserve accounts to deposits is the basic
measure of safety. For all MSBs it averaged 7.9 percent at the end of
1973 (Table 4–1). This ratio tends to fall during periods of rapid

---

[1] National Association of Mutual Savings Banks, *National Fact Book, 1974,* p. 56.
[2] In our balance sheet data, reserves against securities and mortgages are deducted from the value of assets to which they belong.

deposit expansion and good loan demand and rise when the opposite holds.

TABLE 4–1.   Combined Deposits and Reserve Accounts of
Mutual Savings Banks, at Year End, 1955–1973
(billions of dollars)

	1955	1960	1965	1970	1973
Deposits (savings and time)	$28.2	$36.5	$52.4	$71.6	$ 96.5
General reserves	2.8	3.6	4.7	5.7	7.6
Total	$31.0	$40.0	$57.1	$77.3	$104.1

Sources: *Federal Reserve Bulletin;* National Association of Mutual Savings Banks, *National Fact Book of Mutual Savings Banking* (New York, annual).

From 1955 through 1973, the total deposits of mutual savings banks increased from $28.2 billion to $96.5 billion, representing a compounded growth rate of over 7 percent per year. Deposit turnover was traditionally slow, averaging 33 percent per year, or once in every three years, or about one-half that of the savings accounts at commercial banks. Recently the turnover rate for mutual savings banks has increased to over 50 percent as rapidly changing interest rates have caused savings depositors to seek higher yielding investments elsewhere.[3]

Deposit growth, particularly since 1966, has been very erratic, tending to be high (1) when overall interest rate levels are relatively low, (2) when MSBs are paying about 1 percent more than commercial banks on savings deposits, or (3) when rates paid on savings deposits have been increased by all institutions. Deposit growth has been low, or even declining, when opposite conditions hold in the financial markets. In 1973–1974, for example, a massive loss of deposits to other types of investments was caused by high interest rates on competing securities.

During the postwar period, growth of MSB deposits fell behind the growth in savings accounts of commercial banks, the reserves of life insurance companies, and sharply behind the growth of accounts in savings and loan associations. This stems from mutual savings banks' lack of national exposure, from the specialized functions they perform, and from the lower interest rates paid on deposits.

In order to meet the competition of commercial banks and other institutions, MSBs and S&Ls in some states have been allowed to offer differentiated time deposits with varying yields depending on the amount deposited and the length of maturity.

---

[3] National Association of Mutual Savings Banks, *Mutual Savings Banking, National Fact Book 1974* (New York, 1974), p. 21.

Deposit Flows and Fluctuations

The annual increases in deposits and net worth accounts from 1965 through 1973 are shown in Table 4–2. As noted earlier, these increases have changed sharply from year to year even though during this period substantial funds have been provided for capital market investments.

TABLE 4–2. Annual Changes in Deposits and Reserves, Mutual Savings Banks, 1965–1973 (billions of dollars)

	1965	1966	1967	1968	1969	1970	1971	1972	1973
Deposits	$3.6	$2.6	$5.1	$4.2	$2.6	$4.4	$ 9.8	$10.2	$4.7
General reserves	0.3	0.2	0.1	0.3	0.3	0.2	0.4	0.6	0.6
Total	$3.9	$2.8	$5.2	$4.5	$2.9	$4.6	$10.2	$10.8	$5.3

Sources: National Association of Mutual Savings Banks, *National Fact Book of Mutual Savings Banks* (New York, annual); *Federal Reserve Bulletin.* (Flow of Funds.)

The decline in deposit flows from $3.9 billion in 1965 to $2.8 billion in 1966, although reflecting a sluggish economy, was chiefly attributable to the turbulence in the money and capital markets that culminated in the "credit crunch" in October of 1966. Available funds dried up, and with commercial banks paying higher rates on certificates of deposits, as well as higher rates on open-market securities, individuals in seeking higher returns transferred savings from thrift institutions to government securities and other financial institutions as interest rates rose to their highest levels in forty years. To meet severe strains on liquidity and earnings in 1966, mutual savings banks drew on the significant reserves built up in previous years and sold U.S. government securities.

In 1967, as a result of declining open-market interest rates, individuals reversed the procedure and shifted substantial funds from open-market instruments into savings accounts. For the year as a whole, the deposits of mutual savings banks increased by over $5 billion.

In 1968 through 1971 a pattern similar to that of the 1966 to 1967 period developed, when interest rates rose sharply in 1968 and 1969 and moderated in 1970 and 1971. The ebb and flow of funds into mutual savings banks followed accordingly. In 1969, as open-market short- and long-term yields reached historical highs, the flow of savings into mutual savings bank deposit accounts declined substantially. In contrast to the $4 to $5 billion annual increase in previous "normal" years, deposits grew only $2 billion in all of 1969. "Disintermediation," or the flow of savings to the open markets, reflected the greater appeal of high-yielding bonds and of equities, especially mutual funds.

The rate of increase in deposit funds in 1971 and 1972 was particularly strong as higher rates paid on deposits coupled with a cooling economy, a higher rate of individual savings as a percentage of disposable income, and general disenchantment with the stock and bond markets caused investors to place more funds in savings institutions.

Again, the same pattern developed in 1973 and 1974. As inflation in the economy and interest rates rose to all-time highs, mutual savings banks suffered a decline in growth of savings deposits to $4.7 billion in 1973 and then an absolute decline in deposits as disintermediation rose substantially. In April and May 1974, alone, savings banks suffered a staggering net deposit withdrawal of over $1.1 billion or more than one percent of total assets. This was followed by moderate net inflows in the last half of 1974.

Reserves of mutual savings banks have not kept pace with the growth in deposits because of the sharply increased tax liabilities that resulted from the 1969 tax act, the decline in earnings due to the higher interest rates paid on savings deposits during tight money periods, and government policies that have allowed lower reserve ratios aimed at encouraging home building.

Annual sources of funds for capital market investment   Deducting from the figures in Table 4–2 the net changes in cash and miscellaneous assets produces the following annual sources of new funds available for investment in capital market assets:

1965	1966	1967	1968	1969	1970	1971	1972	1973
$3.7	$2.5	$5.2	$4.3	$2.8	$3.7	$8.8	$9.7	$4.5

Such data on net changes do not represent the amount of funds actually used in capital-market transactions. The amortization of mortgages and the maturing of bonds, together with investment income, produce substantial additional funds for reinvestment.

General Investment Policy

The basic purposes of savings banks require that conservative policies of lending and investment be followed. Maximizing earnings is of secondary importance to safety of principal.

Although deposits turn over slowly, a substantial degree of liquidity must be maintained. The importance of the ultimate safety of assets explains the legal requirements that govern investment in securities and mortgages in the various states.[4] These regulations specify the eligible instruments, the standards of quality applied to each (except federal obligations, which automatically qualify), and the limitations on some major instruments as percentages of total assets or total deposits. In two states (Maryland and Delaware), the prudent-man rule applies; this rule, in theory, permits broad discretion but in fact results in the acquisition of high-grade investments. Legal restrictions limit the demand for certain securities (such as industrial bonds) and for mortgages, especially those originating out of state. These limitations restrict the flow of funds through the national capital markets and contribute to the differential yields among different categories of investments. Compared to savings and loan associations, however, mutual savings banks have considerably more latitude in their choice of investments.

Table 4–3 shows the amounts and distribution of industry assets for selected years beginning in 1960. During this period, major shifts took place in the investment powers of savings banks and in their role in the capital markets. Their most important impact is seen in the decline in the relative position of federal securities and mortgages as a result of improved yields among alternative capital-market instruments, especially corporate bonds.

The decline in federal securities is particularly evident. In 1950, federal securities amounted to $10.8 billion, or 48 percent of mutual savings banks assets. At the end of 1973, on an asset base of over $106 billion, they totaled only $3.0 billion or less than 3 percent of total assets.

The primary beneficiary of the decline in federal securities was mortgages, which rose from $8 billion in 1950 to $73.2 billion at the end of 1973. The percentage of assets held in mortgages rose from 36 percent in 1950 to a high of 76.2 percent in 1965 and then declined to 69 percent at the end of 1973. Thus, although the absolute amount invested in mortgages by mutual savings banks has continued to increase yearly since 1965, there has been a relative decline in the percentage of new funds placed in mortgages.

The data in Table 4–3 do not reveal the interim cyclical changes in flow of funds into assets that reflected variations in relative yield differentials among alternative capital-market instruments, especially the differences between the changing yields on corporate and municipal bonds and the relatively inflexible yields on mortgages. During periods of credit stringency, such as 1966 through 1969, and 1973 and 1974, the emphasis on new investment was in the former category as the

---

[4] For a convenient discussion of legal lists, see National Association of Mutual Savings Banks, *Mutual Savings Banking: Basic Characteristics and Role in the National Economy,* a monograph prepared for the Commission on Money and Credit (Englewood Cliffs, N.J.: Prentice-Hall, Inc., 1962), Chap. 5.

TABLE 4–3. Combined Assets of Mutual Savings Banks, Amounts and Percentages, at Year End, 1960–1973 (billions of dollars)

	1960		1965		1970		1973	
Cash assets	$ 0.9	2.2%	$ 1.0	1.5%	$ 1.3	1.6%	$ 2.0	1.9%
Mortgage loans (net)	26.9	66.2	44.4	76.2	57.8	73.0	73.2	68.6
U.S. government obligations	6.2	15.3	5.5	9.4	3.2	4.1	3.0	2.8
Bonds of federal agencies and corporations	0.5	1.2	0.8	1.4	1.7	2.2	2.3	2.2
State and local government bonds	0.7	1.7	0.3	0.5	0.2	0.3	0.9	0.8
Corporate bonds	3.8	9.4	2.9	5.3	8.3	10.5	13.1	12.3
Other securities	—	—	—	—	0.2	0.2	2.0	1.9
Preferred stocks	0.3	0.8	0.4	0.7	0.7	0.9	1.2	1.1
Common stocks	0.5	1.2	1.0	1.8	1.8	2.3	2.8	2.6
Other assets	0.8	2.0	1.8	3.2	3.8	4.9	6.2	5.8
Total	$40.6	100 %	$58.2	100 %	$79.0	100 %	$106.7	100 %

Sources: *Federal Reserve Bulletin*; National Association of Mutual Savings Banks, *National Fact Book of Mutual Savings Banking* (annual).

spread in yields declined; during periods of credit ease and of lower yields, the emphasis moves towards mortgage investment.

In recent years, mutual savings banks have placed large amounts of their new funds into corporate bonds as the yields on these instruments rose to match or exceed mortgage yields. The liquidity offered by corporate bonds compared to mortgages was also an important factor. More recently, mutual savings banks have been adding significant amounts of tax-exempt state and local issues in response to sharply increased income taxes. With rising income tax rates for mutual savings banks as a result of the 1969 tax act, tax-exempt securities should become considerably more important as an investment holding.

The relative importance of major types of assets varies considerably among banks domiciled in different states because of differences in legal list requirements, strictness of supervision, need for liquidity, rate of supply of funds, and local investment opportunities. For example, of the major states, the banks in Connecticut have the highest percentage of assets in mortgages (73 percent in 1973) and those in Pennsylvania the highest percentage in corporate securities (23 percent in 1973); those in Maryland have the highest percentage in United States government securities (7 percent in 1973).[5] A major drive for federal chartering of mutual banks (not yet approved) was to broaden and unify investment powers and to make funds available in a wider national market.

Securities Investments

Historically, savings banks have played a relatively minor role in the securities markets, which include bonds of all types and stocks. Although these securities have grown in importance due to their higher yields, they still constitute only about 24 percent of total savings bank assets. As noted earlier, within this group (until 1974) there has been a shift away from low-yielding federal securities towards a new emphasis on corporate bonds. Lower liquidity reserve requirements than for commercial banks meant that less emphasis need be placed on cash and that secondary reserves could consist of longer-maturity bonds. The pressure for ultimate safety requires high standards for corporate bonds; however, shifting between bonds and mortgages and among bonds does occur, reflecting the availability of funds and changes in the relative yields on different investments.

Unlike life insurance companies, which acquire large amounts of corporate bonds by private placement, savings banks obtain these securities mainly in the open market and so turn to that market for funds when resale is indicated.

---

[5] National Association of Mutual Savings Banks, *National Fact Book of Mutual Savings Banking* (1974), p. 9.

United States government securities   Federal obligations were typically held for safety, liquidity, and income. They reached their peak of popularity at the end of World War II because of the efforts of the banks to aid in war financing and the lack of a good supply of mortgages and corporate bonds. As noted earlier, the great postwar movement into the higher-yielding mortgages reduced the combined holdings of federal obligations from 63 percent of total assets in 1945 to only 2.8 percent at the end of 1973.

Savings banks have traditionally held federal securities for liquidity rather than for earnings. Bonds with a maturity of five years or less constitute more than 75 percent of total federal securities held (1973). Savings banks' holdings of long-term federal securities continued their long decline in 1973 and 1974 due to the more favorable yields available on other short-term instruments.

Corporate bonds   Holdings of corporate and foreign bonds have increased both relatively and absolutely in the postwar period. At the end of 1973 they totaled $15.1 billion or 14.2 percent of total assets. This was almost double the holdings of corporate bonds in 1970 and represented a change in holdings of $6 billion for this period. This was second only to the change of $15 billion in mortgages during this time (but mortgages declined to 68.6 per cent of total assets). The high rate of interest paid on corporate bonds in recent years has been responsible for the continued relative shift from mortgages to bonds. As of December 1974, the composite rate on corporate bonds was 9.50 percent versus an average rate of 9.80 percent on new home mortgages. Because of their liquidity compared to mortgages, corporate bonds serve as secondary liquidity sources and often are sold in periods of outflows as in 1973–74.

Other securities investments   Holdings of other securities investments by savings banks represent a small percentage of total assets.

As noted previously municipal bonds have increased in importance as savings banks sought to minimize the effects of the 1969 tax act. These securities, although representing less than 1 percent of total assets at the end of 1973, have more than doubled in size since 1970. Similarly, federal agency securities have increased in importance due to their high yields, low risk, and increasing abundance as federal programs have encouraged functions financed by federal agencies. The purchase of corporate stocks was fostered in 1951 by the imposition of income taxation on mutual savings banks, giving dividend income (which is 85 percent exempt) a special appeal and by changes in state laws that made modest amounts of selected common stocks eligible for purchase. At the end of 1973, savings banks held $2.8 billion in common stock and $1.2 billion in preferred stock. Given the fiduciary responsibility of savings banks, however, it is not likely that preferred or common stock, regardless of the potential yields, will ever amount to anything more than a token investment for savings banks.

Mortgage Investments—General Policy

Sound mortgages as part of a larger portfolio are good investments for savings banks except in times of rapid inflation when high interest rates cause disintermediation resulting in cash flow problems. Normally, liquidity is provided by holdings of federal securities and by careful management of cash flows. When disintermediation occurs, sales of all kinds of investments including sales of mortgages in the secondary market are frequently necessary to generate the needed liquidity. At the end of 1973, mutual savings banks held $73.2 billion, or 11.5 percent, of the total outstanding mortgage debt of $635.1 billion and $44.2 billion, or 11.4 percent, of the $386.5 billion of the one-to-four family residential debt outstanding. Real estate loans constituted 69 percent of their combined assets in 1973, a drop of four percentage points since 1970 (see Table 4–4).

TABLE 4–4. Mortgage Loans Held by Mutual Savings Banks, at Year End, 1960–1973 (billions of dollars)

	1960	1965	1970	1973
Farm	a	a	$ 0.1	$ 0.1
Residential:				
One-to-four family	$18.4	$30.2	$37.5	44.2
Multifamily	5.9	10.1	12.4	16.8
	$24.3	$40.3	$49.9	61.0
Commercial and industrial	2.6	4.3	7.9	12.1
Total	$26.9	$44.6	$57.9	73.2
Conventional and other	$10.9	$19.4	$29.8	44.5
FHA-insured	7.0	13.8	16.1	15.8
VA-guaranteed	9.0	11.4	12.0	12.9
Total	$26.9	$44.6	$57.9	$73.2

ª Less than $100 million.
Sources: *Federal Reserve Bulletin;* National Association of Mutual Savings Banks, *National Fact Book of Mutual Savings Banking* (1974).

The big postwar growth in mortgages (see Table 4–4) reflects a number of factors: (1) the increase in deposits and, therefore, of assets, (2) the great postwar demand for housing credit, (3) the development of amortized federally-underwritten liens, (4) the relatively attractive yields on mortgages as compared to other securities, (5) the liberalization of regulations governing investment in mortgages whereby loan-to-value ratios for conventional mortgages have risen to 80 percent in most states, (6) the growth of private mortgage insurance, and (7) the increasing practice of out-of-state lending, which began between 1949 and 1950 and has been facilitated by greater use of local mortgage company correspondents. In 1974 the rate of lending slowed down dramatically, reflecting the low level of housing starts and the tightness of mortgage money.

In the past, mutual savings banks sought to maximize earnings (and hence the rate paid to depositors) by setting as high a ratio of mortgages to total assets as regulations and local demand allow and by seeking outside outlets for mortgages funds. This has changed somewhat as mortgage yields no longer exceed the levels of several other competing investments.

Residential and Commercial Mortgages

Residential loans have typically accounted for better than 85 percent of total mortgage holdings by savings banks with commercial mortgages representing the remainder. At the end of 1973, residential mortgages totaled $61 billion and commercial and industrial mortgages $12 billion (Table 4–4). The percentage of commercial mortgages in the portfolio has risen in the 1970s as a result of the higher interest rates generally available on these mortgages compared to residential mortgages.

Mutual savings banks are the largest single private source of federally-underwritten home loans. At the end of 1973, they held $28.7 billion of FHA-insured and VA-guaranteed mortgages, or over 21 percent of the combined total. These mortgages have declined in importance since 1968 as savings banks have placed more funds in conventional loans. Prime reasons for this shift were (1) the "maximum" rates allowed on FHA and VA loans that lagged behind conventional rates and were less than the going mortgage market, (2) the delay and extra paperwork in closing FHA and VA mortgage loans, and (3) the rise of conventional mortgage insurance that allowed high mortgage to value ratios, offsetting a previous FHA and VA advantage, with little risk to savings banks.

The increase in the contractual rate on government-insured loans to its peak of 9½ percent in 1974 was designed to maintain investment in federally-sponsored liens, but continued increases in market yields left these liens in a poor competitive position (see Figure 12–1). In addition, efforts have been made to reduce the paperwork and processing delays on government-insured loans. However, as the private sector can now offer most of the benefits of government-insured loans with respect to downpayments and insurance guarantees, it is expected that savings banks will continue to prefer the private market and place most of their mortgage funds in conventional mortgages.

Annual Uses of Funds in the Capital Market

The data in Table 4–5 show the annual changes in capital market investments for 1965 through 1973. The comparatively low net changes in 1966 and again in 1969 reflect the credit squeezes of those years. Large increases in total funds flows in 1971 and 1972 reflect the slowed economy and lower rates on securities competing directly with savings deposits. The sharp use in competing rates in the latter half of 1973 and in 1974 led to the predictable decline in mutual savings banks growth.

Again, the data show a preponderance of total funds placed in mortgages with commercial mortgages receiving considerable sums in recent years. This was attributed to the higher rates on commercial mortgages as well as a lower total supply of home mortgages during this period. High purchases of corporate bonds in 1970–1972 turned to net sales of $1 billion in 1973 as savings banks met liquidity requirements and mortgage commitments.

Savings Banks in the National Capital Markets

Although savings banks are chartered in only seventeen states and Puerto Rico, they have asserted some influence in the mortgage market at the national level. Interstate lending, formerly dominated by life insurance companies, has achieved major proportions. As noted previously, at the end of 1972, approximately $18.6 billion or 28 percent of the savings banks mortgage portfolios were held in the 33 nonsavings bank states. Most out-of-state loans are acquired from mortgage companies that retain the servicing of the loans (see Chapter 12). Relaxed regulations permitting out-of-state loans, together with the growing use of correspondents, have done much to break down geographical barriers. Many smaller banks confine their lending operations to their local communities. But the larger eastern banks are active exporters of capital to capital-deficient areas such as the Southwest and the West.

In addition, savings banks have been participating in the national mortgage market by recently purchasing substantial amounts of Government National Mortgage Association (called "Ginnie Mae") securities (see Chapter 12). These securities are backed by government-insured (FHA and VA and Farmers Home Administration) mortgages and hence are fully guaranteed by the U.S. government. The mortgages are pooled and a covering security is issued. The principal and interest on the Ginnie Mae security is paid by the repayments from the underlying pool of FHA and VA mortgages. Holdings of these investments by savings banks totalled $1.9 billion in 1973; this represents the second largest investment in GNMA-guaranteed mortgage-backed securities among financial institutions.

TABLE 4–5. Annual Flow of Funds into Capital-Market Assets of Mutual Savings Banks, 1965–1973
(billions of dollars)

	1965	1966	1967	1968	1969	1970	1971	1972	1973
U.S. government securities	$-0.3	$-0.7	$-0.6	$-0.5	$-0.5	$-0.2	$0.2	$0.2	-$0.5
Federally-sponsored agency securities	—	0.2	0.3	0.3	—	0.5	0.2	0.5	-0.1
State and local government securities	-0.1	-0.1	—	—	—	—	0.2	0.5	—
Corporate bonds	-0.1	0.3	1.8	1.0	0.4	1.1	3.3	2.1	} -1.0
Foreign bonds	-0.1	—	0.2	0.3	0.2	0.1	0.1	0.1	
Corporate stocks	0.2	—	0.2	0.3	0.2	0.3	0.5	0.6	0.4
Home mortgages	2.7	1.6	1.8	1.5	1.4	1.0	1.4	3.0	2.6
Other mortgages	1.4	1.1	1.4	1.3	1.3	0.9	2.8	2.6	3.1
Total	$3.7	$2.5	$5.2	$4.3	2.8	$3.7	$8.8	$9.7	$4.5

Sources: National Association of Mutual Savings Banks, *National Fact Book of Mutual Savings Banking* (1974); Bankers Trust Company *Credit and Capital Markets* (New York, annual). (Some columns do not add to totals because of rounding.)

Savings and Loan Associations

Savings and loan associations are the most important single source of home mortgage credit and, in addition, the only major financial institution whose express purpose is to make home-mortgage loans. They typically hold more than 80 percent of their assets in mortgages of all types. At the end of 1973, mortgages totaled $232.1 billion or 85 percent of their total assets of $272.4 billion. Hence, associations operate almost exclusively in the long-term markets, with activity confined mostly to the financing of local housing.

As we will see later, this heavy emphasis on mortgages, especially during tight money, high interest rate periods, has caused considerable problems for these associations and their functioning in the capital markets. It is not surprising that their recent efforts have been aimed at greater flexibility in the capital markets and reducing their dependence on mortgages as an almost singular source of revenues. Additional efforts have been made towards achieving a better hedged position between their assets and liabilities.

General Nature and Functions

Savings and loan associations are organized under both federal and state charters. The savings accounts of all federally-chartered associations are insured (to $40,000 per account) by the Federal Savings and Loan Insurance Corporation. State-chartered associations may join the corporation also. Federal and insured state associations are regulated by the Federal Home Loan Bank Board and state regulatory departments.

At the end of 1973 there were 2,040 federally-chartered associations with assets of $152.2 billion and 3,204 state-chartered associations with assets of $120.1 billion. This represents a drop of over 1,243 state, and an increase of 167 federal associations since 1960. The consolidation in associations was the result of mergers, liquidations, and conversions by many state associations to federal charters.

All federally-chartered associations were initially organized as mutual associations without stockholders. In the past, some mutual associations converted to stock associations in order to sell shares to the public. Subsequently, in 1963, a moratorium was placed on conversions and has now been in existence for several years. In 1974, the moratorium was again extended for two more years; however, up to thirty associations were allowed to convert to stock ownership under a test program.

Many associations desire to convert from mutual, or depositor-owned, associations to stock corporations so they can raise capital by selling stock. This could be helpful during tight money periods when interest rates are high and disintermediation is likely to occur.

There are already existing stock associations in twenty-two states that permit such arrangements and 678 were in existence before the moratorium was declared. Three states—California, Ohio, and Texas —control over 82 percent of all stock association assets.

General Sources of Funds

In a significant step, in 1968, federally-chartered associations (and state-chartered mutual associations where state laws permitted) were allowed classification as "deposit institutions." Holders of "savings accounts" were to be considered creditors in every sense of the term. (Depositors would, however, retain their voting privileges.)

Previously, depositors were considered "savings shareholders" and payments made to savers had to be referred to as dividends or earnings. Consequently, a dividend once declared had to be the same for those depositors with equal sums on deposit. The new ruling applying to all associations allowed deposits to be differentiated according to maturity and the amount of deposit such that higher rates could be paid, for example, to those who agreed to keep the funds on deposit for a specified time period.

In addition, a new ruling, in 1971, allowed for flexibility in passbook savings interest rates. Associations can now pay interest at less than the regular rate for several kinds of passbook accounts. Formerly, an association had to pay its declared rate on almost all passbook accounts.

Savings accounts of associations amounted to $227.3 billion at the end of 1973, more than double the $110.4 billion at the end of 1965. This amounted to 32 percent of savings balances in all deposit institutions. Major factors contributing to this substantial increase were (1) the introduction of flexible rates and several new types of savings accounts, (2) aggressive promotion, (3) an upward increase in the savings rate of individuals from 6.0 percent of disposable income in 1965 to over 8 percent in 1971–1972, (4) rising rates paid on savings accounts relative to competing institutions at least to 1972, and (5) poor investor experience in the securities markets, particularly in common stocks.

The introduction of the certificate account as a second major type of savings instrument—besides the passbook account—greatly aided the growth in total deposits. Certificates are issued in fixed amounts for a specified fixed maturity and earn a higher interest rate than is paid on passbook accounts. Almost the entire increase in deposits, noted above, could be accounted for by increases in certificate accounts. In 1968, certificates accounted for 23 percent of total savings deposits with the remaining 77 percent in passbook accounts. By the end of 1973, certificates had grown to over 50 percent of total savings.

Savings accounts of $227.3 billion constituted 83 percent of total liabilities in 1973. Other liabilities were: advances from Federal Home Loan Banks and other debt, $17.1 billion, up sharply from $5.3 billion in 1968; net worth, $17.1 billion, and miscellaneous liabilities including loans in process and property taxes held in escrow, $6.2 billion.

The protection to savings and loan account holders afforded by reserves and capital (7.5 percent of savings accounts in 1973) is about the same as that provided by commercial banks (see Chapter 3).[6] However, safety is better measured by the quality and liquidity of assets than by the dollar relationship of assets to liabilities.

Annual Sources of Funds

Annual sources of net funds for 1965 through 1973, derived by changes in balance sheet items, are shown in Table 4–6. The data reflect a similar pattern to that of mutual savings banks; namely,

TABLE 4–6. Sources of Net Funds, Savings and Loan Associations, 1965–1973 (billions of dollars)

	1965	1966	1967	1968	1969	1970	1971	1972	1973
Savings accounts	$ 8.5	$3.6	$10.6	$7.4	$3.9	$10.9	$27.8	$32.6	$20.5
Net worth	0.8	0.4	0.4	0.8	0.9	0.8	1.2	1.6	1.9
Borrowing	0.8	1.0	−2.7	1.0	4.1	1.2	−1.9	0.8	7.3
Loans in process	—	−1.0	1.0	0.2	—	0.6	2.0	1.2	−1.5
Total	$10.0	$4.0	$ 9.3	$9.0	$9.4	$13.4	$29.3	$36.2	$28.2

Sources: United States League of Savings Associations, *Savings and Loan Fact Book* (annual); *Federal Reserve Bulletin;* Bankers Trust Company, *Credit and Capital Markets* (New York, annual). (Some columns do not add to totals because of rounding.)

---

6 Beginning in 1966, the Federal House Loan Bank Board (FHLBB) required that associations with adjusted net worth (actual net worth less an allowance for delinquent mortgages) between 8 and 10 percent of specified assets (conventional loans plus 20 percent of FHA and VA loans) to allocate 5 percent of net income to reserves each year. These regulations were substantially revised during 1971 and 1972. Required reserves are now equal to a minimum of 5 percent of total savings but these can be accumulated over a period of time. Furthermore, required reserve allocations can be suspended by the FHLBB especially when associations have difficulty in meeting the requirements due to a heavy inflow of savings, or when they want to encourage mortgage lending. Additional changes were made in computing the net worth requirement; the major change tied the net worth requirement to the amount of risk exposure in the assets. The higher the percentage of risky assets in the portfolio, the higher the net worth requirement.

savings flows decrease in tight money periods such as 1966 and 1969 and increase substantially in periods of monetary ease and when personal saving increases. The rapid rise in savings flows in 1971 and 1972 was also aided by changes in the rates paid on savings accounts.

Borrowing from the Federal Home Loan Banks varies according to (1) money situations, (2) demand for mortgages, (3) savings flow, and (4) government programs encouraging home building. In tight money periods such as 1969 and 1973 S&Ls borrowed heavily from the FHLBs amounting to $4.1 billion and $7.3 billion, respectively, which helped to offset the drop in corresponding savings inflows of only $3.9 billion and $20.5 billion (1969 and 1973). In periods of monetary ease and slack mortgage demand the process is generally reversed and association borrowings reduced, such as in 1967 and 1971.

Deducting annual changes in cash and miscellaneous assets from the figures in Table 4–6 provides data on the funds available for capital market investment:

1965	1966	1967	1968	1969	1970	1971	1972	1973
$9.6	$4.2	$9.2	$10.1	$9.8	$11.4	$29.2	$36.3	$25.9

Uses of Funds: General Investment Policy

That savings and loan associations are primarily mortgage-lending agencies is revealed by Table 4–7, which shows the composition of industry assets from 1965 through 1973. The percentage of total assets invested in mortgages by associations has remained rather constant at about 84 percent since World War II. This is in direct contrast to mutual savings banks, who built up their mortgage portfolios in the 1950s and 1960s from a low of about 36 percent in 1950 to a high of 76 percent of total assets in 1965 which has since declined to 69 percent at the end of 1973. It also reflects the legal restrictions that constrain savings and loans to investment in mortgages. Associations added considerably to their cash and liquid investment in 1973. This dropped the mortgage portfolio to 81 percent of total assets from 85 percent the previous year. The prime reasons for this were (1) higher yields on acceptable legal investments compared to mortgage loans, (2) concern by associations regarding disintermediation as interest rates generally rose in the last half of 1973 and in the first three quarters of 1974, (3) changing reserve requirements, and (4) a slack mortgage demand caused by high interest rates and overbuilding in multifamily units.

The generally low liquidity ratios of saving and loan associations coupled with their poor unhedged position in assets and liabilities— short-term liabilities, long-term assets—would be a matter of deep concern if it were not for the availability of funds from the regional Federal Home Loan Banks. As noted earlier, borrowing by associa-

TABLE 4-7. Combined Assets of Savings and Loan Associations, Amounts and Percentages, at Year End, 1960–1973 (billions of dollars)

	1960		1965		1970		1973	
	Amount	Percent	Amount	Percent	Amount	Percent	Amount	Percent
U.S. government securities [a]	$ 4.6	6.4	$ 7.4	5.7	$ 4.4[b]	2.5	$ 5.0[b]	1.8
Federally-sponsored agency securities [a]	0.6	0.8	0.2	0.1	1.5[b]	0.8	2.0[b]	0.7
Other liquid investment	—	—	—	—	3.1	1.8	8.0[b]	2.9
Mortgage loans:								
Home	55.4	77.5	94.2	72.8	125.0	70.9	186.8	68.6
Other	4.7	6.6	16.1	12.4	25.4	14.4	45.3	16.6
Federal Home Loan Bank stock	1.0	1.4	1.3	1.0	1.5	0.9	2.0	0.7
Cash	2.7	3.8	3.9	3.0	3.5	2.0	4.0	1.5
Other assets	2.5	3.5	5.1	4.9	11.8	6.7	19.3	7.1
Total	$ 71.5	100	$129.4	100	$176.2	100	$272.4	100

[a] Beginning in 1968 S&L associations no longer itemize U.S. government, agency, or municipal bonds or other liquid investments. Accordingly, the figures for 1970 to 1973 are estimates of government and sponsored agency holdings.
[b] Estimated.

Sources: Federal Home Loan Bank Board, *Source Book* (annual); *Federal Reserve Bulletin*; United States League of Savings Associations, *Savings and Loan Fact Book* (annual).

tions from the FHLBs increased by $7.3 billion in 1973. Outstanding obligations due the banks totaled $15.0 billion at the end of 1973, an all time high. This represented almost 6.6 percent of savings balances held by associations, up from 4 percent in 1968.

All federally-chartered associations and most state-chartered associations, together representing 98 percent of the assets of the industry, are members of the Federal Home Loan Bank system. Loans from the Federal Home Loan Banks are used to smooth irregularities among savings inflow, withdrawals, and mortgage-lending activity. Reliance on the bank of their district varies greatly among associations. In addition to lending to member S&Ls at varying rates of interest, the banks serve as general regulatory agencies. Their policies with respect to the amount of credit extended and the rates charged, as well as their dictates on reserves and maximum interest to be paid on member savings accounts, have a very substantial inflence on member lending policies.

Liquidity requirements are also determined by the seasonal pattern of deposits and withdrawals and by the flow of cash derived from maturing mortgages. These factors differ considerably among associations, but the average association experiences strong seasonal inflows in January, June, July, and December. Outflows are typically greatest in January, April, July and October and are closely related to interest periods. The saver tends to wait until the interest payment period before withdrawing his funds.

This withdrawal/deposit procedure tends to be disruptive to the association mortgage lending policies as they must continually focus on estimated net flows to avoid liquidity problems. The willingness of FHLBs to lend funds and the different maturities offered by the associations on savings accounts have helped to ease the liquidity problem and smoothed the net flow of funds from month to month. This is important to associations who need a fully invested position in mortgages or high-yielding, liquid securities in order to pay the high promised yields on savings deposits and still earn a modest profit.

Finally, an important and constant-to-increasing source of cash to associations is mortgage inflows. These flows are received by associations from (1) payments on amortized principal, (2) mortgage prepayments, and (3) loan liquidations resulting from sale of mortgaged properties. In addition, associations also achieve liquidity by selling whole loans and loan participations from their existing mortgage portfolios.

Cash flows from the existing mortgage portfolios of associations have been significant in recent years and have served to dampen the effects of wildly fluctuating net savings flows. This is illustrated in Table 4–8, which shows the flow of funds from these two major sources, net savings and mortgage portfolio inflows. The sharp drops in net savings in

1966 and 1969 are again indicative of the tight money situation that existed during these times. The significant rises in inflows in 1971 and 1972 are a result of the large net savings inflow and the high level of mortgage activity. The large increase in outstanding mortgages coupled with high interest rates on these loans, making mortgage amortization payments larger, contributed to the substantial increases in portfolio inflows in 1971 and 1972. Tight money and disintermediation of savings from S&Ls led to only moderate increases in mortgage portfolio inflows and a sharp decline in net savings receipts in 1973–74.

TABLE 4–8.   Major Sources of Cash for All Savings and Loan Associations, 1965–1973 (billions of dollars)

	1965	1966	1967	1968	1969	1970	1971	1972	1973
Net savings recipts	$ 8.5	$ 3.6	$10.6	$ 7.4	$ 3.9	$10.9	$27.8	$32.6	$20.5
Mortgage portfolio inflows	17.0	14.3	14.6	15.0	14.5	14.8	23.0	30.1	30.9
Net income after interest	0.8	0.6	0.5	0.8	0.9	0.8	1.2	1.6	1.9
Total	$26.3	$18.5	$25.7	$23.2	$19.3	$26.5	$52.0	$64.3	$53.3

Sources: Federal Home Loan Bank Board, *Source Book* (annual); United States League of Savings Associations, *Savings and Loan Fact Book* (annual).

Mortgage Lending

The spectacular postwar rise in total mortgage investments has been a result of a national emphasis on home ownership, increases in population and personal income, and the concomitant increases in personal savings and financial institutions to finance this growth.

Table 4–9 shows that the bulk of mortgage loans financed by associations continues to be conventional loans on one-to-four-family housing units. Changes in relative amounts since 1965 are seen as an increase in the proportion of multifamily to total residential loans and in an increase in federally-underwritten loans. Nevertheless, at the end of 1973, loans on one-to-four-family homes still constituted 81 percent of total mortgages (and 69 percent of total assets).

Savings and loan associations specialize in amortized, conventional, residential loans for the following reasons: (1) the associations are geared by law and tradition to local lending, (2) local demand in most areas has been sufficient to absorb the increase in local savings attracted by the generous rate paid on accounts; (3) associations are permitted a high loan-to-value ratio on conventional loans (up to 95 in some cases); (4) the paperwork, and rate limitations on FHA and VA loans limit the appeal of this form of financing; and (5) the growth of private mortgage insurance that essentially gives conventional lending the low

TABLE 4–9.   Mortgage Loans Held by Savings and Loan Associations,
at Year End, 1965–1973 (billions of dollars)

	1965	1968	1970	1973
Residential:				
1-4 family	$ 94.2	$110.3	$125.0	$188.1
Multifamily	7.6	10.6	13.8	22.5
	$110.8	$120.8	$150.4	$210.6
Commercial and other	8.5	9.9	11.6	21.5
	$110.3	$130.8	$150.4	$232.1
Conventional	$ 98.8	$117.1	$131.8	$202.4
FHA-insured	5.1	6.7	10.2	
VA-guaranteed	6.4	7.0	8.4	29.7
Total	$110.3	$130.8	$150.4	$232.1

Sources: *Federal Reserve Bulletin;* United States League of Savings Associations,
Savings and Loan Fact Book (annual).

downpayment-large mortgage possibilities previously available only
through government financing.[7]

The aversion of associations to government loans should not be
overshadowed by the rather sharp increases in FHA and VA loans in
1971 and 1972. The $10.8 billion increase during these years was
caused primarily by the large savings inflows and the associations purchasing, outright, government-backed loans in the secondary market,
although they still tended to avoid *origination* of FHA and VA loans.

Associations have steadily increased their share of total home
financing. In 1973, they held $188 billion, or 49 percent, of the na-
tional total of $387 billion of loans on one-to-four-family dwellings.

Association loans on multifamily structures and on commercial and
industrial properties have played an increasing role in recent years,
reflecting a search for diversification and higher-yielding assets, as well
as increased demand by business enterprises for long-term financing.

More recently, lending authority for associations has been broadened
to include loans for acquisition and development of residential land,
for participation in mortgages held by other institutions, and for home
improvements.

Association loans to consumers for nonmortgage purposes, although
closely allied to homeownership, more than tripled from 1968 to 1973
to 1.8 percent of total assets. These loans include financing for mobile

---

[7] In August 1971, the FHLBB authorized federal associations to make 95 percent
conventional loans on single-family homes if the principal balance over 90 percent
of the loan was backed by private mortgage insurance or an added association
reserve.

homes, home improvement loans, and loans secured by savings accounts.[8] Consumer loan growth in recent years can be attributable to liberalization of federal and state regulations governing thrift associations and the higher yields associated with these properties. Total outstanding mobile home and home improvement loans were both up sharply in 1973 over previous years and amounted to $1.8 and $1.5 billion, respectively, at year end.

Other Investments

Federally-chartered associations invest in federal securities, obligations of certain federal agencies, and, primarily for safety and liquidity (since 1964), the four top grades of state and municipal bonds. The proportion of these holdings to total assets had been in the neighborhood of 6 percent for several years.

The emphasis in these obligations has been on short- and intermediate-term maturities to reduce price risk and to offset the long maturities of the moragage portfolio. At the end of 1973, over 70 percent of the investment securities held had maturities of five years or less.

Liquidity requirements were substantially revised by an amendment to the Federal Home Loan Bank Act. Regulations now specify the required liquidity ratio as a percentage of total withdrawable savings account balances and short-term borrowings. Acceptable liquid investments include cash, demand deposits held at commercial banks and at the FHLB, federal securities, and government agency issues. By law, the board is allowed to vary the required reserve ratio from 4 to 10 percent.

In 1974, the required ratio was 5 percent, yet qualifying liquidity assets totaled over $22 billion or just under 8 percent of assets. This reflected the high yields on these legal securities and anticipated liquidity problems as disintermediation rose in early 1974 and continued during most of the year.

Annual Uses of Funds in the Capital Market

Annual data on long-term uses of funds for 1965 through 1973 are shown in Table 4–10.

The rate of acquisition of new home mortgage loans fell off sharply in 1966, reflecting the decline in institutional savings, the drop in housing starts, and the rise in mortgage interest rates in a period of

---

[8] Current regulations permit associations to invest up to 10 percent of their assets in loans on mobile homes. These loans are generally made to consumers to finance purchase of a new or used unit or to mobile home dealers to help carry inventories.

TABLE 4–10. Annual Flow of Funds into Capital-Market Assets, Savings Associations, 1965–1973 (billions of dollars)

	1965	1966	1967	1968	1969	1970	1971	1972	1973
U.S. government securities [a]	$0.4	$0.3	$1.4	$0.4	$–1.0	$–0.4	$ 1.4	$ 1.0	$–1.0
Federally-sponsored agency securities [a]	0.1	0.1	0.2	0.4	1.3	1.5	3.9	3.4	1.0
Home mortgages	7.0	2.9	6.0	7.2	7.7	7.2	17.3	24.8	21.0
Other mortgages	2.0	0.9	1.5	2.1	1.8	3.0	6.6	7.1	4.9
Total	$9.6	$4.2	$9.2	$10.1	$ 9.8	$11.4	$29.2	$36.3	$25.9

[a] Estimated. Includes GNMA mortgage-backed securities.
Sources: Federal Home Loan Bank Board; United States League of Savings Associations, *Savings and Loan Fact Book* (annual).
(Some columns do not add to totals because of rounding.)

72

tight money. In 1971 and 1972, years of relative monetary ease, there was a sharp recovery in lending volume and home mortgage funding reached an all-time high. The $17.3 billion, $24.8 billion, and $21.0 billion net addition to home mortgages in 1971, 1972, and 1973, respectively, were two to three times the net additions for any previous years. Volume fell off in 1974 as a result of a decline in deposits and high interest rates that cut mortgage demand.

Throughout the period, amounts invested in other mortgages, including commercial mortgages, increased substantially, reflecting the high rates obtainable on these loans and the demand from commercial borrowers. Undoubtedly, much of the demand for loans from commercial borrowers in 1971 through 1973 was a "spillover" effect from other markets where unsecured loans were difficult to obtain and interest rates to corporate borrowers remained high.

The rapid rise in ownership of federally-sponsored agency securities was the result of higher liquidity requirements under new FHLB Board rules, and the generally high yields on these bonds compared to mortgages and U.S. government debt securities.

Influence of Monetary Policy

As savings and loan associations specialize in mortgage assets with long-term maturities and associations are not controlled by the same reserve requirement as commercial banks, it was often thought that monetary policy had little effect on association operations. Reasons advanced for this thesis were that (1) once committed, the rate earned on a mortgage remains unchanged, and (2) rates paid to savers, the same to both new and old, change only at intervals that may be months or even a year or two apart. Thus, it was concluded that much of the associations' asset and liability base was "locked in" and, as a result, variations in market rates resulting from tighter or easier Federal Reserve policy affected only new lending and savings activity—the earned and paying rates—whose changes normally lagged behind open-market yields anyway.

The sobering experiences of many associations since the mid-1960s, particularly during tight money periods, have tended to refute this hypothesis and have led to the conclusion that monetary policy does have a significant effect on association operations although such effects may be more indirect.

A tight monetary policy affects the volume of new housing starts and new mortgage commitments as well as increasing the cost of borrowings from the Federal Home Loan Banks who in turn must obtain their own funds at open-market yields.

Furthermore, the significant changes in competition for savings deposits with commercial banks and with other securities has had a major impact on association operations. When money is tight and interest rates, including those paid on savings deposits, rise, the heavy commitment to long-term mortgages at fixed rates tends to work against savings associations. That is, because the S&Ls are "locked in" at a specified interest rate or are operating in a market that is interest-rate sensitive, they are limited—legally and competitively—by the rates they can pay on savings accounts With rates rising on other competitive securities, substantial disintermediation is likely to occur and association operations are likely to be seriously affected. In order to mitigate these deficiencies over the business cycle, several savings and loan associations have opted for variable rate mortgages; but so far such plans have met strong consumer resistance.

Role in a National Mortgage Market

Savings and loan associations operate mainly in local markets. Unlike other lenders—mutual savings banks and life insurance companies in particular—they have not made frequent use of agents or correspondents in originating or servicing their loans.

Associations do, however, contribute to a national flow of funds in several ways. They purchase and sell mortgages from other associations, commercial banks, insurance companies, mortgage companies, and brokers, and they participate with each other and with other lenders in large loans. In 1973, insured associations purchased $7.2 billion worth of loans and participations and sold $3.5 billion worth. The difference in net purchases of $3.7 billion was down sharply over the $6.9 billion difference in 1972 as S & L's inflows in 1973 moderated from 1972.[9] In addition, by borrowing from Federal Home Loan Banks, associations tap national sources of capital for local employment. And finally, savings funds are attracted from out-of-town areas where yields on deposit investments are lower. For instance, California associations have aggressively advertised on a national basis to attract funds by offering the highest yields available. The fact that most accounts are insured (to $40,000) by the Federal Savings and Loan Insurance Corporation is a major factor in inducing investors to shift funds to distant associations.

Until recently, savings and loan associations had not been active in the general secondary-mortgage market. However, the rapid development of the secondary mortgage market (see Chapter 12) with improved marketability of conventional mortgage loans as well as FHA and VA loans promises to be of considerable importance to savings associations in the future.

---

[9] United States League of Savings Associations, *Savings and Loan Fact Book* (1974), p. 91.

Competition for Savings—
Impact on Savings Institutions

At least since the 1950s, there have been a number of developments and changes in the capital markets that have tipped the scales in favor of one financial institution or another. The effect of these changes has had a profound influence on savings growth in general, and on the savings and profitability experience of savings and loan associations in particular.

Commercial banks, of course, are the primary competitors of savings associations and savings banks. Table 4–11 shows the annual change in savings deposits for savings asociations, mutual saving banks, and commercial banks. The table shows (1) the fluctuating year-to-year changes, particularly since 1965, in total savings, and (2) the improvement in savings gains in recent years by commercial banks at the expense of savings associations.

TABLE 4–11.   Annual Change in Time and Savings Deposits, 1956–1973
(billions of dollars)

Year	Savings Associations [a]	Mutual Savings Banks [b]	Commercial Banks [c]	All Others [d]	Total
1956	5.0	1.8	2.2	0.2	9.2
1957	4.8	1.7	5.2	0.2	11.9
1958	6.1	2.3	6.2	0.3	14.9
1959	6.6	1.2	3.1	0.3	11.2
1960	7.6	1.4	4.1	0.5	13.6
1961	8.7	1.9	9.9	0.5	21.0
1962	9.4	3.1	14.3	0.5	27.3
1963	11.1	3.3	11.9	0.9	27.2
1964	10.6	4.2	13.7	0.9	29.4
1965	8.5	3.6	20.0	1.0	33.1
1966	3.6	2.6	13.3	0.8	20.3
1967	10.6	5.1	23.7	1.2	40.6
1968	7.4	4.2	20.6	1.1	33.3
1969	3.9	2.6	−9.4	1.4	−1.5
1970	10.9	4.4	37.3	1.7	54.3
1971	27.8	9.8	41.2	2.9	81.7
1972	32.6	10.2	42.6	3.4	88.8
1973	20.5	4.7	50.1	2.9	78.2

[a] All types of savings.
[b] Regular and special savings accounts.
[c] Time and savings accounts of individuals, partnerships, and corporations.
[d] Primarily credit unions.

Sources: Federal Reserve *Flow of Funds*, Federal Home Loan Bank Board; Federal Deposit Insurance Corporation; U.S. Department of Commerce; National Association of Mutual Savings Banks; CUNA International, Inc.; and United States League of Savings Associations.

From 1956 through 1960, associations added a total of $30.1 billion in net new savings; commercial banks added only $20.8 billion during the same period. From 1961 through 1973, however, the success in attracting savings was dramatically reversed with commercial banks recording net new savings of $287 billion while savings and loan associations attracted only $166 billion.

The improved performance of commercial banks in the 1960s was, for the most part, a direct result of the relaxation in laws restricting interest payments on savings deposits and the general encouragement by regulatory agencies in fostering more competition for savings deposits. The procedure was to allow interest rates on savings deposits of all types to rise, while at the same time allowing the differential on maximum rates paid by commercial banks and savings and loans to be reduced. In the past (1950s) when savings and loans paid considerably higher rates than commercial banks and aggressively sought savings funds, commercial banks were seriously hindered in their efforts to attract deposits. When maximum rates were liberalized and the interest rate differential narrowed, commercial banks did considerably better, largely at the expense of savings and loan associations.

Figure 4–1.   Average Annual Yield on Savings at Major Financial Institutions

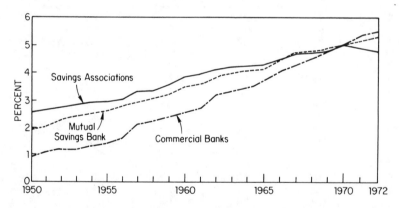

Sources: Federal Home Loan Bank Board; Federal Deposit Insurance Corporation; National Association of Mutual Savings Banks; United States League of Savings Associations.

Figure 4–1 shows the average annual yields paid on savings deposits by savings associations, mutual savings banks, and commercial banks. The figure reveals the narrowing spread in rates paid by the three institutions from 1950 until 1973 when commercial banks paid higher average interest rates on their savings and time deposits than

S&L's. In 1950, the average annual yield on savings accounts in savings associations was 2.5 percent, topping by 1.6 percent the 0.9 percent paid by commercial banks. In 1973, the 5.55 percent yield on savings accounts in savings associations was 15 basis points lower than the 5.70 percent average for commercial banks.

The President's Commission on Financial Structure and Regulation (called the Hunt Commission after its chairman, Reed O. Hunt) as one of its responsibilities studied the problem of rate regulations. Its December 1971 report concluded that rate regulations should be retained and that thrift institutions, including savings banks and associations, should be allowed a rate advantage on savings deposits until legislation is passed to allow broader lending powers for thrift institutions.[10] Although a rate differential is not currently required by law, the typical differential in favor of thrift institutions is one-half of one percent on savings accounts and one-quarter of one percent on certificates up to $100,000. There are, however, no maximum rates for any institutions on time deposits of $100,000 or more; thrift institutions are limited to 7¾ percent for time deposits up to six years maturity.

The net result of increased competition for savings has been a reduction in savings and loan associations' relative profitability. In the decade ending in 1964, their average rate of return on net worth amounted to 11.6 percent. In the period 1965 through 1973, the return on net worth dropped to 8.3 per cent. On the other hand, commercial banks' average net income after security gains and losses improved during the same period from 9.0 percent on net worth to 10.8 percent.

Hunt Commission Report

In recognition of the need for a detailed examination of the structure of the private financial system, the President's Commission on Financial Structure and Regulations (Hunt Commission) was formed in 1970 [11] and their recommendations published in 1971.

Among other things, the commission's report noted that, through the years, several artificial barriers had been erected that limited the effective and efficient operations of financial institutions and markets. Accordingly, the Hunt Commission recommended a reduction in these barriers and opted for a more competitive environment among financial institutions.

It was necessary to temper the recommendations in light of the current realities among existing financial institutions and markets as

---

[10] *Report of the President's Commission on Financial Structure and Regulation.* Superintendent of Documents, (Washington, D.C.: Government Printing Office, December 1971), pp. 23–24.

[11] *Ibid.*

well as acknowledging the dual objectives of safety and viability of financial institutions in a competitive environment. In this regard, some of the more important recommendations by the Hunt Commission directly affecting financial institutions were that:

1. thrift institutions be given third party transfers;
2. thrift institutions receive broadened powers in consumer credit and mortgage lending, and in purchasing corporate bonds;
3. the rate differential on savings deposits be maintained until savings institutions had adjusted their portfolios to reflect the new guidelines;
4. current state-chartered institutions be allowed a federal charter alternative; and
5. tax rates and charges should be made uniform for thrift institutions and commercial banks.

Most of the Hunt Commission recommendations have not, as yet, been incorporated into law, but a legislative trend toward transforming several currently insular and diverse financial institutions into "full service" operations seems clear.

A major step toward "full service" operations among saving institutions would be allowing third party transfer privileges similar to checking accounts at commercial banks. In some states (Massachusetts and New Hampshire) third party transfer is a reality in the form of negotiable order of withdrawal (NOW) accounts. NOW accounts allow transfers of funds from no-passbook savings accounts to other parties by means of negotiable orders of withdrawal. These instruments are not demand deposits in the strict sense of the word and hence do not violate federal prohibition of interest payments on demand deposits. Nevertheless, they are of sufficient concern to banks that bills have been introduced in Congress to prohibit savings institutions from allowing withdrawals by negotiable instruments for the purpose of making transfers to third parties from any account on which interest is paid.

Some of the other recommendations have been partially adopted and previous rulings regarding investments and loans by savings associations modified in light of the Hunt Commission report. Thus, there is no doubt that the public attitude at this time is one of favoring open and freer competition among financial institutions for savings deposits, loans, and investments. In this regard, the public is doing nothing more than reaffirming the role of an intermediary discussed in Chapter 2, namely, that of accepting funds from surplus units and reinvesting them at a higher rate in earning assets and doing it in the most efficient manner.

With proper safeguards, it appears that financial institutions will continue to have wider latitude in determining the earnings assets in which the funds entrusted to them are invested.

```
5555555555555555555555555555555555555555555555555555555555555555555555555555555555555555
5555555555555555555555555555555555555555555555555555555555555555555555555555555555555555
555555555555555555555555555555555555   5555555555   5555555555555555555555555555555555
5555555555555555555555555555555555555   5555555555   5555555555555555555555555555555555
55555555555555555555555555555555555555   555555555   5555555555555555555555555555555555
555555555555555555555555555555555555555   5555555   5555555555555555555555555555555555
5555555555555555555555555555555555555555   55555   5555555555555555555555555555555555
55555555555555555555555555555555555555555   555   5555555555555555555555555555555555
555555555555555555555555555555555555555555   5   5555555555555555555555555555555555
5555555555555555555555555555555555555555555   5555555555555555555555555555555555555
55555555555555555555555555555555555555555555   555555555555555555555555555555555555
5555555555555555555555555555555555555555555555   5555555555555555555555555555555555
5555555555555555555555555555555555555555555555555555555555555555555555555555555555555555
5555555555555555555555555555555555555555555555555555555555555555555555555555555555555555
```

Insurance Companies

IN this chapter we deal with the two major insurance institutions: legal reserve life insurance companies and property and liability companies. The two types perform quite distinct functions, draw on different sources of funds, and employ their funds somewhat differently in the capital market. Many holding companies and insurance groups, however, do control firms that provide both types of service.

Life Insurance Companies

Nature and Functions

Life insurance companies are one of the largest media for individual savings in the United States. Their total assets have grown from $64 billion in 1950 to $252 billion at the end of 1973 and consist chiefly of a variety of capital-market instruments. Their annual rate of asset growth approximates $15 billion, or 6 percent per year compounded.

Life insurance companies provide financial protection for beneficiaries against death and longevity (life insurance and annuities). They can, however, be classed as financial intermediaries as the policies they issue (other than renewable term and industrial) have included in the premium a reserve or savings element that represents an amount in excess of the need for current death losses. This is invested and compounded to cover death losses at later ages. The level annual premiums on annuities include amounts accumulated to provide a life income based on actuarial life expectancy.

Thus, life insurance companies perform two major functions: (1) protection of beneficiaries against premature death (insurance) and unusual longevity (annuities) of the policyholders; (2) investment of funds representing policy reserves (and other funds) in a wide variety of capital-market instruments.

General Relations to the Capital Market

Because the contracts of life insurance companies involve, for the most part, long-term liabilities, the savings they accumulate are placed mainly in capital-market rather than money-market instruments in order to be sufficiently hedged on assets and liabilities. Except for those held for liquidity purposes, the securities and mortgages in the investment portfolio are ordinarily held to maturity as long as they meet required standards of quality. Investment policy emphasizes long-term safety and the achievement of a return that produces the rates built into premium calculations at which reserves must be compounded.

At the end of 1973 about $210 billion, or 83 percent, of the total assets of life insurance companies consisted of capital-market instruments including federal, state, and municipal bonds; corporate and foreign bonds; mortgages; and corporate stock.

Capital-market investments have been growing at the rate of about $10 to $12 billion each year. The net premium and investment income, plus funds from maturing bonds and mortgages, provides an annual discretionary cash flow of $27 to $29 billion, making the industry a very potent factor in the capital markets.

Sources of Funds

The major sources of external funds are the accumulating reserve liabilities derived from net premium income and the compounding of investment income. Between 1960 and 1973, policy reserves grew from $98 to $204 billion. Accumulated policy "dividends" (rebates), reserves for future dividends, and other obligations provide additional funds. The total of these last three sources grew from $11 to $29 billion in the same period. Net worth accounts, including special and unassigned surplus and the capital stock accounts of stock companies, increased from $10 to $20 billion. As most of these sources represent long-term obligations, capital-market assets are appropriate investments.

The annual sources of new funds for capital-market use from 1965 through 1973 are derived by deducting from the annual increase in total assets, the changes in miscellaneous assets, net cash, real estate, and policy loans (data in billions of dollars):[1]

1965	1966	1967	1968	1969	1970	1971	1972	1973
$7.7	$6.6	$7.5	$7.8	$5.3	$6.0	$10.2	$12.5	$13.3

[1] Source: Institute of Life Insurance, *Life Insurance Fact Book* (annual).

Cash flow from sale of securities and maturing mortgages, totaling about $16 to $18 billion annually, was also available for reinvestment annually in recent years.

Factors Determining General Investment Policy

Before examining actual investment policy, we should note the major factors stemming from the nature of the business and its regulation that determine the general character of the investments.

(1) Contracts with policyholders are essentially long-term obligations. Although some mature every day, the cash drain can be forecast with considerable accuracy, as can the cash inflow from net new premiums, the maturing and sales of securities and mortgages, and investment income. Most life insurance contracts provide for an accumulation of cash surrender values payable or loaned on demand. However, experience with policy loans and liquidation of cash values shows that only under extreme conditions (as during the early 1930s) are large permanent withdrawals likely to occur. And for the growing insurance company, steady cash inflow more than exceeds the cash drain for death benefits, expenses, and withdrawals.

The emphasis can therefore be placed on acquisition of long-maturity instruments, and the general practice is to hold these to maturity, unless changes in market yields cause shifts in broad categories of investments or unless a loss of quality of individual investments requires their liquidation.

(2) Some liquidity is, however, required to provide for day-to-day needs, to meet large emergency death losses, and to permit changes among investment categories without sudden sale of assets. Liquidity is provided by working cash balances, federal bonds, and amortization of mortgages and loans.

(3) Premiums are written on the assumption of a minimum rate of return at which funds representing reserves will be compounded (for example, 4 to 4½ percent). A steady and adequate yield is therefore required. Investment policy must emphasize fixed-income assets of high quality and stable income. It is also desirable to earn a rate of return in excess of the "guaranteed" rate and so distribute premium rebates in "dividends."

(4) Their position as trustees of savings requires that life insurance companies invest funds for ultimate safety. This is achieved by re-

stricting investments to instruments that meet the standards of quality established by policy and regulation. Diversification by type of investment, industrial category, maturity, and degree of marketability is also a means of protecting against losses of principal.

(5) Actuarial commitments require insurance companies to remain fully invested, keeping cash balance to the minimum set by estimated cash inflows and outflows. This requirement explains the use of forward commitments for business loans and mortgages; it also explains the use of mortgage company correspondents to originate and service mortgages in capital-seeking areas to which surplus funds can be directed (see Chapter 12).

(6) Valuation of assets for statement purposes has a considerable effect on investment policy. Mutual companies are permitted to build up only limited surplus accounts, and competition prevents stock companies from accumulating large excess premium deposits. Substantial declines in asset values must therefore be avoided. Quality must be emphasized, and bond accounts so managed as to prevent large writedowns of assets because of shifts in market rates of interest.

(7) Life insurance income is not tax free, although the federal income-tax rate is substantially less than that applying to business corporations. The increase in the effective rate in 1959 (from 7 to 8 percent to 21 to 22 percent) in 1973 has led to some interest in the obligations of state and local governments.

(8) Because commitments to policy holders are in fixed dollars, little attention need be paid to actual or potential inflation. Rising operating costs can be met by gradual changes in premiums. Common stocks and real estate are acquired more for their greater long-run income than for their potential value as inflation hedges. (This is not true of pension fund commitments, however, as future payments are usually tied to wage and salary levels, implying a need for inflation protection.)

(9) The effect of state regulation on life insurance investments is important enough to warrant special discussion.

Regulation

In all fifty states, the investments of life insurance companies are heavily affected by regulation specifying the categories of investments that can be acquired and the standards of quality that holdings in each permitted category must meet.[2] Companies domiciled in one state

---

[2] For a convenient discussion of regulation and a summary of the specific regulations in nineteen representative states, see Life Insurance Association of America, *Life Insurance Companies as Financial Institutions,* a monograph prepared for the Commission on Money and Credit (Englewood Cliffs, N.J.: Prentice-Hall, Inc., 1962), Chap. 5 and Appendix.

and doing business in others must conform to the standards required of domestic insurers insofar as locally-generated reserves are concerned, as well as those of the state of domicile. Corporate bonds must meet standards as to type and value of collateral or interest coverage or both; the latter requirement is stricter for unsecured obligations. Conventional mortgages must meet maximum loan-to-appraised-value ratios (as high as 75 percent on one- or two-family dwellings in New York and some other states). Preferred stocks must meet specified tests of dividend coverage and payment. Common stocks, now permitted in limited amounts in the majority of states, must ordinarily be listed and meet specified earnings and dividend tests. Income-producing real estate is restricted as to type and use of property.

The individual states establish what percentage each category of investments may be of total assets and also restrict the percentages of assets invested in the obligations of one (private) borrower. Geographic limitations on investments also apply, as do requirements in a few states that a certain percentage of reserves be invested in instruments originating in that state. Fortunately, the latter requirement is not widespread, as it would prevent companies from directing their funds to the areas of greatest need and best yields.

Annual Investment Policy

Table 5–1 shows the combined assets and percentages of legal reserve companies by major categories from 1965 through 1973 (at year end).

United States government securities   In 1945, direct federal obligations totaled $20.6 billion, or 46 percent of total insurance company assets. Since that time holdings of federal securities have declined in both amount and percentage such that at the end of 1973 they represented only $3.4 billion, or less than one and one-half percent, of total assets.[3]

The primary beneficiaries of the movement away from federal securities in the last three decades have been corporate bonds and mortgages of all types. The reason for this big shift can be traced to the higher yields available on these latter securities. One of the factors contributing to the accord between the Treasury and the Federal Reserve banks in 1951, when the prices and yields of Treasury securities were "unpegged" (see Chapter 8), was the massive sales of federal securities by insurance companies. In the later 1950s and the 1960s, net sales of these securities continued at a varying pace depending on the availability of, and yields on, alternative investments.

---

[3] Direct federal obligations only. $4.4 billion at the end of 1973 including the bonds of federally-sponsored agencies.

TABLE 5–1. Combined Assets of Legal Reserve Life Insurance Companies, Amounts and Percentages, at Year End, 1960–1973 (billions of dollars)

	1960		1965		1970		1973	
	Amount	*Percent*	*Amount*	*Percent*	*Amount*	*Percent*	*Amount*	*Percent*
U.S. government securities	$ 6.4	5.4%	$ 5.1	3.2%	$ 4.0	1.9%	$ 3.5	1.3%
Federally-sponsored agency securities	0.1	—	0.2	0.1	0.5	0.2	0.9	0.3
American municipal bonds	3.6	3.0	3.5	2.2	3.3	1.6	3.4	1.3
Canadian municipal bonds	1.0	0.8	1.9	1.2	2.8	1.4	3.0	1.2
Foreign central government bonds	0.4	0.3	0.9	0.6	0.6	0.3	0.7	0.3
Corporate bonds	47.0	39.4	58.6	37.0	73.1	35.3	91.8	36.8
Mortgages	41.8	35.0	60.0	37.8	74.4	35.9	81.4	32.2
Preferred stocks	1.8	1.5	2.9	1.9	3.5	1.7	6.3	2.5
Common stocks	3.2	2.7	6.2	3.8	11.9	5.7	19.6	7.7
Policy loans	5.2	4.3	7.7	4.8	16.1	7.8	20.2	7.9
Real estate	3.8	3.2	4.7	3.0	6.3	3.0	7.8	3.1
Cash and other assets	5.3	4.4	7.2	4.5	10.8	5.2	13.9	5.4
Total assets	$119.6	100 %	$158.9	100 %	$207.3	100 %	$252.4	100 %

Source: Institute of Life Insurance, *Life Insurance Fact Book* (annual).

At the end of 1973, life insurance companies held $3.5 billion worth of direct federal securities, representing less than 1.0 percent of total federal debt outstanding. Their emphasis has been on intermediate- and long-term maturities with more than 90 percent of their holdings in securities having maturities of more than one year.

State and local government bonds   The holdings of American state and local government bonds have risen only modestly in the last two decades. At the end of 1973, state and local obligations amounted to $3.4 billion, comprising less than 1½ percent of total insurance company assets.

Because they are in effectively lower tax brackets than other financial institutions, the tax-exempt feature of state and local issues is less appealing to insurance companies. Consequently, insurance companies have shown a distinct preference in their investment policies for the higher yields on corporate bonds and mortgages.

General obligation bonds of American state and local governments do not have as much appeal to insurance companies as revenue bonds as the latter issues, which are tax exempt, may sell at yields often equal to those on fully taxable high-grade corporate bonds. At the end of 1973, revenue bonds constituted about 70 percent of insurance company holdings of American municipal bonds. Life insurance companies share of American state and municipal long-term securities amounted to less than 2 percent of all state and local debt of $197 billion (December 1973).

Corporate bonds   Corporate bonds are attractive to insurance companies because of their superior yield, quoted prices (save for those acquired through private placement), marketability, and variety. One of the most important features of insurance company investments since World War II has been the increase in corporate bond holdings. In 1945, these totaled $10.1 billion, or 22.5 percent of total assets. By 1973, they had increased to $91.8 billion and 36.8 percent of total assets. Corporate bonds have constituted 36 to 40 percent of total assets since 1949. The funds for this expansion were provided in the early years by the switch from United States government bonds and later by the large growth in net cash flow.

The composition within the bond portfolio has undergone a marked change. The waning investment status of railway bonds led to the decline in their percentage of total assets from 4.9 percent in 1950 to less than 2 percent in 1973. Utility bond holdings have increased in absolute amount, but have declined to around 10 percent of total insurance company assets (from 12 percent in 1950). The increase in holdings reflected the postwar expansion of the utility industries, especially gas and electric power, and their improved investment status. They have become relatively less important in recent years because they are usually issued through competitive bidding, in which insurance companies seldom participate.

The industrial bond category has grown substantially from $9.5 billion, or about 2 percent of assets, in 1950 to about $62 billion, or about 25 percent, in 1973. This growth reflects the upgrading of the investment status of industrial obligations—especially in such rapidly growing fields as oil, chemicals, and finance—and the fact that the great bulk of high-grade issues are acquired through direct placement, in which life insurance companies play the leading role (see Chapter 10). The industrial bond category also includes long-term loans similar to, but with longer maturities than, bank term loans.

The life insurance industry is extremely important in the industrial corporate bond market. Net investment in these assets increased by $34 billion from 1965 through 1973. At the end of 1973, insurance companies owned 47 percent of all industrial corporate bonds outstanding (at market value).

Mortgages   The large holdings of mortgages by the life insurance industry (see Table 5–2) reflect the following characteristics of these assets: (1) relatively attractive yields (1 to 2 percent above high-grade bonds); (2) safety as required by strict regulation; (3) long-term maturities; (4) steady amortization of principal, which contributes greatly

TABLE 5–2.   Mortgage Loans Held by Legal Reserve Life Insurance Companies, at Year End, 1960–1973 (billions of dollars)

	1960	1965	1970	1973
Farm	$ 3.0	$ 4.8	$ 5.6	$ 6.1
Residential:				
1–4-family	24.9	29.9	26.7	22.0
Multifamily	3.9	8.4	16.0	18.4
	$28.8	$38.3	$42.7	$40.4
Commercial and other	10.0	16.9	26.1	34.9
Total	$41.8	$60.0	$74.4	$81.4
Conventional and other	$25.8	$41.6	$57.7	$67.8
FHA-insured (nonfarm)	9.0	12.1	11.3	9.2
VA-guaranteed	6.9	6.3	5.4	4.4
Total	$41.8	$60.0	$74.4	$81.4

Sources: *Federal Reserve Bulletin;* Institute of Life Insurance, *Life Insurance Fact Book* (annual); United States League of Savings Associations, *Savings and Loan Fact Book* (annual); Federal Home Loan Bank Board, *Savings and Home Finance Source Book* (annual).

to liquidity; (5) growing geographical diversification through the use of the mortgage correspondent and wider-spread direct investment; (6) growing diversity of types; (7) the special appeal of FHA-insured and VA-guaranteed loans; (8) loan-to-value ratios on conventional residential liens as high as 75 percent in some states; (9) rising real estate value increasing the safety of mortgages on property; and (10) an opportunity to structure apartment and industrial mortgage loans to include participation in the equity or profits of the underlying assets. These advantages are somewhat offset by the costlier management, the poorer marketability of mortgage investments as compared with listed securities, the risks associated with investments as compared with listed securities, and the risks associated with investments in new construction or newer properties with sharply higher costs.

Total mortgage investments have increased annually since World War II and have risen from $16.1 billion, or 25 percent, of total assets in 1950, to $81.4 billion, or 32 percent, of total assets in 1973. The rate of net mortgage growth has been about $2 to $5 billion yearly since 1965, depending on the demand for mortgages and the level of interest rates. If rates are high, single family mortgage demand tends to diminish, resulting in only moderate increases in mortgages outstanding.

Thus, characteristically, the annual investment in residential mortgages has been irregular and has followed the cyclical rises and falls in housing starts (for example, large increases in 1964, 1968 and 1971 through 1973, and decreases in 1966, 1969 and 1974).

Mortgages, in general, compete mainly with bonds, and moreover, each major category of mortgages also competes with other types. The ebb and flow of funds into federally-supported mortgages has also been irregular, varying with relative interest rates on competitive investments. The investment in these federally-underwritten loans has seen the most variation because their nominal interest rates are pegged and changed only at rather long intervals. Life insurance companies have not been enthusiastic about buying such investments at a discount when the nominal rate is inadequate (see Chapter 12).

Similar to other financial institutions investing heavily in mortgages, insurance companies have placed increasing amounts in multifamily and commercial mortgages at the expense of single-family housing. Table 5–2 shows that investment in one-to-four-family units by insurance companies declined sharply from $26.7 billion to $22.0 billion in the 1970 to 1973 period. The primary reason for this shift was the emphasis on higher yields. Other reasons were the decline in housing starts, competition for mortgages from other institutions (most notably, savings and loan associations), and the increase in policy loans made at low rates of interest that forced a search for higher-yielding investments.

Insurance companies have particularly favored multifamily and commercial properties over single-family residences because substantial funds can be placed more conveniently in large projects and the expected yields are often considerably higher. In 1973 and 1974, it was common for loans on commercial properties to carry a 10 percent interest rate plus a percentage of the equity or profits from the project; rates on single-family homes were in the vicinity of 8¾ percent. The holdings of commercial properties ($26.1 billion in 1970) rose to $34.9 billion in 1973, representing 43 percent of total mortgages held by life insurance companies.

As a group, life insurance companies are the second most important institutional owner of residential mortgages, surpassed only by savings and loan associations (see Chapters 4 and 12). Like other institutions, they have also tended to prefer conventional loans to government-guaranteed FHA and VA loans. FHA-insured and VA-guaranteed loans fell from 41 percent of mortgage assets in 1950 to 17 percent in 1973 as insurance companies sought higher yields and lower loan processing costs.

Farm mortgage investments totaled $6.1 billion at the end of 1973, or less than 3 percent of total assets. Nevertheless, the industry is the largest private institutional owner of such loans, holding 15 percent of total farm mortgages at the end of 1973.

Life insurance companies rely heavily on local mortgage correspondents for the origination of their mortgage loans, especially residential liens (see Chapter 12). Customarily, about 40 percent of their total mortgages and about two-thirds of their single-family home-mortgage loans have been obtained in this fashion. This figure has declined in recent years due to the decrease in home financing. (The contribution of mortgage companies to a growing national market in mortgages and to greater geographical uniformity in interest rates is indicated in Chapter 12.)

Corporate Stocks   The traditional lack of interest by insurance companies in common stocks has been attributed to (1) the need for a steady and secure income, (2) the necessary safety of principal, and (3) the lack of a strong need for inflation hedges in their investments. Tradition, law (restricting common stock investment to a small percentage of assets or of policyholders' surplus and limiting the amount of investment in any one company), and the valuation at year-end market price also discourage greater holdings of this type of asset.

Holdings of common stocks have, however, increased in amount, and have steadily increased in percentage of total assets for several years. This figure was $10.3 billion in 1968, grew to $21.8 billion at the end of 1972 but declined to $19.6 at the end of 1973, or less than 8 percent of total assets. These figures reflect the appreciation in market value and subsequent depreciation as well as investment policy. Preferred stocks, whose appeal is for current income, totaled $6.3 billion, or 2.5 percent of total assets at the end of 1973.

The interest of life insurance companies in common stocks is likely to increase in the future. Indirect interest derives from participation in the operation of mutual (open-end) investment funds. Direct interest reflects the mounting importance of insured pension plans invested in equities, with the portfolios segregated from general assets, and the relaxation of state rules to permit a higher proportion of life insurance reserves to be invested in equities.

Although $21 to $22 billion is no small amount, it suggests that the influence of this institution in the stock market lags far behind that of others. At the end of 1973, insurance companies owned only 2.4 percent of the value of stocks listed on all stock exchanges.[4]

Annual Uses of Funds

The annual capital-market uses of life insurance company funds from 1965 through 1973 are shown in Table 5–3. The influences indicated earlier in this chapter are clearly revealed by these data: the selloff of federal bonds and home mortgages, the steady accumulation of corporate bonds, and the increase in commercial and multifamily liens.

As insurance companies are well-hedged on their asset and liability accounts, the changes shown in Table 5–3 are largely a result of their efforts to place funds in assets yielding higher returns while holding the maturity of the assets more or less constant.

From 1965 through 1973, corporate bonds accounted for over 47 percent of the increase in capital-market assets at balance-sheet value and multifamily and in commercial mortgages, for 35 percent.

Influence in the National Capital Markets

Life insurance companies direct between $27 and 30 billion of new and internal funds into the capital markets each year. They are the dominating force on the demand side for corporate bonds and are second only to savings and loan associations in the mortgage market. Their decisions concerning investment of this great stream of capital greatly affect yields in some markets. Likewise, changes in market yields influence the direction of their funds toward different categories of assets.

In the later 1960s and early 1970s, the movement toward all-purpose financial combines included the acquisition, by a number of life in-

---

4 See Table 11–5 for total of all listed stocks.

TABLE 5–3. Annual Flow of Funds into Capital-Market Assets, Life Insurance Companies, 1965–1973
(billions of dollars)

	1965	1966	1967	1968	1969	1970	1971	1972	1973
U.S. government securities	$-0.5	$-0.3	$-0.2	$-0.2	$-0.3	$-0.1	$-0.2	$-	$ 0.1
Federally-sponsored agency securities	—	—	—	0.1	0.1	0.1	0.1	0.1	—
State and local government bonds (domestic)	-0.2	-0.4	-0.1	0.2	—	0.1	—	0.1	0.1
Foreign securities	0.4	0.2	0.2	0.2	0.2	0.3	0.1	0.3	0.2
Corporate bonds	2.4	2.2	3.7	3.6	1.5	1.2	5.4	6.8	5.6
Corporate stocks	0.7	0.3	1.0	1.4	1.7	2.0	3.6	3.5	3.6
Home mortgages	1.1	0.6	-0.5	-0.7	-1.1	-1.3	-2.1	-2.1	-0.5
Other mortgages	3.8	4.0	3.4	3.2	3.1	3.6	3.2	3.9	4.3
Total	$7.7	$6.6	$7.5	$7.8	$5.3	$6.0	$10.2	$12.5	$13.3

Source: Institute of Life Insurance, *Life Insurance Fact Book*: (annual); Bankers Trust Company, *Credit and Capital Markets* (annual); *Federal Reserve Bulletin* (Flow of Funds). (Some columns do not add to totals due to rounding.)

surance companies or their parents, of mutual fund management companies, mortgage banking firms, and property insurers. The consolidated statements of such groups lose the characteristics of those of insurance companies, and their flows of funds become less and less typical of the life insurance industry as such.

Property and Liability Insurance Companies

Nature and Scope of Industry

The property-liability insurance group contains over 2,000 companies, with assets in excess of $83 billion consisting mainly of capital-market securities. Unlike life insurance companies, property and liability companies do not collect savings. They sell a service, and their liabilities do not represent firm dollar obligations to policyholders. They acquire their assets almost exclusively in the secondary markets. Their aggregate resources include a very respectable percentage of outstanding government and corporate instruments, and so investment policies exert an important influence on the market for outstanding long-term securities. Although our discussion, in the main, pertains to the whole industry, two important subclassifications should be recognized: (1) mutual and stock companies; and (2) insurers of property loss due to events such as fire, and insurers of personal liability.

Mutual companies do not issue stock but are owned by their policyholders. Their net worth is appropriately called "policyholders' surplus." The net worth of stock companies (capital stock and surplus) also constitutes protection to policyholders and so is also called policyholders' surplus, using the term in a broad sense. The distinction between the two types of ownership has an important influence on investment policy.

Insurers against loss to property from fire and other causes sell contracts that provide for indemnification of damage losses up to the limits of the policy. The actual losses depend on the cost of repair or replacement. Casualty insurance companies (auto, workmen's compensation, and so on) are primarily concerned with losses caused by injuries to persons and by damage to property of others. Many casualty companies also write fidelity and surety insurance.

"Multiple-line" companies, offering a variety of lines of property or casualty insurance or both, are found in both the mutual and stock categories.

Two minor types of organizations are *reciprocal exchanges*—cooperatives formed to provide coverage for members at cost—and *domestic Lloyds*—associations of unincorporated individuals that underwrite unusual risks.

Sources of Funds

Investment funds are derived mainly from (1) premium income allocated to two types of reserves for possible payment to policyholders—reserve for losses and reserve for unearned premiums; and (2) increases in policyholders' surplus consisting of capital (stock) and surplus and voluntary reserves of stock companies; and guarantee funds, net surplus, and voluntary reserves of mutuals. Loss reserves represent liability for claims that have been filed and that are anticipated (a 60 to 65 percent loss ratio is assumed). Premiums are collected in advance and are not fully earned until the policies expire (one, three, or five years for fire, one year for casualty), and so the unearned premium reserve represents the amount that would be returned to policyholders for the unexpired terms if all policies were canceled.

The actual net worth of a company is higher than reported because part of the unearned premium reserve represents funds in excess of actual need. Acquisition costs have already been incurred, and the risks could be reinsured for less than the prepaid premium. Typically, analysts transfer 35 to 40 percent of this reserve in calculating adjusted actual net worth.

TABLE 5–4.   Reserves and Net Worth, Property-Liability Insurance Companies, 1960–1973 (billions of dollars)

	1960	1965	1970	1973
Loss reserves:				
Stock companies	$ 5.4	$ 8.7	$14.0	$22.1
Mutuals	2.1	3.4	6.6	7.2
	$ 7.5	$12.1	$20.6	$29.3
Unearned premium reserves:				
Stock companies	$ 6.6	$ 8.3	$11.2	$14.2
Mutuals	1.6	2.3	3.3	3.7
	$ 8.2	$10.6	$14.5	$17.9
Policyholders' surplus:				
Stock companies	$ 9.5	$13.7	$14.0	$20.0
Mutuals	2.1	3.1	4.0	6.2
	$11.6	$16.8	$18.0	$26.2
Total reserves and net worth	$27.3	$39.5	$53.1	$73.4
Total assets:				
Stock companies	$22.8	$31.3	$42.6	$62.2
Mutuals	6.6	9.4	14.1	18.7
	$29.4	$40.7	$56.7	$80.9

Source: Alfred M. Best Co., Inc., *Best's Aggregates and Averages, Property-Liability* (annual).

The distinction between reserves and policyholders' surplus is important in determining investment policy. The data in Table 5–4 show the amounts and relative proportions of these accounts, along with total assets, from 1965 through 1973. (Net worth is unadjusted.) The data exclude reciprocal and domestic Lloyds companies and represent about 97 percent of the industry in the United States.

For both types of companies, the relative size of policyholders' surplus compared with reserves has steadily increased, reaching 39 percent of total assets in 1973, compared with 53 percent provided by reserves. This cushion against decline in asset values and calamitous losses has been consistently greater for stock companies than for mutuals.

Annual Sources of Funds, 1965–1973

The annual sources of new funds from 1965 through 1973 are shown in Table 5–5. The increase in unearned premium reserve accumula-

TABLE 5–5. Sources of Funds, Property-Liability Insurance Companies, 1965–1973 (billions of dollars)

	1965	1966	1967	1968	1969	1970	1971	1972	1973
Unearned premium reserves	$0.6	$0.7	$0.7	$0.7	$1.1	$1.7	$1.1	$1.3	$1.9
Loss reserves	1.0	1.2	1.4	1.8	2.1	2.2	2.7	3.7	3.8
Policyholders' surplus a	0.3	1.0	0.6	0.6	0.3	1.3	2.4	2.5	−1.1
Total	$2.0	$2.9	$2.7	$3.0	$3.6	$5.1	$6.2	$7.6	$4.6

a Net of changes in market values of assets.
Sources: Alfred M. Best Co., Inc., *Best's Aggregates and Averages, Property-Liability* (annual); Bankers Trust Company, *Credit and Capital Markets* (annual). (Certain columns do not add to totals because of rounding.)

tion, particularly in 1970, reflects favorable loss experience. After deducting the annual changes in cash and miscellaneous assets from the figures in Table 5–5, the following sums were available for capital-market use (in billions of dollars):

1965	1966	1967	1968	1969	1970	1971	1972	1973
$1.2	$2.2	$2.2	$2.5	$2.3	$4.0	$6.2	$6.2	$2.5

Differences among sources of funds play an important part in investment policy. Reserve liabilities have short and intermediate maturity, depending on the length of policies (one to five years). If an insurance company were to stop writing new business, it would pay out on existing claims approximately the amount of its loss reserve plus that portion of unearned premium credited to loss reserves as the policies neared expiration. This payment coverage would require extreme liquidity. Actually, however, most companies can meet both expenses and losses from new premium income. This income relieves the pressure for liquidity, but it does not remove the price risk on the portfolio. The possible need to sell securities in large amounts to meet calamitous losses requires not only a thick equity cushion, but also limited vulnerability to fluctuations in the market value of portfolio assets.

Uses of Funds

Two major functions are performed: underwriting of risk and investment of funds in a diversified portfolio of securities. The two are, however, closely related. The substantial holdings of federal securities and other high-grade assets reflect the obligation of the companies to meet all underwritten losses when incurred. Unlike life insurance companies, fire and casualty companies are unable to estimate future claims with a high degree accuracy.

Table 5–6 shows the combined percentage distribution of the assets of property-liability companies from 1960 through 1973.[5] The data conceal substantial variations within the group resulting from factors discussed below, but it is interesting to note that since 1965 the percentage composition of assets for all property-liability companies has remained relatively constant. The decline in relative holdings of U.S. government securities and corporate bonds has been absorbed by additional investments in municipal bonds and preferred stock.

Futhermore, the investment policies of property-liability companies contrast sharply with those of life insurance companies. The table shows that the former invest substantial sums in corporate stocks and very little in mortgages while the opposite result holds for life insurance companies. A greater need for liquidity by property-liability companies helps to explain the differences in security holdings. There is a substantial variance, however, in the investment policies of mutual and stock property-liability companies, which is briefly discussed below.

Factors Affecting Investment Policy

Various factors determine the investment policy of property and liability insurance companies.

Type of organization   Mutual companies lack the investment of stockholders as a cushion against losses in asset value. Policyholders' surplus belongs to the clients rather than to proprietors, and consequently, the investment policy of mutual companies is more con-

---

[5] The total asset figures exceed those given in Table 5–4 because the assets of reciprocal and domestic Lloyds are included.

TABLE 5–6. Combined Assets of Property-Liability Insurance Companies, Amounts and Percentages at Year End, 1960–1973 (billions of dollars)

	1960		1965		1970		1973	
U.S. government securities	$ 5.8	19.3%	$ 6.0	14.4%	$ 5.0	8.5%	$ 5.3	6.4%
Federally-sponsored agency securities	0.2	0.7	0.5	1.2	0.4	0.6	0.3	0.3
State and local government bonds:								
General	5.2	17.3	5.7	13.6	8.4	14.5	12.6	15.2
Revenue	3.0	10.0	5.5	13.2	8.4	14.5	15.5	18.7
Corporate bonds	1.7	5.6	2.6	6.2	8.1	14.0	7.7	9.3
Preferred stock	0.8	2.7	1.1	2.6	1.6	2.8	3.3	4.0
Common stock	8.6	28.6	14.1	33.7	16.0	27.6	24.3	29.2
Mortgages	0.1	0.3	0.1	0.2	0.2	0.4	0.2	0.2
Premium balances	2.0	6.6	2.6	6.2	4.3	7.5	6.4	7.7
Cash	1.4	4.6	1.3	3.1	1.4	2.4	1.5	1.8
Other assets	1.3	4.3	2.3	5.5	4.2	7.2	6.0	7.2
Total	$30.1	100%	$41.8	100%	$58.0	100%	$83.1	100%

Source: Alfred M. Best Co., Inc., *Best's Aggregates and Averages, Property-Liability* (annual).

servative. Bonds and preferred stock constituted 50 percent of total assets at the end of 1973. The relative importance of federal bonds has, however, declined substantially in the postwar period.

Type of business written   Property insurance policies may cover terms as long as five years and tend to have highly variable losses, whereas liability policies typically cover one year and losses are more stable from year to year. Consequently, companies writing property insurance often need greater liquidity.

Regulations for safety and liquidity   State laws governing investments vary considerably. In general, they require (1) investment in high-grade bonds of funds representing reserves and *minimum* required policy holders' surplus or capital; (2) adequate diversification; (3) observance of quality standards (for example, for stocks, a certain dividend history).

Sources of funds   Ability to meet all claims under any conditions requires avoidance of substantial price risks. Premiums are collected in advance, and funds representing reserves must be available at all times. In 1973, cash plus premium income in process of collection plus bonds equaled 59 percent of total assets. Loss reserves and unearned premiums represented 58 percent of total assets.

The proportion of liquid assets has declined in recent years. This decline reflects chiefly the increase in book (year-end market) value of stocks held, together with a decline in the relative importance of safety in terms of federal and corporate bonds.

Tax relief   Stock companies pay the corporate income-tax rate on net investment income and net underwriting profits. Mutuals are taxed (since 1962) on substantially the same basis.[6] As a result corporate bonds, with their fully taxable interest, are not in favor. By contrast, tax-exempt direct obligations of state and municipal governments and tax-free revenue bonds constituted 34 percent of the total assets of mutuals at the end of 1973. Stock companies had a smaller percentage in these assets because of the larger relative importance of common stocks in their portfolios.

Need for inflation protection   At the end of 1973, stock companies had 33 percent and mutuals 20 percent of total assets in common

---

[6] Mutual companies are permitted to establish pretax protection against loss accounts in an amount equal to 1 percent of insurance losses during the year and 25 percent of ordinary underwriting income for a period of five years. Mutual companies that elect to distribute their underwriting profit to policyholders are allowed full deduction for these "dividends."

stocks. Much of the shift to common stock in recent years reflects the need for price appreciation as protection against increasing costs of repair and replacement. In addition, 85 percent of dividend income is tax exempt. Nevertheless, there is a wide variation in policy; some companies emphasize common stocks, while others own relatively small amounts.

Liquidity   Liquidity needs are provided by cash and high-grade bonds. Recently, the main interest in federal bonds has been in the short- and intermediate-term categories because of their lesser price risk and because their yields are (in 1974) slightly above those of long maturities (see Chapter 8).

Volume of business and loss experience   Both rapidly rising volume of premiums written and an adverse record of underwriting losses require a conservative investment policy. The combination of insurance and investment "exposure," together with the other factors mentioned above, sets the pattern for the individual company.

Annual Uses of Funds, 1965–1973

The data in Table 5–7 show the net disposition of funds in capital-market assets in recent years. As noted earlier, federal bonds are not as attractive to property and liability companies as they are to some other institutional investors; the others need less liquidity and require investment income to offset underwriting losses and to provide earnings for dividends. The major emphasis has been on tax-free state and municipal bonds, except when deficit underwriting operations make nontaxable bonds less attractive. Net acquisitions of corporate stocks (mostly common) have been important in the 1970s.

Corporate bonds have drawn increasing investor funds as their attractive yields have compared favorably with other capital-market instruments.

Property and casualty insurance companies, with $83 billion in assets of which $69 billion consisted of securities at the end of 1973, are not nearly as large as the other major institutions—commercial banks, life insurance companies, and savings and loan associations—in asset size. Yet, due to their specialization in limited types of securities, they are a significant institutional factor in the stock market and in the market for state and local government obligations.

TABLE 5–7. Annual Flow of Funds into Capital-Market Assets, Property-Liability Insurance Companies at Year End, 1965–1973 (billions of dollars)

	1965	1966	1967	1968	1969	1970	1971	1972	1973
U.S. government securities	$—	$0.2	$—0.8	$—0.1	$—0.3	$—	$—	$—0.5	$0.8
Federally-sponsored agency securities	0.2	0.1	—	0.1	—	0.1	—0.2	—0.1	0.1
State and local government securities	0.5	1.0	1.5	0.8	1.1	1.3	3.5	3.5	4.3
Corporate bonds	0.6	0.7	0.6	1.2	0.8	1.5	0.3	0.8	—1.5
Corporate Stocks [a]	—0.1	0.2	0.9	0.6	0.7	1.1	2.5	2.5	—1.2
Total	$1.2	$2.2	2.2	$2.5	$2.3	$4.0	$6.2	$6.2	$2.5

[a] Stocks are shown net of change in market values.

Sources: Alfred M. Best Co., Inc., *Best's Aggregates and Averages, Property-Liability* (annual); Bankers Trust Company, *Credit and Capital Markets* (annual). (Some columns do not add to totals because of rounding.)

```
66666666666666666666666666666666666666666666666666666666666666666666666666666666666666
66666666666666666666666666666666666666666666666666666666666666666666666666666666666666
6666666666666666666666666666666  6666666666666  666  66666666666666666666666666666666666
6666666666666666666666666666666  6666666666  6666  66666666666666666666666666666666666
6666666666666666666666666666666666  66666666  66666  66666666666666666666666666666666666
6666666666666666666666666666666666  6666666  666666  66666666666666666666666666666666666
6666666666666666666666666666666666  66666  6666666  66666666666666666666666666666666666
66666666666666666666666666666666666  666  66666666  66666666666666666666666666666666666
66666666666666666666666666666666666  6  666666666  66666666666666666666666666666666666
666666666666666666666666666666666666  6666666666  66666666666666666666666666666666666
6666666666666666666666666666666666666  666666666  66666666666666666666666666666666666
66666666666666666666666666666666666666666666666666666666666666666666666666666666666666
66666666666666666666666666666666666666666666666666666666666666666666666666666666666666
```

Pension and Retirement Plans

Dᴜʀɪɴɢ the postwar period, pension and retirement plans of all types
have become very important investors in the capital markets. In this
chapter we are concerned chiefly with trusteed (noninsured) private
pension funds and state and local government retirement funds. A
short section on federal retirement funds is also included.

As the liabilities of pension funds are long-term commitments to
employees, it is not surprising, from a hedging viewpoint, that all types
of long-term capital market instruments are found in the growing
accumulations of retirement systems. Perhaps the most important
development in pension funds (until 1973–1974) has been the greater
emphasis on common stocks—except in the case of the federal accounts, which acquire Treasury obligations only—in an attempt to
obtain greater growth in the investment portfolios. The weak stock
market and poor economic outlook in 1973, and especially 1974, caused
many funds to put new money into high-yielding short- and long-term
debt instruments.

Trusteed Private Pension Funds

Nature and Scope

The importance of pension funds to the economy and to the capital
markets is tremendous. At the end of 1973, the assets of all public and
private pension and retirement funds totaled $344 billion. Although

both public and private pension funds have increased substantially since World War II, the most substantial growth has been in the private sector. Private plans numbered over 165,000 and had reserves totaling $183 billion (at book value) at the end of 1973.

Private pensions plans differ widely in a number of aspects, such as employees covered, service and age requirements for eligibility, retirement provisions, and vesting privileges. Our chief interest, however, lies in the sources and uses of funds and in their impact on the capital markets.

For our purposes plans can be classified as follows: (1) total private pension and profit-sharing plans (including those of companies, unions, and nonprofit organizations) versus corporate pension plans in particular; and (2) insured versus uninsured, or trusteed, corporate plans. The funds of insured corporate plans are invested in annuities and so are comingled with the other assets of life insurance companies.[1] Uninsured plans are usually administered by, or are at least in the custodianship of, bank trustees.

Table 6–1 shows the growth of total private plans since 1960. Their expansion reflects: (1) growth in employment; (2) the increase in the number of persons approaching retirement age and needing protection; (3) the increase in number of plans, indicating acceptance by employers of responsibility for their employees' retirement years; (4) the use of retirement plans—both fixed and profit-sharing—as incentives to improve work quality and lower employee turnover; (5) the need for inflation protection for retirement income; (6) inclusion of pensions in labor union contracts; and (7) the tax advantages of company plans that meet the eligibility requirements of the Internal Revenue Code, under which contributions are tax exempt to the company and to the employee until retirement.

Persons covered by private plans of all types in early 1974 amounted to 44 percent of wage and salary workers in private industry. Trusteed plans are more important than insured plans because they are larger, offer greater flexibility of investment policy, and hence are more involved in the capital markets.

Assets for all private noninsured funds, including those of nonprofit organizations, multiemployer funds, and union-administered funds, totaled $126.5 billion (at book value) at the end of 1973. The reserves

---

[1] Under a ruling by the Securities and Exchange Commission early in 1963, life insurance companies are exempt from its jurisdiction if they restrict annuity arrangements with employers to those involving fixed-income contracts. They may avoid SEC jurisdiction and still segregate the assets representing pension contracts and have their investment free from the usual restrictions on the acquisition of common stocks, providing the risk of market fluctuations is borne by the employer and does not affect the dollar amount of the employees' annuities.

TABLE 6–1.   Selected Data on All Private Retirement Plans,* at Year End,
1960–1973 (billions of dollars)

	1960	1965	1970	1972	1973
Persons covered a					
(number in 000)	21,200	25,300	29,700	27,500	‡
Contributions	$ 5.5	$ 8.4	$14.0	$18.5	‡
Benefit payments	$ 1.7	$ 3.4	$ 7.4	$10.0	‡
Reserves (book value):					
Insured plans	$18.8	$27.3	$40.1	$50.3	$56.0
Uninsured plans	33.1	59.2	97.0	117.5	126.5
Total reserves	$51.9	$86.5	$137.1	$167.8	$182.5

* Includes multiemployer and union-administered plans and those of nonprofit
organizations. Excludes federal railroad retirement program.
a Excludes those receiving benefits. Data prior to 1972 are being revised by the
Social Security Administration.
‡ Not available.
Sources: U.S. Department of Commerce, Bureau of the Census, *Statistical Ab-
stracts of the United States;* Department of Health, Education and Welfare, Social
Security Administration, *Social Security Bulletin;* Securities and Exchange Commission, *Statistical Bulletin.*

of insured plans aggregated only $56.0 bilion (see Table 6–1) or less
than half the total of noninsured plans.

Sources of Funds: Private Plans

Private plans derive their funds from employer and employee contributions and from net investment earnings. In many cases, all contributions are made by employers in amounts based on wages and
salaries, or company profits, or both. Excluding investment income,
employers as a whole contribute about 90 percent of the total yearly
contributions to pension plans [Table 6–2].
As shown in Table 6–1, total contributions to all private plans increased from $5.5 billion in 1960 to $18.5 billion in 1972. From 1968
through 1973, the average annual input was over $10 billion. Invest-
ment income, exclusive of profit on sale of assets, has provided about
27 percent of total receipts.

Annual Sources of Funds
of Noninsured Private Plans

Noninsured (trusteed) private plans exclude private plans administered by insurance companies but include nonprofit organization and labor unions. Funds available for investment consist of em-

TABLE 6–2.   Receipts of Private Noninsured Pension Plans, 1965–1973 (billions of dollars)

	1965	1966	1967	1968	1969	1970	1971	1972	1973
Employer contributions	$5.6	$6.4	$ 7.0	$ 7.7	$ 8.5	$ 9.7	$11.3	$12.7	$14.4
Employee contributions	0.7	0.7	0.8	0.9	1.0	1.1	1.1	1.2	1.3
Investment and other income [a]	2.4	2.7	3.0	3.3	3.7	4.0	4.2	4.4	5.0 est.
Total receipts	$8.7	$9.8	$10.8	$11.9	$13.2	$14.8	$16.6	$18.3	$20.7
Benefit payments and expenses	2.9	3.5	4.0	4.6	5.4	6.2	7.3	8.5	9.6
Net receipts	$5.8	$6.3	$ 6.8	$ 7.3	$ 7.8	$ 8.6	$ 9.4	$ 9.8	$11.1

[a] Not including profit (or loss) on sale of securities.

Sources: Social Security Administration, *Social Security Bulletin*; Securities and Exchange Commission, *Statistical Bulletin*; Bankers Trust Company, *Credit and Capital Markets* (annual).

ployer and employee contributions and investment income, net of benefits and expenses. The annual data from 1965 through 1973 in Table 6–2 reveal the steady growth of private plans, now at around $10 billion per year, or double the 1960 rate. Because the coverage of most plans is growing and will continue to do so for several years, receipts will be well in excess of expenditures and the excess will be invested primarily in capital-market instruments. It should be noted, however, that even though net receipts have continued to increase, benefit payments and expenses have risen from 33 percent of total receipts in 1965 to over 46 percent in 1973. Until 1963, investment income, alone, was sufficient to cover benefit payments; in 1973 benefit payments and expenses exceeded investment income by $4.6 billion.

Investment income in 1973 of 5.0 billion was about 24 percent of total receipts—a drop from 28 percent in 1965. This reflects the increased role of employer contributions in funding the pension plan. Investment income, as we use the term here, excludes realized and unrealized profits or losses on assets. If we include realized net capital losses of $920 million and relate investment income to book value, the rate of return was 3.3 percent in 1973. Excluding losses, the rate of return was 4.1 percent.

Deducting from the above sources the annual changes in cash and miscellaneous assets, we have the following sums available for capital-market investment (billions of dollars):

1965	1966	1967	1968	1969	1970	1971	1972	1973
$5.2	$5.9	$5.9	$6.9	$6.2	$7.1	$7.8	$6.8	$8.8

Uses of Funds: Investment Policy

The growing accumulation of corporate pension fund capital reflects the increase in the number of plans, the number of persons covered, and the increase in net receipts of established plans. The asset expansion of trusteed corporate plans in recent years is indicated in Table 6–3. Assets grew about $12 billion per year from 1965 through 1973, a yearly compounded growth rate of better than 10 percent. The market drop in 1973, however, caused stock values to drop by more than 14 percent and total assets of uninsured private pension funds dropped from $154.3 billion in 1972 to $132.2 billion in 1973. The decline accelerated in 1974. Nevertheless, the large yearly flow of funds into pension funds makes them a major demand component in the capital market for years to come.

Similar to those of insurance companies, the group figures hide the wide range in investment policy of individual funds. Some hold only federal bonds; others consist entirely of common stocks. But it is apparent that there is a continued swing into common stocks. At the end of 1968, stocks constituted about 62 percent of total assets. At the end of 1973, even in a declining market, common stocks were 68 percent of total pension fund assets.

Trusteed funds are normally managed by bank trust departments or investment advisors and are invested within the framework of trust regulations. The trust agreement may allow complete freedom in choosing investments. Even in nondiscretionary funds, however, wide latitude is provided by the agreements and by the "prudent-man" rule in effect in several states. In general, investment policy permits sufficient flexibility to take into account changes in the markets and the business cycle. These factors are especialy important to funds emphasizing common stocks; even in these the steady inflow of cash permits the use of dollar cost averaging. Some funds buy stocks every day. Others vary the proportions in cash, fixed-income securities, and equities according to a rough or an exact formula.

Investment policy is also affected by the sources of funds and by whether the benefits are to be fixed or variable. More risk can be taken with company-contributed funds and in plans whose benefits are not determined on an actuarial basis. If inflation hedging is an important goal, a substantial investment in common stocks has been considered appropriate (at least until 1974).

The high rate of inflation and the sharp increase in future pension benefits have, until recent years, caused pension administrations to focus more on common stocks in hopes of securing higher returns. A mere one-quarter of one percent improvement in annual return enables a company to cut its contributions or increase benefits by 4 to 6 percent per year. The market decline in 1973–1974, however, resulted in disillusionment with the belief that equities would provide this improvement.

Cash position   Funds differ greatly in the degree of liquidity maintained. Cash held (including commercial paper) affects the rate of return on the portfolio and for this reason represents less than 2 percent of total pension fund assets. In periods of continued weakness in the bond and stock market, cash balances usually increase as a percentage of assets.

United States government securities   The proportion of total pension fund assets held in federal securities has declined over the years to where they now represent only 3 percent of total assets. This decline reflects recognition of three factors: (1) that growing funds need little liquidity as payouts lag far behind cash receipts and both receipts and benefits are subject to forecasts; (2) that the rate of return on assets is important—the assets of the fund are expected to grow through compounding of income as well as through new contributions; and (3) that other securities may provide higher returns over the long run.

TABLE 6–3. Market Value of Assets of Uninsured Private Pension Funds,[a] 1960–1973 (billions of dollars)

	1960		1965		1970		1973	
	Amount	Percentage	Amount	Percentage	Amount	Percentage	Amount	Percentage
Cash and deposits	$0.9	2.4%	$0.9	1.2%	$ 1.8	1.7%	$ 2.3	1.7%
U.S. Government securities	2.7	7.2	2.9	4.1	3.0	2.9	4.4	3.3
Federally-sponsored agency securities (est.)	0.4	1.1	0.7	0.8	0.9	0.9	0.8	0.6
Corporate bonds	14.2	37.9	21.2	29.1	24.0	22.9	27.0	20.4
Preferred stock	0.7	1.9	0.8	1.1	1.6	1.5	1.0	0.8
Common stock:	15.8	42.2	40.0	54.8	65.5	62.6	89.5	67.7
(Own company)	(2.0)	(5.3)	(4.4)	(6.0)	(5.9)	(5.6)	(6.9)	(5.2)
(Other companies)	(13.8)	(36.9)	(35.6)	(48.8)	(59.6)	(56.9)	(82.6)	(62.5)
Mortgages	1.3	3.5	3.4	4.7	3.6	3.4	2.4	1.8
Other assets	1.4	3.8	3.0	4.1	4.3	4.1	4.8	3.6
Total	$37.1	100 %	$72.9	100 %	$104.7	100 %	$132.2	100 %

[a] Includes all corporate funds except those administered by insurance companies; includes nonprofit organization and multiemployer plans. (Some columns do not add to totals because of roundings.)

Sources: Social Security Administration, *Social Security Bulletin*; Securities and Exchange Commission, *Statistical Bulletin*; *Federal Reserve Bulletin* (Flow of Funds).

Corporate bonds   Fixed-income securities such as corporate bonds continue to occupy an important place in most portfolios even though they have declined as a percentage of total assets in recent years. Their steady income, plus cash from spacing of maturities, helps to provide for current expenses and benefits. They are especially important to funds that guarantee the repayment of employees' contributions, for large withdrawals in profit-sharing plans, and for the payment of vested benefits on death, withdrawal, or early retirement of participants.

At the end of 1973, corporate bonds including small amounts of federal agency securities (less than 1.0 billion) totaled $27.8 billion, or 21 percent of total pension fund assets.

The sharp decline in bond prices in 1966, 1969, and 1974, reflecting sharply increased yields, has caused a new look at the management and safety of these securities in an inflationary economy; however, if the high bond yields prevailing in 1974 persist and if the prices of common stocks fail to regain a substantial upward march after previous weaknesses, corporate bonds should attract more funds than has been the case in recent years.

Common stock   As suggested previously, pension funds have had their greatest impact in the area of common stocks where they are the largest institutional holder, owning about 10 percent of the value of all net domestic common stocks outstanding. In 1972, more than 70 percent of their net receipts went into stocks. This percentage dropped to less than 55 percent in 1973 as disenchantment with the stock market spread to pension funds and interest rates on alternative competing securities made these attractive alternative investments.

The funds' investment policies, characterized by a relatively slow portfolio turnover but large investment purchases, have contributed to a thinning of the market for selected issues, to the sharp changes in stock prices, and to modest stock yields as funds prefer long-term capital gains and growth.

Some stock activity by pension funds will likely continue in the future despite the disillusionment with the market in 1973–1974 as a result of the need for high returns over time to pay for future retirement benefits and vesting privileges for employees. Moreover, large wage increases and rapid inflation will place a greater premium on growth because retirement benefits are usually tied to a percentage of an employee's earnings and there will likely be more demands for benefits to cover the effects of inflation.

Unfortunately, stocks have not been the inflation hedges that some institutions had hoped and thus have not generated the expected capital gains, particularly from 1964 to 1974. It is not surprising that pension funds have to some degree switched to other types of investments in their search for higher returns.

Other investments   Preferred stocks do not appeal to tax-exempt institutions and thus continue to be in relative disfavor due to market yields that are as low as those on many high-grade bonds. This is a result of the tax exclusion on dividends paid to other corporate owners. Furthermore, their dividends are not assured, and they have no fixed maturity.

Nor are low-yielding, tax-free municipal bonds attractive to the qualified fund whose income is exempt under the Internal Revenue Code.

Types of investments that may have increasing emphasis are direct ownership of real estate and mortgages. The latter totaled only $2.4 billion, or less than 2 percent of total trusteed funds, at the end of 1973. In large funds, the attractive yields on mortgages offset their higher costs of management and lack of good marketability. Also, servicing can be left with originating mortgage companies and a secondary market for mortgages is becoming better established.

Annual Uses of Funds

The data in Table 6–4 show the annual net flows of investable funds into capital-market assets from 1965 through 1973. The trends indicated previously are apparent: the dramatic flow of funds into common stocks almost to the exclusion of all other capital-market instruments; the substantial variations in the flow of funds into corporate bonds; and the decrease in investment in federal obligations. As noted earlier, only in 1973–1974 did pension funds deviate from this established pattern. The funds have their greatest influence in the secondary corporate bond and stock markets. (Their impact on the stock and bond markets are discussed later in Chapters 10 and 11.)

Pension Reform Act of 1974

In the future, pension fund managers are likely to face an even greater need to improve fund performance because provisions in the Pension Reform Act of 1974 will sharply increase the cost of pensions to corporations. All existing and new corporate pension plans must conform to the requirements of the Act as of January 1, 1976. The major changes in the Act concern (1) earlier employee coverage under a plan, (2) a more uniform accrual of pension credits, (3) a guaranteed pension or vesting rights, (4) increased funding of past service liabilities, (5) insured pension benefits, and (6) increased retirement allowances for self-employed persons. (It should be noted, however, that the

TABLE 6–4. Annual Net Flow of Funds into Capital-Market Assets, Private Pension Funds, at Year End, 1965–1973 (billions of dollars)

	1965	1966	1967	1968	1969	1970	1971	1972	1973
U.S. government securities	$—0.2	$—0.5	$—0.4	$0.4	$ —	$0.3	$—0.2	$ 1.0	$ 0.5
Federally-sponsored agency securities	—	—	—0.2	0.1	—0.2	0.0	—0.1	0.1	0.5
Corporate bonds	1.7	2.1	1.6	1.7	0.8	2.1	—0.6	—0.8	2.2
Preferred stocks	0.1	2.1	0.2	0.4	0.1	—	0.4	—	—0.2
Common stocks	3.0	3.7	4.4	4.3	5.3	4.6	8.9	7.1	6.0
Home mortgages	0.2	0.2	0.1	—	0.1	0.1	—0.7	—0.7	—0.2
Other mortgages	0.4	0.3	0.1	—	0.1	—	0.1	0.1	—
Total	$ 5.2	$ 5.9	$ 5.9	$6.9	$ 6.2	$7.1	$ 7.8	$ 6.8	$ 8.8

Sources: Securities and Exchange Commission, *Statistical Bulletin*; Bankers Trust Company, *Credit and Capital Markets*. (Some columns do not add to totals because of rounding.)

new law does not require a firm to have a pension plan.) Some of the more important aspects affecting pensions are discussed below.

In the past, new employees often had to wait several years before becoming eligible for pension plans. Under the new law, with few exceptions, any person who is at least 25 years old, and who has been with a company for one year, is automatically covered under a company plan, if it has one. If an employee commenced work several years before age 25, he must be given up to three years credit for past service. Furthermore, the accumulation of pension credits must be done in an orderly and fair manner. The benefit credits to an employee in any one year cannot exceed $1\frac{1}{3}$ times the amount credited in any other year. This prevents a firm from accumulating few credits in early years and then sharply increasing credits after several years for the long-term employee. In this manner, a person leaving the employment of a firm receives a more proportional "vesting" of his retirement benefits.

The accumulation of these pension credits over time has often meant very little because in the past these credits were not "vested" with the individual. Very often, all pension benefits contributed in an employee's name were returned to the company if he left the firm before his earliest retirement date. Under the new Act, companies are given several options of ultimately vesting benefits with the employee. The plans allow for either partial vesting, immediately, or full vesting after as early as ten years or as late as fifteen years, and full vesting— i.e., a claim to all accrued credits in the employee's name—after age 45.

In the past, even if a plan had full vesting privileges from the start, there was no guarantee an employee would receive the benefits rightfully due him. Such a situation often resulted when a firm failed, or merged with another company, or merely dropped the plan. As of January 1, 1976, all plans must be funded on a current basis. Past service liabilities—obligations already accrued—must be authorized in an orderly and consistent fashion, and pension fund assets must be made independent of the firm itself. Accordingly, if a firm fails the employees will not lose the benefits accumulated for them in the pension plan. Finally, effective July 1, 1974, a new corporation, the Pension Benefit Guaranty Corporation, will insure all vested benefits up to certain specified limits. As of this date, the guarantee amounts to a maximum of $750 per month and up to one hundred percent of the employee's wages in his five years of highest earnings. The insurance company has an automatic "draw" of $100 million from the Treasury, but the bulk of the funds come from annual premium assessments of $1 per employee for corporations (50¢ for union plans).

From the new Act the implication is clear: more funds and investment income will be needed to cover the added cost. Annual contributions in 1974, running at the rate of over $20 billion, need to be placed in investment securities, which necessarily means that the capital market will be one of the prime beneficiaries.

State and Local Government Retirement Plans

The wide attention given to corporate and other pension funds has obscured the fact that public retirement funds have also grown rapidly in the postwar period. Total assets of the over 2,100 state and local employee retirement systems have increased from $4.7 billion in 1950 to $80.7 billion at the end of fiscal 1973. These resources are to provide retirement income to over 1½ million persons.

State and municipal pension funds differ in scope of coverage, employee contributions, vesting provisions, actuarial assumptions, and many other factors. We are concerned chiefly with investment policy.

Sources of Funds

Government and employee contributions and investment income provide the funds for these systems. The estimated annual sources of funds for *calendar years* 1965 through 1973 were as shown in Table 6–5. In comparison to pension funds where more than 90 percent of total contributions (excluding investment income) were paid by the employer, government contributions amounted to about 63 percent.

Although the net receipts have been substantial (in 1973, 67 percent of total receipts were brought down to net), many plans are relatively mature, and in recent years the rate of asset growth has lagged behind that of corporate and other private pension funds. Nevertheless, the annual supply of funds to the capital markets is very significant. Deducting the funds allocated to cash and miscellaneous assets, the figures are as follows:

1965	1966	1967	1968	1969	1970	1971	1972	1973
$3.2	$3.7	$3.9	$4.5	$5.1	$6.4	$6.9	$7.8	$9.3

Uses of Funds: Investment Policy

In 1950, federal, state, and local bonds comprised more than 87 percent of total assets. The percentage of relative investment declined sharply after that time and in 1973 the two categories together represented less than 10 percent of total assets. During this same period, the percentage of assets invested in corporate bonds rose from 11 percent in 1950 to 60 percent in 1973. The shift to corporate bonds reflected a declining need for liquidity and the superior yields available on high-grade corporates. At the end of 1973, the funds owned about 20 percent of all corporate bonds outstanding. Federal bonds and federal agency bonds worth $4.6 billion constituted about 5.6 percent of their total assets.

State and local retirement funds still own nearly $1.5 billion of tax-

TABLE 6–5. Annual Sources of Funds, State and Local Government Retirement Plans, 1965–1973 (billions of dollars)

	1965	1966	1967	1968	1969	1970	1971	1972	1973 [a]
Government contributions	$2.5	$2.8	$3.3	$3.8	$4.3	$4.9	$5.6	$6.4	$7.2
Employee contributions	1.7	1.9	2.1	2.3	2.6	3.0	3.4	3.8	4.2
Investment income	1.3	1.5	1.7	2.0	2.3	2.7	3.1	3.9	4.2
Total receipts	$5.5	$6.2	$7.1	$8.1	$9.2	$10.6	$12.1	$14.1	$15.6
Benefit payments	2.1	2.4	2.6	3.0	3.4	3.9	4.4	5.0	5.6
Net receipts	$3.4	$3.8	$4.5	$5.1	$5.8	$6.7	$7.7	$9.1	$10.0

[a] Estimated.

Sources: Bankers Trust Company, *Credit and Capital Markets* (annual); U.S. Department of Commerce, Bureau of the Census, *Government Finances*, and *Finances of Employee-Retirement Systems of State and Local Governments* (annual). (Some columns do not add to totals because of rounding.)

111

TABLE 6–6.   Book Value of Assets of State and Local Government Retirement Funds, Amounts and Percentages, Calendar Years 1960–1973 (billions of dollars)

	1960		1965		1970		1973	
	Amount	Percentage	Amount	Percentage	Amount	Percentage	Amount	Percentage
Cash	$ 0.2	1.0%	$ 0.3	0.9%	$ 0.6	1.0%	$ 1.0	1.2%
U.S. government securities	5.7	29.1	7.1	21.4	5.1	8.8	3.2	3.9
Federally-sponsored agency securities	0.2	1.0	0.5	1.5	1.6	2.7	1.4	1.7
State and local government securities	4.4	22.4	2.6	7.8	2.0	3.4	1.4	1.7
Corporate bonds	6.7	34.2	16.6	50.0	33.1	57.0	49.0	60.0
Preferred stock	—	—	0.2	0.6	0.4	0.7	0.5	0.6
Common stock	0.4	2.0	1.4	4.2	7.6	13.1	18.1	22.2
Mortgages	1.5	7.7	3.7	11.1	6.9	12.0	6.7	8.2
Other assets	0.5	2.6	0.8	2.4	0.8	1.4	0.4	0.5
Total	$19.6	100 %	$33.2	100 %	$58.1	100 %	$81.6	100 %

Sources: U.S. Department of Commerce, Bureau of the Census, *Governmental Finances* (annual) and *Finances of Employee-Retirement Systems of State and Local Governments*; Securities Exchange Commission, *Statistical Bulletin* and *Statistical Series*.

free municipal securities although they do not need the the tax advantage because they pay no taxes. Political pressure apparently requires investment in such securities in a number of jurisdictions, particularly when unsold municipal issues exist. However, their influence in the municipals market will likely continue to decrease as fund managers aim for higher portfolio yields.

In about 40 percent of the states, fund managers are now permitted to invest in high-grade listed common stocks, reflecting the need for potential inflation protection and the minor importance of liquidity. Since 1965 mortgages have shown the greatest relative growth. Mortgages are likely to be even more attractive in the future as the need for higher yields increases, legal barriers are removed, and fund managers become more familiar with mortgage instruments and make greater use of the services of mortgage correspondents.

Annual Uses of Funds

Table 6–7 shows the net annual additions to capital-market assets from 1965 through 1973. The data show the declining investment in federal and municipal bonds and the steady accumulation of corporate bonds and stocks. The rate of growth of state and local government retirement funds has been exceeded only by that of corporate pension funds and that of savings and loan associations. Although there are some signs of maturity, as government employment, salaries, and benefits continue to increase, these funds will likewise grow. Their increasing interest in high-grade corporate bonds has already made them the most important buyer of publicly-marketed securities of this type, especially in very recent years. Their influence in the stock market will likely continue to increase due to the increased pressure for portfolio performance and growth.

Federal Retirement Funds

The federal government manages several trust funds that may be divided into two broad categories: retirement/disability funds and agency funds. Included as retirement funds are (1) Old Age and Survivors Insurance Trust Fund (OASI)—Social Security, (2) Disability and Insurance Trust Fund, (3) Civil Service Retirement and Disability Fund (covering 1.2 million persons), and (4) Railroad Retirement Fund. The federal government manages a variety of other trust funds, acting as an agent in a fiduciary capacity. These include insurance funds, department trusts, and budgeted agency funds. Our concern in this chapter is with federal retirement funds.

TABLE 6–7. Annual Flows into Capital-Market Assets, State and Local Government Retirement Plans, 1965–1973
(billions of dollars)

	1965	1966	1967	1968	1969	1970	1971	1972	1973
U.S. government securities	$ 0.2	$—0.1	$—1.0	$—0.2	$—0.5	$—0.3	$—1.2	$—0.5	$—0.1
Federally-sponsored agency securities	0.1	0.1	0.1	0.4	0.1	—	—0.3	—0.1	0.3
State and local government securities	—0.3	—0.1	—0.1	—0.1	—0.1	—0.3	0.1	—0.1	—0.6
Corporate bonds	2.1	2.5	3.7	2.6	3.1	4.2	4.8	5.3	5.9
Corporate stocks	0.4	0.5	0.7	1.3	1.8	2.1	3.2	3.5	3.9
Mortgages	0.7	0.8	0.5	0.4	0.6	0.8	0.3	—0.3	—0.1
Total	$ 3.2	$ 3.7	$ 3.9	$ 4.5	$ 5.1	$ 6.4	$ 6.9	$ 7.8	$ 9.3

Sources: Bankers Trust Company, *Credit and Capital Markets* (annual); U.S. Department of Commerce, Bureau of the Census sources; *Federal Reserve Bulletin* (Flow of Funds). (Some columns do not add to totals because of rounding.)

Combined Assets of Federal Retirement Funds

Federal retirement funds have grown substantially in the postwar period reflecting the expanded benefits over time, the increasing number of employees covered by the retirement plans, and the growth in net receipts. Benefits have increased sharply as a result of competition from private pension funds, inflation and political popularity.

Table 6–8 shows the asset sizes for federal retirement funds in representative years 1960 through 1973. In total, the funds have not grown as rapidly as private pension plans or state and local retirement funds. Social Security assets, for instance, actually declined from 1955 through 1965 because of the increased benefits granted without commensurate increases in contributions. The rapid growth since 1965 has resulted from much higher contributions due to higher social security taxes.

TABLE 6–8.   Assets of Federal Government Retirement Funds, Years 1960–1973 (billions of dollars)

	1960	1965	1970	1973
Old Age Survivor's Insurance	$20.3	$18.2	$32.5	$36.5
Disability and Insurance	2.3	1.6	5.6	7.9
Civil Service Retirement and Disability	10.4	15.9	23.1	31.5
Railroad Retirement	3.7	3.9	4.4	3.8
Total	$36.7	$39.6	$65.6	$79.7

Sources: *Treasury Bulletin;* Securities and Exchange Commission, *Statistical Bulletin.*

The assets of federal retirement funds include some marketable federal securities, but the bulk of their holdings consists of special nonmarketable securities issued by the federal government (see Chapter 8).

In order to avoid intergovernmental transactions, changes in federal retirement trust holdings are excluded from the data on annual changes in the ownership of federal debt on page 137, and from the master schedule of sources and uses of funds in Chapter 13. But federal trust fund and agency ownership of U.S. debt is included in Table 8–5 (p. 140).

It is also important to distinguish the operations of these trust funds from Treasury management of a variety of federally sponsored agencies. The role of these agencies in supplying and using capital-market funds is discussed in Chapter 8, and their operations are included in the master data in Chapter 13.

```
777777777777777777777777777777777777777777777777777777777777777777777777777777777777777777777
777777777777777777777777777777777777777777777777777777777777777777777777777777777777777777777
7777777777777777777777777777    7777777777777   777    777    7777777777777777777777777777777
77777777777777777777777777777   7777777777777   77777  777    7777777777777777777777777777777
777777777777777777777777777777777  777777777   77777  777    7777777777777777777777777777777
7777777777777777777777777777777777  7777777   77777   777    7777777777777777777777777777777
77777777777777777777777777777777777  77777  7777777   777    7777777777777777777777777777777
77777777777777777777777777777777777777  777  7777777   777    7777777777777777777777777777777
777777777777777777777777777777777777777  7  777777777  777    7777777777777777777777777777777
7777777777777777777777777777777777777777777  777777777  777    7777777777777777777777777777777
77777777777777777777777777777777777777777777  7777777777  777    7777777777777777777777777777777
777777777777777777777777777777777777777777777777777777777777777777777777777777777777777777777
777777777777777777777777777777777777777777777777777777777777777777777777777777777777777777777
```

Investment Companies

THE great growth in investment company assets in the postwar period
prior to 1972 was one of the outstanding successes among all financial
intermediaries. This growth was abruptly reversed in the 1972 to 1974
period, however, as investment companies experienced considerable
problems due to investor disenchantment with the stock market and
competition from higher rates of return available on other securities.
Open-end investment companies, particularly, experienced heavy net
withdrawals of funds during this latter period as well as their sharp-
est decline in assets ever.

Serving as media through which individual investors acquire a stake
in bonds and stocks, investment companies have had a great influence
on investor habits and the securities markets. Their role has been to
funnel savings into outstanding securities in the secondary markets
rather than to finance new capital investment.

In recent years, since 1968, a new financial institution, the real
estate investment trust (REIT), has gained prominance (and notoriety)
in the capital markets. As the name suggests, these specialized institutions have emphasized real estate loans in their portfolios and in a
short period of time have grown to be the fifth largest institutional
holder of real estate mortgages. They, likewise, experienced considerable difficulty in the 1973 to 1974 period due to loan foreclosures and
general investor dissatisfaction that led to a precipitous decline in

market prices for most REITs. Real estate investment trusts are discussed in greater detail at the conclusion of this chapter.

General Nature and Types of Investment Companies

The investment company pools the funds of investors, obtained through the sale of shares (and in some cases bonds) in a portfolio of securities. The portfolio is presumably managed to obtain for the shareholders the benefits of diversification, professional selection and supervision of securities, and skilled timing of purchases and sales that hopefully will lead to better performance than the shareholder could do on his own through direct investment.

For these companies, investment is the primary function. Funds are obtained and managed for this purpose in contrast to other financial institutions (such as banks and insurance companies), which invest funds in order to meet their obligations, or holding companies, which acquire stocks for purposes of control.

Investment companies differ widely in size, objectives (such as income versus appreciation), methods of operation, composition of portfolios (securities held and range of diversification), degree of risk undertaken, and relations with investors. A classification of main types from the standpoint of organization and financing is as follows:

(1) Fixed. Here (using the trust form of organization) shares represent ownership of a portfolio over which management has little or no discretion.

(2) Management. This group, to which our discussion will be confined, involves companies whose managements, within the limits of announced policy and legal regulation, adjust the portfolio to obtain superior results for shareholders. There are two major categories:

(a) Open-end, or "mutual" funds. Such organizations make a continuous offering of new shares at prices to net the issuer their net asset value. The share capitalization is "open." Shares are redeemable at net asset value on very short notice. Such companies do not issue bonds or preferred stock. The investor in the shares of mutual funds acquires them from the company or from distributing dealers. There is no open-market trading. The market for their sale is the issuing company, through the privilege of redemption.

(b) Closed-end. Such companies have a fixed capitalization. Funds are obtained originally from the sale of common stock and, in the case of "leverage" companies, bonds or preferred stock (or both) and bank loans. Shares are traded on the listed and over-the-counter markets.

In recent years a number of new types of investment companies, focusing on one particular segment or aspect of the securities markets, have been formed. This category would include such funds as specialized income funds (open- and closed-end), emphasizing short- and/or long-term, high-income securities; "money-market" funds, stressing short-term instruments; and funds specializing in government securities —both federal and municipal—such as federal and agency bonds and tax-exempt bonds.

The financial statements of open-end (mutual) and of most closed-end companies show their securities portfolio at market value. Changes in asset values of an individual fund thus represent (a) excess (or deficit) of shares issued, sold to existing and new shareholders, over shares redeemed; and (b) any change in the market value of the portfolio. The open-end company must engage in constant sales activity to prevent redemptions from shrinking the asset value of the fund. Dollar growth of a closed-end company reflects occasional new financing and the rising market value of portfolio assets.

A minor type of mutual fund sells face-amount certificates, designed to reach a set dollar amount at the maturity of the contract.

The degree of diversification, types of securities held, amount of risk assumed, and investment purposes of the company are interrelated and are all reflected in a funds securities portfolio. Closed-end companies are classifiable into two major types: (a) diversified, with portfolios consisting of a broad array of securities, mainly common stocks; and (b) those whose portfolios consist mostly of special situation investments.

Since the late 1960s a number of funds have been started that specialize in certain income or capital gain arrangements or else emphasize a particular type of asset. These funds may be of either the open-end or closed-end variety and would include dual funds, funds that invest in money market instruments, or funds that purchase tax exempt securities only.

A newer form of a closed-end fund, the dual fund, first appeared in 1967. These funds are capitalized at equal amounts of common stock (capital shares) which receive all the capital appreciation, and income shares which receive all net investment income and have a cumulative dividend requirement. The funds have a redemption date varying from ten to fifteen years after issue. In 1973 and 1974, a number of other closed-end funds were launched, mostly as income funds specializing in "money-market" instruments.

A unique characteristic of most closed-end funds in recent years is that they have been selling at sharp discounts—up to 40 percent—of their underlying asset values. That is, the shares of the closed-end funds are traded and not redeemed—except upon "maturity" for dual funds—and their prices can vary substantially from underlying per share asset values. Lackluster performance and low yields relative to returns on other competing securities are usually given as reasons for the sharp price discounts of closed-end shares.

Open-end (mutual) funds as a group have the greatest variety of investments. One classification of such companies, by general portfolio distribution, at the end of 1973 is shown in Table 7–1.

TABLE 7–1.   Composition of Open-End (Mutual) Funds, 1973
(billions of dollars)

Type	Number	Net Assets Amount	Net Assets Percentage
Common Stock:			
Maximum capital gain	164	$ 5.7	11.7%
Growth	165	15.2	30.9
Growth and income	109	17.3	35.1
Specialized	22	0.5	1.1
Balanced	24	5.4	10.9
Income	63	3.2	6.3
Tax-free exchange	20	0.9	1.8
Bond and/or preferred	26	1.1	2.2
	593	$49.3	100 %

Source: Arthur Wiesenberger Services, Inc., *Investment Companies* (New York, 1974). International funds are excluded.

Growth and Size

The number of all investment companies had grown from 366 at the end of 1945 to over 800 at the end of 1973 with total assets increasing from $3 billion to $56 billion. Although investment companies were in existence in the 19th century almost all of their growth has occurred since 1945. Largely responsible for this growth were the open-end, or mutual, funds with total assets of $49.3 billion at the end of 1973.

Based on estimates by the Investment Company Institute, there were over 10.3 million individual and institutional investors holding investment company shares at the end of 1973.

This postwar expansion reflects a number of factors: the general economic progress of the period, the growth in total savings, the rise in stock market values, the aggressive sales promotion of mutual fund shares, and their appeal for a variety of reasons including the desire (through common stocks) to offset inflation. Other factors include the increase in the number and types of funds and the appeal of a growing number of conveniences and services such as accumulation plans and dividend reinvestment arrangements. On the other hand, the decline in mutual fund popularity in 1972 through 1974 paralleled the general disenchantment with stock market securities, and the increased criticism of poor mutual fund performance, especially after the "go-go" era of 1969–1970 and in the 1973–74 period of sharply falling prices.

Basic Sources of Funds

Closed-end companies, as a group, grow relatively slowly because of their fixed capitalizations. Occasionally new funds such as dual funds are offered and new securities are sold, but these developments are frequently offset by redemptions or partial liquidations of existing securities. The major factor in their asset growth has been the general rise in market value of stock holdings. Net assets of closed-end companies totaled $6.6 billion at the end of 1973, an increase from less than $1 billion at the end of 1945. About half of this growth was represented by increased market values.

Conversely, mutual funds can expand by selling more shares than they redeem. They stand ready to buy back shares at net asset value or sell shares at net asset value plus a commission. In every postwar year until 1972, mutual funds as a group sold more shares than were redeemed. Table 7–2 shows, however, that redemptions sharply exceeded sales in 1972 and 1973 and also continued into the first quarter of 1974. The large number of redemptions in 1973, together with slumping stock market prices, produced a whopping $10.3 billion drop in mutual fund assets from the previous year, or a decline of 17 percent.

From 1955 through 1973, the assets of open-end companies increased by $43.5 billion. Of this increase, $24.4 billion was attributable to net

TABLE 7–2. Net Assets and Net Sales, Mutual Investment Companies, 1955–1974 (millions of dollars)

	Total Change in Net Assets	Excess of Sales Over Redemptions	Asset Change Attributable to Market
1955–1959	+$ 9,709	5,266	+$4,443
1960–1964	+ 13,298	7,105	+ 6,193
1965	+ 6,104	2,396	+ 3,708
1966	— 391	2,666	— 3,057
1967	+ 9,872	1,926	+ 7,946
1968	+ 7,976	2,981	+ 4,995
1969	— 4,386	3,057	— 7,441
1970	— 683	1,638	— 2,321
1971	+ 9,076	397	+ 8,679
1972	+ 3,137	—1,671	+ 4,808
1973	— 10,278	—1,293	— 8,985
1974 (10 mos.)	— 9,403	— 780	—10,883

Sources: Arthur Wiesenberger Services, Inc., *Investment Companies* (annual); Investment Company Institute, *Mutual Fund Fact Book* (annual); *Federal Reserve Bulletin.*

sales of new shares.[2] The asset changes in the last column of Table 7–2 show how risky investment in common stocks can be even with diversified portfolios. From 1965 through 1973, four out of the nine years had mutual funds assets declining in value before adding net sales. It is the former figure that is important to existing mutual fund holders; therefore, the exodus from common stocks and mutual funds is not surprising when these recurring market developments exist.

Annual Sources of Funds

Table 7-2, column 3, shows the excess of sales of capital shares over redemptions (investment income is all distributed in dividends) for 1965 through 1973. A disconcerting trend for the mutual funds is the general decline since the late sixties in the sale of new shares and the rise in redemptions. Even if mutual funds are able to reverse the trend, it is likely to be some time before they enjoy anything close to the banner years of the late 50s and early 60s. Again, the relative decline in flows to mutual funds, even at a time when savings of individuals were at all-time highs as in 1971 through 1973, could be traced to: (1) poor investment performance, (2) high rates of return available on other securities, (3) public criticism of mutual funds, and (4) recent Securities and Exchange Commission rulings on sales of contractual plans that give the purchaser time to rescind the contract without penalty.

If we deduct changes in cash and other assets (net of liabilities) from yearly flows, the sources of funds available for capital market investment were:

1965	1966	1967	1968	1969	1970	1971	1972	1973
$1.6	$2.0	$1.2	$2.1	$2.1	$2.0	$0.8	$–0.3	$–2.7

Uses of Funds

Investment companies have operated almost mainly the capital markets. With the exception of short-term bank borrowings of a few closed-end companies, new funds are raised from long-term sources (sale of securities) and are invested mainly in the secondary securities markets, that is, in outstanding rather than in new issues. In contrast to other institutional groups—for example, savings and loan associations, whose members are much alike—investment companies differ very widely in objectives and portfolio composition. No generalizations as to the character of their assets are feasible, except to say that as a group the bulk of their money is placed in common stocks. Funds

---

[2] Data are for members of the Investment Company Institute, which represents more than 90 percent of the industry.

that buy only common stocks or that are predominantly stock funds are in the majority; they are also the very large funds and so dominate the group data. Investment in common stocks ran about $38 billion at the end of 1973, down from $51 billion in 1972 after reflecting the stock market decline.

Mutual funds are a major factor in the secondary securities markets. The emphasis for the group continues to be placed on common stocks, with some slight increase in the proportion of common stocks to total assets in recent years. This proportion is, of course, affected by changes in market value.

The combined balance sheets of mutual funds (ICI members) and their relative proportions at selected year ends are shown in Table 7–3. (Cash is shown net of all liabilities.) Until very recently, th'e burgeoning dollar growth of these funds shows up almost entirely in common stocks; common stocks as a proportion of total net assets reached 81 percent at the end of 1973, down from 86 percent in 1965. One should, of course, remember that group figures are not typical of all individual funds, which differ greatly in portfolio composition, and that funds specializing in common stocks dominate the combined data.

Annual Portfolio Changes

The data in Table 7–4 show the annual net accumulation of capital-market securities by mutual funds from 1965 through 1973. Government bond acquisitions have varied through the years, reflecting the need of the mutual funds for liquidity and their policy with respect to full investment and acquisitions by balanced funds that have bonds as an important part of their portfolio. The data show that in 1972, for the first time in the postwar era, mutual funds were net sellers of common stocks. (The figures in Table 7–4 represent net flows and not changes in market values.) This was caused by the large number of net redemptions, which induced mutual funds to sell securities in order to maintain liquidity.

Preferred stocks have continued to lose favor, being unattractive for income and (except for convertibles) lacking the appreciation possibilities of common stock. In 1974, the general decline in stock prices caused many funds to increase their cash positions in expectation of later buying opportunities.

Influence in the Capital Market

The impact of investment companies is primarily in the secondary market for corporate stocks and particularly those issues on the New York Stock Exchange.

At the end of 1973, listed holdings of mutual companies totalling

TABLE 7–3. Combined Net Assets of Open-End Investment Companies,* Amounts and Percentages, at Year End, 1960–1973 (billions of dollars)

	1960		1965		1970		1973	
	Amount	Percentage	Amount	Percentage	Amount	Percentage	Amount	Percentage
Net cash [a]	$ 0.4	2.4%	$ 1.0	2.8%	$ 2.7	5.7%	$ 2.8	6.0%
U.S. government securities	0.6	3.5	0.8	2.3	0.9	2.0	1.2	2.6
Corporate bonds	1.2	7.1	2.5	7.3	4.3	9.0	4.2	9.0
Preferred stocks	0.7	4.1	0.6	1.7	1.1	2.4	0.6	1.3
Common stocks	14.1	82.9	30.3	85.9	38.5	80.9	37.7	81.1
Total	$17.0	100 %	$35.2	100 %	$47.6	100 %	$59.8	100 %

* Investment Company Institute members only.

[a] Cash and commercial paper less liabilities.

Sources: Investment Company Institute, *Mutual Fund Fact Book* (annual); Arthur Wiesenberger Services, Inc., *Investment Companies* (annual); *Federal Reserve Bulletin*.

TABLE 7–4. Annual Flow into Capital-Market Assets, Mutual Funds, 1965–1973 (billions of dollars)

	1965	1966	1967	1968	1969	1970	1971	1972	1973
U.S. government securities	$ —	$ 0.6	$ -0.5	$ 0.2	$ -0.5	$ 0.2	$ -0.3	$ 0.1	$ 0.5
Corporate bonds	0.4	0.4	0.1	0.4	0.2	0.7	0.7	1.7	-0.9
Preferred stocks	-0.1	-0.1	—	—	0.2	-0.2	—	0.1	0.1
Common stocks	1.3	1.1	1.6	1.6	2.2	1.3	0.4	-1.6	-2.3
Total	$ 1.6	$ 2.0	$ 1.2	$ 2.1	$ 2.1	$ 2.0	$ 0.8	$ 0.3	$ -2.7

Sources: Investment Company Institute; Arthur Wiesenberger Services, Inc., *Investment Companies* (annual); Bankers Trust Company, *Credit and Capital Markets*. Data represent net flows and do not reflect changes in market value. Cash is omitted. (Some columns do not add to totals because of rounding.)

$41.4 billion represented 5.73 percent of the value of all stocks listed on the New York Stock Exchange.[4]

The contribution of mutual funds to stock trading activity, however, is considerably greater than their stock holdings would indicate and has accelerated from the late 1960s to 1974. Purchase transactions have exceeded sales in each year through 1971, but net acquisitions became negative in 1972 and 1973.

The activity rate of stock market trading by the mutual funds was the highest rate for all institutional investors in 1973—39 percent for the year. This rate, however, was the lowest turnover rate for mutual funds since 1966. The rate in 1972 was 45 percent.[5]

The rise in trading until 1973 was caused by the emphasis on performance by fund managers, lower commission fees on stock transactions, and the rapidly changing fortunes of some companies that have precipitated wholesale acquisitions and liquidations of particular common stocks. Lower activity in 1972 and 1973 reflected the negative cash flows and cautious investment policy by most funds.

The influence of mutual investment companies on stock prices has been the subject of much debate. Some have claimed that they have contributed to stability, because in all periods of stock declines, until 1972 and 1973, investors purchased more mutual fund shares than they sold (thus contributing net capital for investment in common stocks), and the companies themselves, on balance, increased rather than decreased their portfolios. Other informants have been less positive and have concluded that it is difficult to say whether mutual funds have been a stabilizing or destabilizing influence because so many other factors are involved, although there is some evidence of a destabilizing influence in a price decline.[6] In any event, the lack of new commitments in stock purchases and the liquidation of stocks by mutual funds to cover their redemptions in 1972 through 1974 has no doubt contributed to the poor market performance. In 1972 and 1973, net redemptions were $1.7 and $1.3 billion, respectively.

Real Estate Investment Trusts

Background and Development

Real estate investment trusts (REITs), although in existence in one form or another since the 19th century, have grown since 1970 from less than $1 billion in assets to over $20 billion (book value) in 1973

---

[4] Investment Company Institute, *Mutual Fund Fact Book 1974.*

[5] Securities and Exchange Commission, *Statistical Bulletin* (April 3, 1974, p. 405). The activity rate is the average of purchases and sales divided by the average market value of stockholdings at the beginning and end of the year.

[6] Wharton School of Commerce and Finance, *A Study of Mutual Funds,* p. 23.

and have become the fifth largest institutional holder of mortgages. The growth in the early 1970s was aided by the tremendous demand for mortgage money during this period and by the lack of available funds from traditional mortgage lenders. The aggressiveness in marketing the REIT concept was also a contributing factor.

The Real Estate Investment Trust Act of 1960 gave the small investor an opportunity to participate and receive the returns from real estate investments without the concomitant management problems. Thus, the REIT investor was to enjoy essentially the same benefits as mutual fund holders. It was not until after 1968, however, that REITs attracted any investor interest and became an important factor in the mortgage market (Table 7–5).

REIT companies are exempt from corporate income taxes if they meet the following qualifications: (1) They derive at least 75 percent of their gross income from rents, interest on mortgages, or capital gains on sales of property. Up to 15 percent of their income can come from regular security holdings and not more than 30 percent of their gross profits can come from sale of securities held less than six months nor real estate held less than four years. (2) At least 75 percent of their assets is in real estate, mortgages, cash, or government securities at the end of each quarter. (3) They distribute at least 90 percent of their income to shareholders, exclusive of capital gains.

REITs compare quite closely with closed-end investment companies in that investors hold the shares of the REIT and trade them on the exchanges and over-the-counter. Consequently, like closed-end funds, they may sell above or below their net asset values. The basic difference, of course, is that REITs are confined primarily to real estate investments, mortgages, and construction loans.

Although several types of real estate investment trusts are in existence, they can be classified as basically "equity" trusts or "mortgage" trusts. Equity trusts purchase real estate and receive the rents from the property. Mortgage trusts invest in mortgages and construction loans and do not own the property outright. Their income derives mainly from interest and loan fees charged the borrowers.

In order to increase profitability, mortgage trusts specializing in construction loans usually leverage themselves by borrowing short-term funds from banks or by issuing commercial paper in amounts up to two or three times their equity base, and lending at a higher rate to builders. This procedure worked well when short-term interest rates were relatively low in 1971 and 1972. As rates rose in 1973 and 1974, however, mortgage trusts found themselves squeezed as a result of (1) the decline in the spread between the short-term rates they paid on borrowed funds and previously committed rates to builders and (2) defaults by builders on loans. These two factors caused a sharp drop in the market prices of REITs such that in 1974, most sold well below book value and most REITs reported large losses.

TABLE 7–5. Combined Book Value of Assets of Real Estate Investment Trusts, 1968–1973 (billions of dollars)

	1968 [a]		1970		1972		1973	
	Amount	Percentage	Amount	Percentage	Amount	Percentage	Amount	Percentage
Home mortgages [b]	—	1%	$0.7	18%	$ 2.8	21%	$ 4.1	20%
Multifamily mortgages [b]	$0.1	33	1.0	26	2.9	22	3.7	18
Commercial mortgages [b]	0.1	33	1.5	40	4.9	38	7.3	36
Other assets	0.5	33	1.5	16	2.5	19	5.1	25
Total assets	$0.7	100%	$4.7	100%	$13.1	100%	$20.2	100%

[a] Insignificant data before 1968.
[b] Mortgages include construction loans.
Source: *Federal Reserve Bulletin* (flow of funds).

127

Investment Policy

Table 7–5, showing the combined assets of real estate investment trusts from 1968 to 1973, indicates the heavy emphasis on real estate mortgages as expected. The largest amount was committed to commercial mortgages wtih multifamily properties also receiving considerable support.

Annual Uses of Funds

Table 7–6 shows the annual uses of funds by REITs from 1968 to 1973. The relative emphasis on commercial and multifamily mortgages is again noted. The growth in home mortgages is largely attributed to the purchases of home mortgages from the Federal National Mortgage Association and the Federal Home Loan Mortgage Corporation in the secondary market.

TABLE 7–6.   Annual Flows into Capital-Market Assets of Real Estate
1968–1973 Year End Totals (billions of dollars)

	1968	1969	1970	1971	1972	1973
Home mortgages a	$ —	$0.1	$0.5	$0.7	$1.2	$1.3
Multifamily mortgages b	0.1	0.3	0.6	0.7	1.9	0.7
Commercial mortgages b	0.1	0.4	1.0	1.1	1.8	2.5
Total	$0.2	$0.8	$2.1	$2.5	$4.9	$4.5

a Insignificant amounts prior to 1968.
b Mortgages include construction loans.
Source: *Federal Reserve Bulletin* (flow of funds).

Sources of Funds

The annual sources of funds for capital market use for 1965 through 1973 are arrived at by deducting changes in miscellaneous assets such as cash and real estate. The growth in assets prior to 1968 was insignificant:

1965	1966	1967	1968	1969	1970	1971	1972	1973
—	—	—	$0.2	$0.8	$2.1	$2.5	$4.9	$4.5

The sharp increase in funds in 1972 and early in 1973 reflected the availability of funds at moderate interest rates and the favorable response that investors accorded the REIT concept. This response was drastically curtailed in the latter part of 1973 and in 1974 as liquidity problems faced most REITs due to "problem" loans and high interest rates.

The sources of funds for real estate investment trusts come from three major areas, corporate securities (bonds and stocks), commercial paper, and bank loans. Table 7–7 shows the sources employed from

TABLE 7–7. Annual Sources of Funds of Real Estate Investment Trusts, 1968–1973 Year-End Totals (billions of dollars)

	1968 a	1970	1972	1973
Commercial paper	—	—	$2.4	$0.7
Bank loans	$0.1	$0.6	1.3	4.0
Bonds issued	—	0.5	0.4	0.6
Mortgages on properties owned	0.2	0.1	0.5	0.3
Common equity	0.4	1.4	1.5	0.7
Other liabilities	—	0.1	0.1	—
Total	$0.7	$2.7	$6.2	$6.3

a Insignificant data before 1968.
Source: *Federal Reserve Bulletin* (flow of funds).

1968 through 1973. As noted earlier, corporate bonds, commercial paper, and bank loans have been used mostly by the mortgage trusts to increase leverage and profitability, but when short-term rates were high, as in 1974, the effect of the short-term borrowings on REITs was devastating. The increase in outstanding mortgage liabilities (Table 7–7) is a result of mortgages on properties owned primarily by equity trusts. The commercial paper total, since it is short-term, is a close approximation to the actual amount outstanding at the year end. Total amounts of commercial paper issued throughout the year are considerably higher.

The strategy used by REITs to expand their operations in 1970–1973 is a prime example of institutions' speculating on differences in the maturity structure of their assets and liabilities (Chapter 2). By borrowing short-term through issuing commercial paper and through bank loans and by lending longer term in construction loans and permanent mortgages, these institutions were in a highly unhedged position regarding their asset and liability structure. When borrowing rates were low and longer term lending rates were high they did exceedingly well. In high interest rate periods, such as 1973–74, when short-term money was above 12 percent they faced a dilemma: they could lend the money at a high rate, but builders faced large losses at such high rates. On the other hand, they could not reduce their short-term debt due to the longer term commitments and the inability of builders to repay their REIT loans on time. The net result was large losses for builders and REITs together, and a badly tarnished reputation for real estate investment institutions.

In order to try to salvage something from their operations and to cut losses, many mortgage lending REITs made application to shed their trust status and become operating companies. In this manner, they would not have to dispose of their foreclosed properties, could manage the properties for the trust's future benefit, and thus gain more freedom to operate. In addition, although it would mean loss of tax exemption on earnings, it would be an opportunity to carry forward losses to future earnings.

```
8888888888888888888888888888888888888888888888888888888888888888888888888888888888888888
8888888888888888888888888888888888888888888888888888888888888888888888888888888888888888
8888888888888888888888888    8888888888888    888    888    888    8888888888888888888888888
8888888888888888888888888    8888888888888    8888    888    888    8888888888888888888888888
88888888888888888888888888    888888888    88888    888    888    8888888888888888888888888
88888888888888888888888888888    8888888    888888    888    888    8888888888888888888888888
88888888888888888888888888888    88888    8888888    888    888    8888888888888888888888888
888888888888888888888888888888    888    88888888    888    888    8888888888888888888888888
8888888888888888888888888888888    8    888888888    888    888    8888888888888888888888888
88888888888888888888888888888888888    8888888888    888    888    8888888888888888888888888
8888888888888888888888888888888888888888    8888888888    888    888    8888888888888888888888888
8888888888888888888888888888888888888888888888888888888888888888888888888888888888888888
8888888888888888888888888888888888888888888888888888888888888888888888888888888888888888
```

The Federal Securities Market

O UR discussion of the federal securities market in this chapter emphasizes the obligations of the United States Treasury. We also discuss the unguaranteed securities of federally-sponsored agencies because they are closely related.

Federal agencies can be classified as financial intermediaries in some cases except that they frequently are the "second tier" of financial institutions that deal primarily with other financial institutions in providing depth and breadth to the capital markets. For simplicity, their roles as suppliers of capital and as users of long-term funds are combined in one section at the end of this chapter.

United States Obligations

The whole subject of federal financing and debt management and its interrelations with monetary policy is very complex. This discussion can include only a summary of federal borrowing policy, along with the demand, ownership, and yield aspects of the federal securities market.

Much of federal debt is intermediate or long term in maturity. But it is difficult arbitrarily to consider this portion separately from the short term. Maturities of all lengths are held by institutions for income and liquidity. Our discussion, however, focuses on the capital market, or long-term aspects of the federal securities market.

Types and Trends of Total Federal Debt

The direct and guaranteed debt of the federal government at the end of selected years is shown in Table 8–1. There are three major types of marketable federal securities: Treasury bills, notes, and bonds. Certificates of indebtedness have not been issued since the early 1960s and their range of maturity (around 1 year) has been covered by bills and notes.

Treasury bills are issued on a discount basis and are sold for cash at auction through the Federal Reserve banks. Their maturity ranges from 3 months to 1 year. One-year bills were first issued in 1959 in an effort to lengthen the maturity of the federal debt, and compete for investors' savings.

Treasury notes are coupon instruments with maturities of from 1 to 7 years. Treasury bonds have original maturities of from 7 to 26 years. Both are issued for cash and for refinancing. Bonds are often callable 5 years before maturity.

Only the fully-marketable issues are eligible for purchase by all investors, but there are minimum purchase amounts on some issues that effectively limit certain marketable federal securities to dealers and large institutions.

The remaining federal obligations are nonmarketable (nonnegotiable) and so their supply has only an indirect effect on market yields. Savings bonds currently being issued are Series E (discount bonds) and Series H (interest paid by check). E bonds yielded (in mid-1974) 6 percent if held to full maturity (5 years), and H bonds, 5.6 percent for the first 5 years and 6.5 percent for the remaining 5 years to maturity. Treasury bond "investment series" are sold to large institutional investors and are convertible into marketable Treasury notes. Foreign series are issued to foreign governments and monetary authorities. Special issues are sold directly to various agencies and government trust funds.

Growth of the Federal Debt

The federal debt rose from $43 billion in June 1940 to its wartime peak of $278 billion in fiscal 1945–1946. This enormous expansion was the result of wartime deficit financing. Peace brought a temporary decline in debt to $253 billion at the end of 1948, but this was followed by increases in all except four years through 1973. During this period, 1948–1973, debt has increased by $216 billion to a total of $469.9 billion at the end of 1973. The debt ratio, as a percentage of gross

TABLE 8–1.   Gross Public Debt of the United States Government,
at Year End, 1955–1973 (billions of dollars)

	1955	1960	1965	1970	1973
Marketable:					
Bills	$ 22.3	$ 39.5	$ 60.2	$ 87.9	$107.8
Certificates	15.7	18.4	—	—	—
Notes	43.3	51.3	50.2	101.2	124.6
Bonds	81.9	79.8	104.2	58.6	37.8
Total	$163.2	$189.0	$214.6	$247.7	$270.2
Nonmarketable:					
Savings bonds and notes	$ 57.9	$ 47.2	$ 50.3	$ 52.5	$ 60.8
Treasury bonds (investment series)	12.3	6.2	2.8	2.4	2.3
Foreign series issues	—	—	2.4	5.7	26.0
Special issues	43.9	44.3	46.3	78.1	107.1
Miscellaneous	0.4	0.1	0.1	0.9	0.4
Total	$114.5	$ 97.8	$101.9	$139.6	$197.6
Noninterest-bearing debt	3.0	3.4	4.4	1.9	2.1
	$280.7	$290.2	$320.9	$389.2	$469.9

Source: *Treasury Bulletin.*

national product, however, has declined from about 80 percent in 1948 down to 36 percent at the end of 1973. The rapid rise in debt since 1968 was caused largely by (1) the Viet Nam war, (2) expanded programs in health, education, and welfare, and (3) rising interest rates on federal debt, and (4) deficit financing.

At the end of 1973, marketable securities constituted $270 billion of the total debt of $470 billion. After deducting the $21 billion of marketable debt held by federal agencies and trust funds (in addition to their holdings of special issues), the debt involved in the money and capital markets, including holdings by the Federal Reserve banks, totaled $249 billion; of this amount, $139 billion had a maturity of less than one year and the remaining "capital-market" debt totaled $110 billion.

Reference to Table 1–2 shows that in the postwar period the federal debt has not increased at the same rate as have other long-term instruments. This lack of growth has facilitated the direction of institutional investment funds into the municipal and private capital markets. The federal government has normally avoided competing for funds in the long-term market in order to aid corporate investment and to minimize the interest costs on the total debt as short-term rates are usually less than long-term rates.

Shifts in Types and Maturities

The variations in total federal debt have not been accompanied by similar changes in marketable debt or its various maturity classes. The data in Table 8–2 show the composition of public marketable debt at selected year ends. From 1955 to 1965, marketable debt rose significantly while total nonmarketable debt fell as the federal government found the marketable approach to financing debt easier and more preferable. With the advent of sharply higher interest rates and the already strained capital markets in the late 1960s and early 1970s, the federal government tapped the source of funds available in the several trust funds that it manages and issued special nonmarketable issues, which more than doubled from 1965 through 1973. Savings bonds, the other major nonmarketable category, have shown little growth and, at the end of 1973, stood only $3 billion higher than in 1955.

TABLE 8–2.   Composition of Federal Marketable Debt at Year End, 1955–1973 (billions of dollars)

	1955	1960	1965	1970	1973
Within a year	$ 60.6	$ 73.8	$ 93.4	$123.4	$141.6
1–5 years	38.3	72.3	60.6	82.3	81.7
5–10 years	31.4	18.7	35.0	22.6	25.1
10–20 years	32.9	13.2	8.5	8.6	15.7
Over 20 years	—	11.0	17.1	10.7	6.1
	$163.2	$189.0	$214.6	$247.7	$270.2
Less debt held by federal agencies and trust funds	4.2	8.1	13.4	17.1	21.0
Total "public marketable" debt	$159.0	$180.9	$201.2	$230.6	$249.2

Sources: *Treasury Bulletin; Federal Reserve Bulletin.* Data are classified by final maturity. It should be noted that these data show the maturity classifications outstanding, not those at time of issue. A bond issued over 19 years ago with a maturity of 20 years would be included in the "within a year category.

The shifting internal composition of the debt has an important impact on yields. A planned increase in the supply of marketable types, resulting in increased yields, is not offset by demand for savings bonds whose yields have become increasingly unattractive. Funds are more likely to move into other savings media or into capital-market securities, and the holdings of special issues in government trust funds are in effect impounded. Yields on government bonds, therefore, reflect changes in marketable debt outstanding rather than in total debt.

The data in Tables 8–1 and 8–2 reveal the increasing importance of debt with maturity of five years or less. Large amounts of marketable Treasury bonds, whose original maturity is over 7 years, have not been issued in recent years because of the former statutory limits on their coupon rates and, as noted previously, a desire to minimize interest costs and not compete with private firms and state and local governments in the over-burdened, long-term bond markets.

As a result of Treasury policy to finance with shorter maturities, debt due within a year increased from 38 to 57 percent of marketable debt from 1955 through 1973. Debt due in 10 years or more constituted less than 9 percent of the total, compared with 20 percent in 1955. Short maturities have been emphasized during periods of economic expansion when long-term rates have been kept relatively low to aid long-term investment. On other occasions, short-term maturities have been emphasized when interest rates are high in order to avoid being "locked into" high long-term rates.

Medium maturities have been emphasized during periods of monetary ease such as 1955, 1957 through 1958, 1967, and 1971 to maintain a position of maximum neutrality in the money and capital market.

Movements in Treasury financing to add or to detract from the supply of different classes have reflected an attempt to balance the debt structure to minimize the total interest bill, aid our balance of payments, long-term investment, and so on. In general, the cyclical debt management policy of the Treasury with respect to maturities, although exerting now an upward and now a downward pressure on long-term yields, has in general followed the climate of the market.

Organization of the Primary Market

The Federal Reserve banks serve as agents of the Treasury in issuing and redeeming government securities. Each new issue is announced by press statements of the Secretary of the Treasury, and the Federal Reserve banks send out descriptive circulars to commercial banks, dealers, and other possible buyers. Only about seventeen important dealers have major activity in the government securities market—five commercial banks and twelve nonbank securities firms.

New issues of Treasury bills are offered at auction regularly through the Federal Reserve banks and their branches. The Secretary of the Treasury invites tenders for purchase on a discount basis below par and accepts bids from the highest price down until the approximate amount of funds stated in the offering circular is obtained. Federal Reserve banks themselves may make bids to the limit of the maturing bills they hold.

Other marketable issues are sold at par at a specified rate of interest determined after analysis of the market and consultation with banks and other institutions. The government enters the market in competition with other users of capital and must pay the required yield, although this yield is influenced by Treasury debt management and Federal Reserve open-market policy. The Federal Reserve banks receive the applications of dealers, banks, and others, and make allotments in accordance with instructions from the Treasury. They also receive payments for the securities and deposit the proceeds to Treasury accounts.

Volume and Buyers of New Federal Government Securities

Each year the Treasury undertakes sufficient financing to cover deficits and refunding and to keep its cash balance satisfactory. In most years, the total volume of financing substantially exceeds that of the combined state and local governments, and in some years, that of corporations. The net increases (or decreases) in outstanding debt (after refunding) do not correspond with Treasury budget surpluses and deficits because these in turn do not correspond with changes in Treasury cash balances. The balances reflect public and intragovernmental cash transactions, including transactions with government trust funds.

Table 8–3 shows the gross proceeds of new issues adjusted for refinancing and redemption (which in some years resulted in debt reduction) and for intragovernmental transfers and changes in Treasury cash balances. By deducting changes in government investment fund holdings (mostly special issues), the net annual changes in publicly-held securities, including, for this purpose, those held by sponsored federal agencies and by the Federal Reserve Banks, are derived. The substantial growth of the federal debt, especially since 1970, in competition with the needs of state and local governments, business, and individuals (for mortgages), has contributed to the high level of interest rates (see Figure 8–1). The drop in total gross debt in 1972 over 1971 (Table 8–3) was a result of increased treasury revenues from higher corporate profitability and personal income taxes and a smaller increase in governmental expenditures, particularly as the Viet Nam War wound down. The change in gross debt in 1973 over 1972 was caused by a need to finance increased governmental expenses, especially in new programs, and interest on the debt.

The discussions of the composition and the changes in the ownership of federal obligations in the previous chapters did not reveal the holdings of various maturities by all categories of investors. Even if the data were available, a discussion of the shift of funds between short- and long-term federal obligations in all institutions would present too many complexities for this short book. The data in Table 8–4 on annual net acquisitions of government securities (excluding those of Treasury trust funds) therefore include the whole range of maturities.

Business corporations change their holdings (short maturities) with

TABLE 8–3. Annual Changes in Publicly-held U.S. Government Securities, 1965–1973 (billions of dollars)

	1965	1966	1967	1968	1969	1970	1971	1972	1973
Gross proceeds, new issues	$ 9.3	$ 8.2	$ 19.4	$ 18.0	$ 4.8	$ 14.8	$ 17.3	$ 17.1	$ 17.9
Less—refinancing, intra-governmental financing, and changes in cash	6.3	−0.2	4.1	4.6	−5.4	−6.1	−17.7	−8.1	−2.7
Change in gross debt	$ 3.0	$ 8.4	$ 15.3	$ 13.4	$ 10.2	$ 20.9	$ 35.0	$ 25.2	$ 20.6
Less—change in U.S. government trust accounts	1.3	7.5	7.1	3.6	11.2	8.0	9.1	6.2	12.7
Change in U.S. government securities not in Treasury trusts [a]	$ 1.7	$ 0.9	$ 8.2	$ 9.8	$−1.0	$ 12.9	$ 25.9	$ 19.0	$ 7.9

[a] Figures may not add to totals due to rounding.

Sources: *Federal Reserve Bulletin*; *Treasury Bulletin*.

TABLE 8–4. Annual Acquisitions of Publicly-held U.S. Government Securities, 1965–1973 (billions of dollars)

	1965	1966	1967	1968	1969	1970	1971	1972	1973
Commercial banks	$-3.0	$-3.4	$ 6.3	$ 2.0	$-9.8	$ 7.0	$ 3.2	$ 2.1	$-8.8
Federal Reserve banks	3.8	3.5	4.8	3.8	4.2	5.0	8.1	-0.3	8.6
Mutual savings banks	-0.3	-0.7	-0.6	-0.5	-0.5	-0.2	0.2	0.2	-0.5
Savings & loan associations	0.4	0.3	1.4	0.4	-1.0	-0.4	1.4	1.0	-1.0
Life insurance companies	-0.5	-0.3	-0.2	-0.2	-0.3	-0.1	-0.2	—	0.1
Property and liability insurance companies	—	0.2	-0.8	-0.1	-0.3	—	—	-0.5	0.8
Private noninsured pension funds	-0.2	-0.5	-0.4	0.4	—	0.2	-0.2	1.0	0.5
State and local government retirement funds	0.2	-0.1	-1.0	-0.2	-0.5	-0.3	-1.2	-0.5	-0.1
Mutual investment companies	—	0.6	-0.5	0.2	-0.5	0.2	-0.3	0.1	0.5
Federally-sponsored credit agencies	0.1	1.0	—	-0.1	-0.4	1.9	-1.2	-0.4	1.3
Business and financial corporations	-1.8	-1.8	-1.1	-0.5	-2.8	-0.2	2.0	-3.1	-3.0
State and local governments	1.6	1.3	—	0.3	2.2	-0.3	0.3	3.3	1.2
Foreign investors	—	-2.2	1.3	-1.5	-2.9	9.2	26.3	8.4	0.3
Individuals and others	1.4	3.0	-1.0	5.8	11.6	-9.1	-12.5	7.7	8.0
Total	$ 1.7	$ 0.9	$ 8.2	$ 9.8	$-1.0	$ 12.9	$ 25.9	$ 19.0	$ 7.9

Sources: Citations in schedules, Chapters 3–7; *Federal Reserve Bulletin*; *Treasury Bulletin*; Bankers Trust Company, *Credit and Capital Markets*. (Some columns do not add to totals because of rounding.)

their changing need of operating cash. Liquidation to meet expansion and, in part, to avoid high interest costs is apparent in 1964 through 1973. In 1966 and 1969 when money was tight and interest rates were high, business and financial corporations were net sellers of federal securities in the amounts of $1.8 and $2.8 billion, respectively. Net additions were made in 1971 as corporate liquidity improved and temporary funds were available for security purchases, but the process was again reversed in 1972 to 1974 as monetary restraint prevailed and funds were used for corporate expansion.

Foreign and individuals' acquisitions also show cyclical variations, although their purchases or sales are likely to be more influenced by interest rates available on alternative securities. In 1971, these groups made opposite investment decisions on their federal security holdings. Individuals and others were large net sellers ($12.5 billion) though foreign investors were large net purchasers ($26.3 billion). This reflected both the relatively higher rates available on other types of alternative domestic securities as well as the lower rates in some foreign markets and the weakness in other foreign currencies that forced some investors to hold federal securities. In 1972 to 1973, individuals and others joined foreigners in continuing to add to their government holdings as rates remained relatively high.

Among the institutional owners, commercial banks show acquisitions of the greatest volatility. Bank funds move into and out of this asset with the changing cyclical demand for loans. In 1969, the net liquidation helped to meet the credit strain of that year (see Chapter 3). Modest purchases of federal securities were made in 1970 to 1972 as time and savings inflows improved substantially and the period became one of monetary ease. Substantial federal securities were sold on balance in 1973 and 1974 as tight money and heavy corporate loan demand prevailed.

As we have seen, life insurance companies, mutual savings banks, and pension funds have steadily reduced their federal investments. In contrast to their influence on the corporate bond and stock markets, institutional investors (other than commercial and Federal Reserve banks) have had a declining impact on the market for federal debt. The steady increase in holdings by Federal Reserve banks reflects the expansion of their deposits and their contribution to the money supply.

Ownership of the Federal Debt

At the end of 1973, the gross direct and guaranteed debt of the federal government was owned as shown in Table 8–5. Almost three-fourths of the debt was held outside the commercial banking system. Although debt held by institutions is not demonetized in the technical sense, it is subject to only indirect fiscal influence. Nearly 40 percent of the total debt was held by federal investment accounts and by individuals; the nonmarketable character of these holdings remove them from any impact on the market. The share of debt held by business corporations and foreign investors constitutes a volatile element and exerts a more than proportional influence on yields.

The changes in the ownership of federal obligations have resulted in an interesting pattern. We have already discussed the shifts in institutional ownership. "Foreign and International" holdings, representing mainly short-term obligations held for liquidity and as a hedge against fluctuating foreign currencies, have become very substantial.

TABLE 8–5.   Ownership of Direct Federal Securities, 1973
(billions of dollars)

		Amount	Percentage
Commercial banks		$ 58.8	12.5%
Federal Reserve banks		78.5	16.7
Mutual savings banks		3.0	0.6
Savings and loan associations		5.0	1.1
Life insurance companies		3.4	0.7
Property-liability insurance companies		5.3	1.1
Uninsured private pension plans		4.4	0.9
Federal insurance and pension funds		97.7	20.8
Federally-sponsored credit agencies		4.0	0.8
Other federal agencies and trust funds		27.9	5.9
Investment companies (mutual)		1.2	0.3
Other corporations		10.9	2.3
State and local government retirement funds (est.)		3.2	0.7
State and local governments (direct)		31.0	6.6
Individuals:			
Savings bonds	$60.3		
Other	16.9	77.2	16.4
Foreign and international		55.6	11.8
Miscellaneous		2.8	0.6
Total		$469.9	100 %

Sources: *Treasury Bulletin, Federal Reserve Bulletin;* adjusted from data in Chapters 3–7.

State and local government holdings represent investment of miscellaneous trust funds and liquid assets. Together with retirement funds, their share is significant. Individuals owned $17 billion of debt in addition to $60 billion of savings bonds. The latter, yielding 5.6 to 6 percent to maturity (in October 1974), have declined in attraction relative to competing savings and capital-market instruments. The federal insurance and pension funds own special nonmarketable issues for the reserves of the insurance and retirement plans managed by the Treasury (see p. 113).

Organization of the Secondary Market in Federal Securities

The secondary market in federal securities is largely a dealer market, both for short-term maturities, which are close substitutes for money, and for the longer-term issues. Yields vary with maturity, and the dealers arbitrage the yields on various maturities to produce spreads satisfactory to the buyers and sellers of the various issues. The market is the mechanism whereby the structure of interest rates affects the flow of savings according to the demands of borrowers and lenders.

Although federal obligations are listed on the New York Stock Exchange, transactions in outstanding securities are made in the over-the-counter market through dealers and a limited number of banks. Operations are conducted by the telephone and teletype. The Federal Reserve Bank of New York also operates a trading desk for open-market operations. Some dealers specialize in certain securities. Although also active in the short-term market, the larger dealers and banks do most of the trading in long-term maturities. They keep in constant touch with the locus of ownership of different issues and with potential buyers, on a national basis. The smaller dealers tend to concentrate more in the New York market than elsewhere.

Dealers act mainly as principals for their own accounts, "making markets" for customers and other dealers by quoting firm prices or spreads at which they are willing to buy and sell. However, in large transactions in longer-maturity issues, the larger dealers also act as brokers. The broker function reflects the smaller size of longer-maturity issues and the frequency of Treasury refundings.

The Federal Reserve System provides important services. As we have seen, it auctions Treasury bills and acts as fiscal agent of the Treasury in the exchange of issues involved in refunding. The Federal Reserve Bank of New York is particularly active, serving as the medium for transactions of the Federal Reserve Open Market Committee with dealers. It also acts as agent for other buyers and sellers. The Federal Reserve banks also finance dealer positions through the use of repurchase agreements, which are, in effect, temporary loans.

Financial institutions, including commercial and Federal Reserve banks, are the dealers' major customers, although a growing volume of business in bills and certificates is done with corporations. The market for federal obligations is the largest security market in the country. In 1974, the dollar volume of transactions conducted by dealers reporting to the Federal Reserve Bank of New York averaged $3½ billion per day.[1]

---

[1] *Federal Reserve Bulletin.*

Prices and Yields

The yields and prices of marketable government securities rise and fall with general changes in short- and long-term interest rates, which in turn reflect the demand of and supply for funds. Because these yields represent the price of riskless money, they are close to being pure interest rates. They are however, subject to two special influences: (1) changing Treasury debt policy with respect to the issue and redemption of different maturities, and its effects, through supply, on the yield pattern; and (2) Federal Reserve policy implemented through open-market operations, which affects both supply and demand and which influences yields on different maturities through shifts in buying and selling between short- and long-term securities.

Figure 8–1 shows the market yields (averages of daily yields) of short-, medium-, and long-term Treasury obligations for selected dates from 1961.

Since 1951, after the Treasury–Federal Reserve Board accord where rates were "unpegged," yields have fluctuated in a pronounced pattern related in part to the general business cycle but, more importantly, to money- and capital-market conditions. After the Federal Reserve Open Market Committee abandoned its "bills only" policy in the late fifties, the actions of the "Fed" in influencing short- or long-term market rates became relatively neutral and interest rates were allowed to respond more naturally to market conditions.

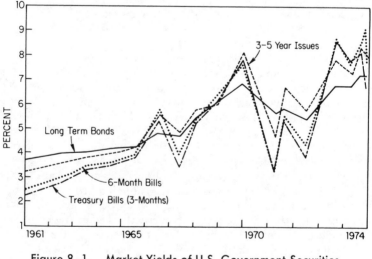

Figure 8–1.   Market Yields of U.S. Government Securities,
1961–1974

Source: *Federal Reserve Bulletin.* For data, see Appendix, Table A–1.

Tight money prevailed in 1959 as the interest rate on Treasury securities rose to more than 5 percent (the magic 5's); thereafter, there was a general decline in yields until May 1961 produced the more typical situation—yields rising with maturities. During the decline, long-term rates fell to less than 4 percent. Then came a long climb in all money and capital-market rates that culminated in the "credit crunch" in the fall of 1966. Demand for both short and long funds by individuals, corporations, governments, and institutions ran far ahead of supply and drove yields to record heights. Short- and medium-term yields substantially exceeded the long term. The process was magnified by the credit policy of the Federal Reserve, which kept the discount rate at 4½ percent from December 1965.

Some weakening of yields until the middle of 1967 and the decline in short-term below long-term rates, encouraged by the reduction to 4 percent in the discount rate in April 1967, reflected an easing in the money and capital markets. Then yields soared again until, by the end of 1968, they had reached all-time highs. The discount rate had been raised to 5½ percent in December. The primate rate, at which city banks lent to their strongest customers, went to 7 percent, and, as we shall see in subsequent chapters, yields on municipal and corporate obligations reached new heights.

The trend continued into 1969. During the first half of the year, yields on all maturities continued to rise as a new "crunch" developed. Efforts of the Federal Reserve to aid in discouraging the expansion of credit and thus to help in controlling inflation included the increase in the discount rate to 6 percent in April, together with increases in member bank reserve requirements. In June 1969, the bank prime rate went to 8½ percent with other rates, notably federal funds and Eurodollars, soaring considerably higher—up to 13 percent.

By December, 90-day Treasury bills were selling to yield 7.2 percent, one-year bills 7.5 percent, and a new issue of 18-month notes required 7¾ percent—the highest coupon rate in 110 years. Long-term yields also set new highs. The average yield on long-term "Treasurys" at the end of November was 6.6 percent. The extreme variation and erosion in the price of long-term Treasury bonds resulting from the increases in yield are indicated by the fact that in July 1954, the average price of taxable Treasury's was 108. By the autumn of 1969, it was at its then all-time low of 62.

The sharp break in interest rates in 1970 and 1971 sent short-term rates considerably below long-term rates and the more normal pattern of rising yields with length of maturity was resumed. The short-term rate (Figure 8–1) dipped over 4 percentage points from 7.87 percent in January 1970 to 3.38 percent in March 1971. Long-term Treasury issues dropped during this same period from 6.86 to 5.71 percent.

Yields were up again in July of 1971 but then fell back by over 1 percent in short-term securities and by about 40 basis points in long-term securities by July 1972. From there rates rose to unprecedented levels, reaching a high of 8.96 percent for short-term securities (90-day bills) in August 1974, while at the same time long-term rates rose to 7.33 percent before declining later in the year.

One conclusion from observing interest rate patterns in the 1960s and early 1970s is that short-term rates have reached higher levels and fluctuated considerably more than in the past. Furthermore, throughout most of the period, from 1965 on, long-term rates have remained relatively near their all-time highs.

The substantial swings and high levels of interest rates have been caused by: (1) the high rate of inflation; (2) the development of international markets that are sensitive to interest rate levels, inflation, political disruptions, and other economic factors—here the interest rate mechanism has been the primary tool in influencing balance of payments, trade deficits, and liquidity crises; (3) the demand for funds by government and business alike (see Chapters 3 to 6); (4) the gradual acceptance of higher interest rates by investors, borrowers and financial institutions; (5) the change in management philosophy and procedures by many financial institutions emphasizing the free interplay of market rates without government interference; and (6) the formula-based methods of calculating prime rates that have tended to cause quick responses to rate changes.

Securities of Federally-Sponsored Credit Agencies

The term *federal agency* covers a broad and changing group of often specialized organizations that serve many different purposes. The various agencies fall conveniently into three groups: (1) federally-sponsored credit agencies, (2) budget agencies, and (3) other specific agencies.

Many of the federal agencies have had an important indirect influence in the capital markets. On the supply side, they have made loans to member organizations that in turn acquired capital-market instruments. On the demand side, they have borrowed from or sold stock to the Treasury and have sold stock to and acquired deposits from member organizations. Some of the funds of the member organizations have thus been diverted from direct employment in the markets.

Federally-sponsored credit agencies are not owned by the U.S. Government, but were initially authorized under its auspices. Their shares are owned either (1) by the institutions that the agency is designed to directly benefit, such as Federal Home Loan Banks shares owned by savings and loan associations, (2) by the investing public, such as the Federal National Mortgage Association (FNMA), whose shares are traded on the New York Stock Exchange, or (3) by another agency, as in the case of the Federal Home Loan Mortgage Corporation, whose shares are owned by Federal Home Loan Banks. The six current agencies, as listed in Table 8–6, are the concern of this chapter.

Budget agencies are owned by the U.S. Government and are operated by various governmental departments. Included in this group are the Federal Housing Administration, the Tennessee Valley Authority, the Government National Mortgage Association, the Export-Import Bank of the U.S., and the Farmers Home Administration.

All of the above, at one time or another, have issued their own securities.

Other special "agencies" are owned by the federal government but have not issued securities to the public. Their funds come from appropriations by Congress and/or from fees that they charge for their services. Included in the former category would be such agencies as the Commodity Credit Corporation and the Small Business Administration and in the latter the Federal Deposit Insurance Corporation and the Federal Savings and Loan Insurance Corporation.

Recognizing the problems associated with the burgeoning number of agencies and agency issues, the Federal Financing Bank was created by Congress in 1974. The purpose of the FFB is to raise its own funds in the capital markets and borrow from the Treasury, if necessary, and lend these funds, in turn, to the various agencies eligible for participation in the FFB. The benefit from the new bank is two-fold: (1) it will be able to borrow at a lower interest rate than any agency could obtain independently, and (2) it should make the capital market more orderly and efficient by reducing the number of separate issues.

The agencies eligible for FFB participation generally include most of the agencies listed in categories (2) or (3) above, but they do not include federally-sponsored credit agencies, which will continue to handle their own financing in the capital markets.

In order to avoid direct competition with the federally-sponsored credit agencies and other institutions—particularly savings and loan associations—in the credit markets, the FFB security issues are designed primarily for large investors and, accordingly, have minimum denominations of $10,000.

Thus, the federally-sponsored credit agencies operate as usual and supply funds to the capital market by acquiring federal obligations, mortgages, municipal bonds, and, to a certain extent, notes and securities of businesses, and obtain funds from the market by selling their own obligations to individual and institutional investors.

Public Borrowing

The direct debentures and notes of the federally-sponsored credit agencies outstanding at the end of selected years are shown in Table 8–6.

TABLE 8–6.   Outstanding Debt Securities of Federally-sponsored Credit
Agencies, 1955–1973 (billions of dollars)

	1955	1960	1965	1970	1973
Banks for Cooperatives	$0.1	$0.4	$ 0.8	$ 1.8	$ 2.7
Federal Home Loan Banks	1.0	1.3	5.2	10.2	15.4
Federal Intermediate Credit Banks	0.7	1.5	2.3	4.8	6.9
Federal Land Banks	1.2	2.2	3.7	6.4	9.8
Federal National Mortgage Association	0.6	2.5	1.9	15.2	23.0
Federal Home Loan Mortgage Corporation	—	—	—	—	2.6
	$3.6	$7.9	$14.1	$38.4	$60.4

Sources: *Federal Reserve Bulletin; Moody's Government Manual; Treasury
Bulletin.*

The public debt of these agencies rises and falls with the volume of
their activities and with their changing reliance on debt financing.
Although their financing through 1968 was rather small, their
growth since that ·time has increased measurably such that in recent
years their annual financing on occasions has exceeded that of many
other major institutions. The primary cause for their rapid growth in
the 1970s has been a result of the difficulty the individuals and institutions they serve have encountered in securing funds from other sources
—especially mortgage money by individuals and savings by savings and
loan associations. These latter groups, particularly in periods of tight
money and high interest rates, have been seeking more and more support directly and indirectly from the appropriate credit agency.

The annual net changes in outstanding publicly-held notes and debentures of the sponsored credit agencies from 1965 through 1973 are:

1965	1966	1967	1968	1969	1970	1971	1972	1973
$2.0	$5.0	$—0.6	$3.2	$9.1	$8.4	$3.8	$6.2	$19.6

These figures do not indicate total activity in the capital markets.
Other sources have been employed, and some funds have been devoted
to farm and urban loans of a specialized or short-term nature and to
loans to member organizations. Nevertheless the data attests to the
emerging importance of credit agencies in the 1970s.

Chief Investments

Federal credit agencies direct funds to the capital markets mainly by acquiring federal securities and mortgages of different types and by different routes. With the exception of the case of the Federal National Mortgage Association, much of the influence of the Federal credit agencies in the mortgage market has been indirect, through member organizations. The chief assets of the sponsored credit agencies were as in Table 8–7 at selected year ends.

Banks for Cooperatives make loans to farmers' cooperatives to finance the handling and packing of farm commodities. The eleven Federal Home Loan Banks advance funds to member savings and loan associations (all federally- and state-chartered associations that choose to join) for mortgage loan purposes (see Chapter 4). The Federal National Mortgage Association (now privately owned) acquires FHA-guaranteed mortgages in both the primary and secondary markets (see Chapter 11). The twelve Federal Intermediate Credit Banks lend on

TABLE 8–7. Principal Assets of Federally-sponsored Credit Agencies, 1955–1973 (billions of dollars)

	1955	1960	1965	1970	1973
Banks for Cooperatives— Loans to Co-ops	$0.4	$0.6	$1.1	$ 2.0	$ 2.6
Federal Home Loan Banks: Advances to members	1.4	2.0	6.0	10.6	15.2
Investments	0.7	1.2	1.6	3.9	3.5
Federal Intermediate Credit Banks—Loans	0.7	1.5	2.5	5.0	7.2
Federal Land Banks—mortgage	1.5	2.6	4.3	7.2	11.1
Federal National Mortgage Association—Mortgages	0.1	2.8	2.5	15.5	24.2
Federal Home Loan Mortgage Corporation—Loans, participations	—	—	—	—	2.5

Sources: *Federal Reserve Bulletin; Treasury Bulletin.* Federal National Mortgage Association (FNMA) data cover secondary market operations only.

farm notes pledged by member production credit associations. The twelve Federal Land Banks provide long-term mortgage credit through local member farm credit associations. The Federal Home Loan Mortgage Corporation sells investment securities backed by mortgages. The annual changes in the investments of federally-sponsored credit agencies in major capital-market assets from 1965 through 1973 are displayed in Table 8–8. The data in Tables 8–7 and 8–8 show that most of the funds received by credit agencies and disbursed by them directly or indirectly, have gone to support those institutions or individuals in the mortgage market.

Annual Changes in Ownership of Federal Agency Securities

The market for federally-sponsored agency securities (excluding participation certificates) is shown by the data in Table 8–9 which covers annual changes in ownership from 1965 to 1973. Individual and consolidated issues of the federal credit agencies have virtually the same market as federal obligations. Because short-term issues generally have higher yields than federal securities, yet comparatively low risk, commercial banks have been their chief buyers; longer-term issues are acquired by a variety of owners.

Savings and loan associations increased their purchases of credit agency securities in 1971 and 1972, as high yields on these securities attracted the S&L's surplus funds during this time. As money became tight in 1973 and 1974, this procedure was reversed and S&L's sold agency securities. Finally, individuals find these securities especially attractive in years of sharp declines in common stock prices, such as in 1962, 1966, 1969 and 1973–4.

Yields

Yields of sponsored agency securities follow closely those of other high-grade obligations and have usually been slightly above those of government bonds and slightly below those of high-grade corporate bonds. Temporary changes in supply and demand produce changes in the differentials. In October 1974, a 7⅜ percent Federal Land Bank bond due in 1993 sold to yield 8.90 percent, while a 6¾ percent treasury bond of the same maturity yielded 8.22 percent. The high yields and the substantial spread reflected the very elevated level of general interest rates at that time.

On occasion, as in the 1971 to 1973 period, the yields paid on credit agency securities exceeded the rates the agencies charged the institutions they lent money to or otherwise supported. This phenomenon has been most often associated with the mortgage-oriented institutions such as savings and loan associations. For instance, in August 1974, the Federal Home Loan Bank issued bonds carrying a coupon rate of about 9½ percent, yet the loans to savings associations and mortgage rates at the time were less than 9 percent.

TABLE 8–8. Annual Changes in Capital-Market Assets, Federally-sponsored Credit Agencies, 1965–1973

(billions of dollars)

	1965	1966	1967	1968	1969	1970	1971	1972	1973
U.S. government securities	$0.1	$1.0	—	$−0.1	$−0.4	$1.9	$−1.2	$−0.4	$1.3
Mortgages	1.1	2.6	1.8	2.1	4.5	5.5	3.5	4.1	7.1
Term loans (Banks for Cooperatives)	0.1	0.1	0.1	0.1	0.1	0.3	—	0.3	0.3
Total	$1.3	$3.7	$1.9	$ 2.1	$ 4.2	$5.7	$ 2.3	$ 4.0	$8.7

Sources: *Federal Reserve Bulletin*; Bankers Trust Company, *Credit and Capital Markets.*

TABLE 8–9. Acquisitions of Federally-sponsored Credit Agency Securities, 1965–1973 (billions of dollars)

	1965	1966	1967	1968	1969	1970	1971	1972	1973
Commercial banks	$ 0.6	$ 0.3	$ 2.9	$ 1.2	$–0.3	$ 3.5	$ 3.8	$ 4.0	$ 7.5
Federal Reserve banks	—	—	—	—	—	—	0.4	0.6	0.7
Mutual savings banks	—	0.2	0.3	0.3	—	0.5	0.2	0.5	–0.1
Savings and loan associations	0.1	0.1	0.2	0.4	1.3	1.5	3.9	3.4	1.0[a]
Life insurance companies	—	—	—	0.1	0.1	0.1	0.1	0.1	—
Property and liability insurance companies	0.2	0.1	—	0.1	—	0.1	–0.2	–0.1[a]	0.1[a]
Private, noninsured pension funds	—	—	–0.2	0.1	–0.2	—	–0.1	0.1	0.5
State and local government retirement funds	0.1	0.1	0.1	0.4	0.1	—	–0.3	–0.1[a]	0.3[a]
Business and financial corporations	0.4	0.4	–1.4	0.8	0.5	0.1	0.1	0.7	1.2
State and local governments (general funds)	0.6	0.1	0.6	1.3	0.5	—	–1.0	0.5	0.2
Foreign investors	—	0.2	0.1	0.1	0.3	0.3	—	0.1	—
Individuals and others	—	3.5	–3.2	–1.6	6.8	2.3	3.1	–3.6	8.2
Totals	$ 2.0	$ 5.0	$–0.6	$ 3.2	$ 9.1	$ 8.4	$ 3.8	$ 6.2	$19.6

[a] Estimated. Savings and loan figures include GNMA mortgage-backed securities.

Sources: Bankers Trust Company, *Credit and Capital Markets*, and sources indicated in Chapters 3 through 7, especially *Federal Reserve Bulletin* and *Treasury Bulletin*. Some columns do not add to totals due to rounding.

150

```
9999999999999999999999999999999999999999999999999999999999999999999999999999999
9999999999999999999999999999999999999999999999999999999999999999999999999999999
9999999999999999999999999999999999999   999   99999   9999999999999999999999999999
9999999999999999999999999999999999999   9999   999   9999999999999999999999999999
9999999999999999999999999999999999999   99999   9   9999999999999999999999999999
9999999999999999999999999999999999999   999999   9999999999999999999999999999999
9999999999999999999999999999999999999   9999999   999999999999999999999999999999
9999999999999999999999999999999999999   999999   9999999999999999999999999999999
9999999999999999999999999999999999999   99999   9   9999999999999999999999999999
9999999999999999999999999999999999999   9999   999   9999999999999999999999999999
9999999999999999999999999999999999999   999   99999   9999999999999999999999999999
9999999999999999999999999999999999999999999999999999999999999999999999999999999999
9999999999999999999999999999999999999999999999999999999999999999999999999999999999
```

The Market for State and Local Government Bonds

STATE and local governments employ three main types of debt: bonds sold to the public, tax anticipation notes sold to banks, and loans from the federal government. Local governments also rely heavily on state grants. Because it is the major source, we are concerned mainly with the first category.

Bonds are typically issued in serial maturities, with designated par amounts due in successive years to final maturity. Investors have a wide choice among short-, intermediate-, and long-term maturities.

The maturities of state and local government bonds have tended to increase in recent years. Many issues of larger units run as long as thirty years and even longer when based on the revenue from specific projects. Such a trend parallels that of other long-term instruments whose buyers are also finding longer maturities acceptable.

With the exception of revenue bonds, the obligations of state and local governments are supported by the "full faith and credit" of the taxing jurisdictions. They all (including revenue bonds) enjoy exemption of interest from federal income taxation.[1] This exemption gives

---

[1] An exception to this statement is the limitation on firms issuing their own debt with interest payments that are tax deductible and using the proceeds to invest in tax-exempt securities. Municipal interest payments are also generally exempt from state and local income taxation in the jurisdictions of issue.

151

them a special appeal to many investors, and their yields reflect the value of the exemption. Their yields are, of course, also influenced by the general supply of, and demand for, funds in the capital market, and by the particular factors affecting supply and demand for municipals.

The legal history of federal income tax exemption and the arguments pro and con constitute a subject too complex to discuss here.[2] The tax-exempt status has, however, had an enormous effect on the ability of state and local governments to attract low-cost funds to finance their enormous expenditures for schools, highways, and other projects.

Classification of Bonds

A convenient classification of bonds combines the issuer and the degree of tax support or other means of payment:

(1) General ("full faith and credit") obligations secured by the general taxing power of governmental units
  (a) Regular:
       States
       Counties and parishes
       Cities, towns, boroughs, and so on
  (b) Special tax districts:
       School districts
       Water districts
       Others
(2) Revenue bonds (nonguaranteed) secured only by special income
  (a) Municipal utilities and similar departments
  (b) Quasimunicipal authorities and commissions
  (c) Regular governmental units supporting the issue from special taxes only or from project income
(3) Housing authority issues further supported by state or federal guarantee of principal and interest (a special type of revenue bond)

Bonds can also be classified as to quality. Security-rating services rate full faith and credit obligations of states from *Aaa* to *B*; local government bonds and revenue bonds show a range from *Aaa* to those in default. The ratings are a function of the (1) ratio of total debt to assessed valuation, (2) prior debt outstanding, (3) intended use of the funds, and (4) economic base of the taxing authority. Some local municipalities have higher ratings than some states have.

---

[2] See D. J. Ott and A. H. Meltzer, *Federal Tax Treatment of State and Local Securities* (Washington, D.C.: The Brookings Institution, 1963).

Regular government units possess broad general powers of taxation, limited only by statute with respect to types of taxes, total general debt in relation to property value, and limitations on the property tax rate. They ordinarily pledge their general credit but may also pledge specific revenues. Special districts, organized to operate a specific activity such as schools, also have the power to tax the property within their borders. Revenue bonds are issued by states, counties, and local units payable from some specific source, and by departments and statutory authorities (quasipublic corporations without the power to tax) organized to operate revenue-producing projects.

Growth and Types of State and Local Debt

In the postwar period, the rate of growth of state and local government debt has outstripped that of the federal government. This growth reflects the expansion of governmental services, the growth of population, and the steady process of urbanization. The growth of state and local debt in relation to federal debt is also revealed by figures of year-end per capita debt: [3]

	1960	1965	1970	1973
Direct federal gross debt	$1,591	$1,631	$1,816	$2,227
State and local gross debt	389	513	707	960

Table 9–1 shows the composition of state and local debt by major types for selected years (as of June 30). Net debt is after deductions for sinking fund.

Revenue bonds (nonguaranteed) increased more than general obligations in absolute amounts in the late 1960s, as industrial revenue bonds, municipal departments, and special commissions and authorities to operate utility, toll-road, airport, bridge, and other facilities, grew substantially.

As of June 30, 1973, nonguaranteed bonds constituted about 42 percent of total "municipal" long-term bonds outstanding. This ratio dropped to slightly over 40 percent in 1973 as the need for revenue bond financing declined relative to total financing, reflecting lower interest rates. In 1974, increased demand for funds resulted in increased yields.

Use of revenue rather than direct borrowing avoids certain statutory limits on "full faith and credit" debt, interest rate ceilings, and the legal restrictions on purposes for which tax revenues can be

---

[3] U.S. Department of Commerce, Bureau of the Census, *Statistical Abstract of the United States* and *Governmental Finances* (annual).

employed. The outstanding long-term debt as of June 30, 1973, by governmental unit, is shown in Table 9–2.

TABLE 9–1. Outstanding Debt of State and Local Governments, 1960–1973, as of June 30 (billions of dollars)

	1960	*1965*	*1970*	*9173*
Long-term debt:				
Full faith and credit	$ 41.7	$ 56.4	$ 75.3	$102.9
Nonguaranteed	25.1	37.8	56.1	69.7
	$ 66.8	$ 94.2	$131.4	$172.6
Short-term debt	3.2	5.3	12.2	15.9
Total debt	$ 70.0	$ 99.5	$143.6	$188.5
Net long-term debt	$ 61.6	$ 86.0	$122.2	$158.7

Sources: U.S. Department of Commerce, Bureau of the Census, *Governmental Finances* (annual).

TABLE 9–2. Long-Term State and Local Debt, 1973 (billions of dollars)

	Full Faith and Credit	*Nonguaranteed*	*Total*
States	$ 28.5	$27.2	$ 55.7
Counties	11.6	2.9	14.5
Municipalities (cities)	28.9	20.4	49.3
Townships	2.6	0.2	2.8
School districts	24.3	—	24.3
Special districts	7.0	19.0	26.0
Total	$102.9	$69.7	$172.6

Source: U.S. Department of Commerce, Bureau of the Census, *Governmental Finances in 1972–1973*.

Purposes of Borrowing

Long-term debt is issued to meet special operating expenses, to finance capital project construction not borne by current revenues or grants from the federal and other governments, and to refund maturing obligations. Although there is no exact relationship between the amount of debt financing and capital expenditures, most of the debt bears part of the capital cost of projects involving fixed assets.[4]

In recent years, the annual increase in long-term debt has been

---

[4] In recent years, federal funds have financed about 20 percent of state and local public construction through loans and grants.

about one-third of total capital outlay expenditures and an even smaller proportion of actual construction costs. Much capital construction by governments is financed from general and special tax revenues—for example, the use of gasoline taxes for highway construction. Revenue bond financing of self-supporting departments and authorities tends to follow more precisely the capital costs of these enterprises.

Organization of the Primary Market

The first step in the issuance of a new state or local government bond issue is its authorization by the governmental unit under the terms of the prevailing statute. The financial officer then prescribes the terms of the issue—denominations, interest rate, serial maturities, and so forth—and, in most states, advertises it for sale under competitive bidding, ordinarily in the *Bond Buyer*. The chief buyers are large investment banking firms, some of which specialize in such securities, and commercial banks, which are authorized to act as underwriters of municipal issues (general obligations only).[5] Less than sixty banks are active in the market for large new issues. Some banks, even large ones, confine their holdings to bonds of issuers within their state. Smaller issues tend to be purchased by local banks.

In most states, individual underwriters or syndicates acquire general obligations by competitive bidding. Competitive bidding is expected to produce lower yields than negotiation; it does, however, deprive the issuer of the initial advice and continuous services of the investment banker. Revenue bonds are frequently sold on a negotiated basis; their more specialized nature and generally lower quality make the aid of a banker in consultation and tailoring of features more important.

Buying syndicates are managed by firms that invite other banks and dealers to participate in the underwriting. The larger underwritings are managed by a limited number of banks or firms, and underwriters often specialize in issues from a particular area or in certain types of obligations.

Bidding for municipal bonds (and their later resale) is on a yield basis on bids of par value or more. The syndicate determines the yields at which the various serial maturities will be absorbed, adds a gross spread to cover buying risk and distribution expense, and arrives at an overall net interest cost. Some invitations to bid require that all maturities bear the same coupon rate; in other cases the coupon may vary with maturity. Under the former arrangement, the

---

[5] Housing Assistance Administration bonds are the exception.

offering price is adjusted above par for the different serial blocks because the market ordinarily requires that yields rise with length to maturity. Where the coupon varies with maturity, the rate may be set very high on early maturities, and these may be resold at substantial premiums.

The gross underwriting spread, or difference between cost and offering price, is the margin within which the successful bidder must be prepared to work. It ranges from less than 1 to 1.5 percent (with the average around 1 percent) and is a function of type, size, quality, marketability, and maturity.

The successful individual bidder or syndicate may retain the issue for its own inventory (as banks do for investment), retail it to its own customers, or reoffer it to dealers at a modest concession from the public offering price. Both in the original bidding and in later trading, the prices of the various maturities are indicated in terms of yield rather than in dollars.

Postwar Volume and Buyers of New Municipal Securities

In recent years, a fairly steady increase in municipal financing has resulted from the expansion of governmental services and the favorable market for "tax-exempt" securities. The data in Table 9–3 show the gross proceeds (at time of delivery) of new long-term issues, including those issues purchased by state and local government retire-

TABLE 9–3. Borrowing by State and Local Governments, 1965–1973
(billions of dollars)

	1965	1966	1967	1968	1969	1970	1971	1972	1973
New capital issues	$11.1	$11.1	$14.3	$16.4	$11.5	$17.8	$24.4	$23.1	$22.7
Less refunding and refinancing	6.0	6.1	8.4	7.0	4.3	8.8	10.2	10.2	12.0
	5.1	5.0	5.9	9.4	7.2	9.0	14.2	12.9	10.7
Federal loans and other debt	1.7	1.3	2.0	0.4	3.5	2.4	2.8	−0.7	−0.2
Increase in debt	$ 6.8	$ 6.3	$ 7.9	$ 9.8	$10.7	$11.4	$17.0	$12.2	$10.5

Sources: Investment Bankers Association of America, *Statistical Bulletin;* Bankers Trust Company, *Credit and Capital Markets* (annual); *Federal Reserve Bulletin,* including flow-of-funds tables.

ment funds. These proceeds are reduced to the net annual increase by deducting the cost of refinancing and retirements. Increases in loans from the federal government are added to produce the annual volume of total new debt.

The data reveal a secular increase in financing and some cyclical variation. In periods of tight money such as 1966, 1969, and 1973 through 1974, characterized by rising yields and lower bond prices, a considerable amount of planned financing was withdrawn or postponed, some of this caused by the maximum interest rate ceilings on issued debt.

In 1969, for instance, the high cost of funds, threats against the tax-free status of bond income, and statutory ceilings on municipal bond coupon rates reduced borrowing substantially and caused deferment of many capital projects. The drop in direct financing was partially offset by sharp rises in the amount of federal loans.

New issues are absorbed primarily by taxed institutions, especially commercial banks, which not only underwrite but also invest (except in revenue bonds) for their own account. Some bonds are placed with government retirement funds (see Chapter 6), and a modest amount with state and local governments proper and business corporations. Individuals seeking tax relief account for most of the balance. The data in Table 9–4 show the annual net changes in ownership since 1965.

Variations in annual net acquisitions by investors are only partly explained by changes in their available funds. Individuals, and especially institutions, switch in and out of municipals as the relative yields on competitive investments rise and fall. Bank acquisitions show the greatest variations in a loose cyclical pattern as banks use these securities for their liquidity requirements. Changes in their reserve position and in the demand for loans, which they prefer, determine their holdings and purchases of these securities. This situation is well illustrated by the drop in acquisition of municipals in 1966 and by the rebound in acquisitions in 1967 and 1968, which soared to record levels in 1971 and 1972. Bank policy was also affected by the heavy influx of savings deposits in 1967 and in the 1970 to 1972 period, part of which was invested in municipal bonds for their advantageous after-tax yields (see Chapter 3). These bonds become even more attractive as tax rates are increased on savings institutions.

The interest of property and liability insurance companies in municipal bonds was stimulated by the increase in their income-tax rates (Chapter 5). Life insurance companies, pension and retirement funds, because of lower or no income taxes, do not find the holding of these securities appealing.

Variations in acquisitions by business corporations, individuals and others are more difficult to analyze. Some countercyclical pattern in net purchases is evident, explained by variations in total savings and by the fact that in years of rapidly rising prices of common stocks, the latter become relatively unattractive for future capital gains. The

TABLE 9–4. Annual Acquisitions of State and Local Government Bonds, 1965–1973 (billions of dollars)

	1965	1966	1967	1968	1969	1970	1971	1972	1973
Commercial banks	$ 5.2	$ 2.3	$ 9.0	$ 8.6	$ 0.2	$ 10.7	$12.6	$ 7.1	$ 5.6
Mutual savings banks	-0.1	-0.1	—	—	—	—	0.2	0.5	—
Life insurance companies	-0.2	-0.4	-0.1	0.2	—	0.1	0.1	0.1	0.1
Property and liability insurance companies	0.5	1.0	1.5	0.8	1.1	1.3	3.5	3.5	4.3
State and local government retirement funds	-0.3	-0.1	-0.1	-0.1	-0.1	-0.3	0.1	-0.1	-0.6
Business corporations	0.9	-1.0	-0.3	0.5	-1.0	-0.6	1.0	1.0	-0.1
State and local governments	-0.1	-0.1	—	—	0.1	0.2	-0.3	0.2	0.2
Individuals and other (residual)	0.9	4.7	-2.1	-0.2	10.4	—	-0.2	1.3	1.0
Total	$ 6.8	$6.3	$ 7.9	$ 9.8	$ 10.7	$ 11.4	$ 17.0	$ 13.5	$ 10.5

Sources: See citations in schedules, Chapters 3–7; Bankers Trust Company, *Credit and Capital Markets* (annual); *Federal Reserve Bulletin.* (Some columns do not add to totals because of rounding.)

higher the income-tax bracket, of course, the more favorable the after-tax rate from municipals.

Ownership of State and Local Government Bonds

At the end of 1973, the estimated ownership schedule was as shown in Table 9–5. The last category, individuals and others, includes partnerships, bank trust accounts, savings and loan associations, dealers and brokers, and foreign owners. Individual ownership, direct and through trusts, accounts for close to 90 percent of that figure. Again the data show that those institutions (banks and property and liability insurance companies) and individuals who have the most to gain by holding tax-exempt issues are the prime holders.

TABLE 9–5.   Ownership of State and Local Government Debt, 1973
(billions of dollars)

	Amount	Percentage
Commercial banks	$ 95.1	47.0%
Mutual savings banks	0.9	0.4
Life insurance companies	3.4	1.7
Property and liability insurance companies	28.1	13.9
State and local government retirement funds	1.4	0.7
State and local government general funds	2.5	1.2
Business and financial corporations	4.0	2.0
Individuals and others (residual)	67.0	33.1
Total	$202.4	100 %

Sources: Secretary of the Treasury, *Annual Report,* adjusted to year end and for data cited in Chapters 3–7. See also *Federal Reserve Bulletin,* annual flow-of-funds tables.

Organization of the Secondary Market

Individual and institutional investors in tax-exempt bonds require a good secondary market when orderly liquidation of their holdings becomes necessary. Trading is done by the original underwriting firms and banks and by dealers who specialize in these securities in the over-the-counter market. The secondary and primary marketing organizations consist largely of the same types of firms. The daily *Blue List of Current Municipal Offerings* may list 2,500 to 3,000 available issues. Although no firm data are available, the interdealer volume of transactions is known to be substantial but the total volume of trading is probably much lower than the volume of new offerings. However, with annual gross financing of $22 to $24 billion and with a total of over $200 billion outstanding as of 1973, even a modest turnover of the latter may eventually produce a volume equal to the new issue volume.

Yields

The yields on state and local government bonds as a class are a function of (1) the level of interest rates in general; (2) the value to investors of the tax-exempt privilege; (3) the supply of new and outstanding securities of this type; (4) the supply of funds available for purchase of such investments; and (5) the appeal of alternative investments. Yields on individual issues are further affected by their size, quality, maturity, and marketability. Tax-exempt yields have fluctuated in a wider range than have other high-grade yields, mainly because of changes in supply in relation to that of federal bonds, and in bank demand. The market for tax-exempt bonds is more restricted than that of federal and corporate debt and is consequently more erratic. Figure 9–1 shows the annual average yields for Moody's U.S. Treasury long-term bond series compared with Moody's *Aaa* and *Baa* state and local government bonds series. The annual averages disguise the interim variations but are suitable for our purpose. Although all yields rose and fell in a common pattern, the spread between the yield on long-term Treasury bonds and the *Aaa* state and local government series has shown considerable variation. In general, in periods of prosperity yield spreads tend to narrow as risk factors become less of a consideration. Spreads also tend to narrow when overall market rates decline.

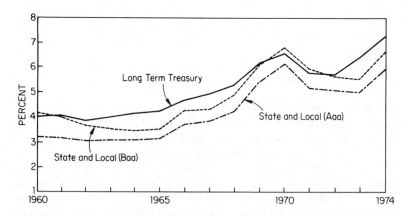

Figure 9–1.   U.S. Government and Municipal Bond Yields, 1960–1974
(average yearly before—tax yield)

Sources: *Federal Reserve Bulletin; Moody's Bond Survey.* For data, see Appendix, Table A–2.

The modest increase in yields on Treasury bonds beginning in 1962 was accompanied by smaller increases in yields on high-grade municipals, so that by 1964 and 1965 the yield spread had widened to over 100 basis points. Then in 1966 came the "credit crunch," which saw all yields setting record levels. Pressure for loan funds reduced bank investment in municipals in early 1966, but as the rise in yields continued, banks became aggressive buyers of municipals in later 1966 and 1967. The lessening pressure in the corporate market that produced somewhat lower yields was not experienced in either the long-term government or municipals market in 1967. Yields continued to rise and in November 1969 the 6.3 percent yield on the composite group far surpassed previous levels. All elements of demand in the bond market sought an increasing share of a diminishing supply of funds.

The high level of market yields in 1969 posed a problem; in many states statutory limits on state bond coupons are lower than required yields. Therefore, much new long-term financing was virtually stopped or postponed in 1969.

Rates subsequently declined from late 1969 through 1973 as available savings funds reduced demand by governments and corporations due to improved cash flows, and generally easier monetary policy combined to relieve pressure on the long-term bond market. This process was again reversed in 1974, however, as stringent monetary policy and high inflation caused rates to rise along a broad front.

The spread between taxable and tax-free yields is the price investors are willing to pay for the privilege of tax exemption. This price changes with the general level of yields and with the changing constituency of buyers. The continuing high spread in the latter 1960s reflected high general yields caused in part by inflation, higher income taxes, and large numbers of investors seeking tax relief.

The yield curve for state and local bonds has not been shaped like, nor has it necessarily followed, that for Treasury obligations (see Chapter 8). Longer maturities produce substantially higher rates, and the typical term structure of interest rates normally prevails. For example, late in April 1974, *Aaa*-rated 20-year general obligations bore an average yield of 5.75 percent, while 5-year maturities sold to yield 5.30 percent and 1-year maturities, 5.10 percent. In the same month, yields on Treasury obligations of similar maturities were 8.23, 7.99, and 7.04 percent, respectively. The chief buyers of municipal bonds, commercial banks, prefer short- and intermediate-term obligations; the longer bonds are most appealing to individual investors.

Yields on individual municipal issues are also a function of quality, size, and marketability. Quality tends to correlate roughly with size—

the big name issues finding the best market. The previous data reveal, however, that the differential of *Baa* over *Aaa* yields has been declining steadily in recent years. As the tax-free privilege became more valuable to more investors, they were willing to accept a lower premium on lesser-grade issues. However, the hectic pressure for funds in 1966 through 1969 and 1973 to 1974 drove all yields to record highs, and investors began to require a higher spread on lesser-grade obligations.

101010101010101010101010101010101010101010101010101010101010101010101010101010101010
101010101010101010101010101010101010101010101010101010101010101010101010101010101010
101010101010101010101010101010101010101 10101 1010101010101010101010101010101010
101010101010101010101010101010101010101010 010 01010101010101010101010101010101010
101010101010101010101010101010101010101010101 1 101010101010101010101010101010101010
101010101010101010101010101010101010101010101010 01010101010101010101010101010101010
101010101010101010101010101010101010101010101010101 1010101010101010101010101010101010
101010101010101010101010101010101010101010101010 01010101010101010101010101010101010
101010101010101010101010101010101010101010101 1 101010101010101010101010101010101010
101010101010101010101010101010101010101010101010 010 01010101010101010101010101010101010
101010101010101010101010101010101010101010101 10101 1010101010101010101010101010101010
101010101010101010101010101010101010101010101010101010101010101010101010101010101010101010
101010101010101010101010101010101010101010101010101010101010101010101010101010101010

The Market for Long-Term Corporate Debt

Definitions and Reasons for Use

Our definition of the capital markets as the markets for funds of over
1 year in maturity suggests a rather broad definition of corporate
intermediate- and long-term debt. It technically includes longer-term
trade payables, mortgages, term loans, corporate 1 to 5 year notes sold
in the open market, and corporate bonds. Because precise data on
some of these categories are lacking and because we are interested
mainly in debt whose yields are determined in open competition,
attention is confined to corporate term loans and bonds.

Term loans are business debts with more than 1 year maturity,
negotiated directly with banks and insurance companies and ordinarily amortized on a serial basis. They are used to finance both
working capital and fixed-asset requirements, and the repayment
schedule is related to the future cash flow of the borrower. The
latest available data on the volume of bank term lending are shown
in Table 3–5. Insurance companies class their term loans as "industrial and miscellaneous" bonds, or as mortgages, and do not report
separate figures for this investment.

Corporate debt finance rose to eminence in external corporate
financing in the late 1960s and 1970s as the stock market declined
and low stock prices made stock sales an impractical source of
financing for most industrial firms. The heavy debt financing came

at a time when inflation escalated, causing interest rates to climb to all-time highs and construction costs for new plant and equipment to burgeon, thereby compounding the need for new funds. All of this developed against a backdrop of stagnant to declining corporate profitability from 1969 to 1972. Although corporate profitability improved in 1973 and 1974, the energy crisis and general uncertainty continued to undermine stock market prices.

Historically, corporate bonds have been issued for a variety of reasons. The most important of these are to reduce the cost of financing and to increase the rate of return on total capital by applying the principle of leverage. The after-tax cost of long-term debt, assuming a judicious use of debt, is lower than that of equity capital because of its preferred risk position and the fact that interest payments are tax deductible. Bond financing also avoids possible dilution of control.

As many managers found out in 1969, and later, however, debt financing has many disadvantages. The contractual payments and the restrictions on working capital and retained earnings contained in the indenture agreement are among the factors inhibiting corporate flexibility and diminishing the appeal of debt financing. Management temperament is also a major factor determining the pattern of business financing. There is often a resistance to borrowing that may be based on rational risk avoidance or simply on innate conservatism. In regulated industries, limits to borrowing are imposed by the controlling commissions. For all companies, investors' standards with respect to appropriate debt burden have, of course, a powerful influence. Finally, very high interest rates in 1973 and 1974 tended to reduce corporate profitability and discourage borrowing.

General Corporate Financing

Sources of corporate funds from 1965 through 1973 are presented in Table 10–1. The data summarize the net financing after eliminating trade payables in order to avoid double counting of nonfarm, nonfinancial business corporations. (The data do not represent the total volume of actual capital-market activity in that they exclude refinancing and redemptions.)

Internal sources of funds have exceeded external sources for every year, and customarily account for about 55 to 60 percent of all financing sources. Although internal funds are invested directly in corporate assets, they nevertheless affect the capital markets. To the extent that corporations can finance their needs in this manner, the need for securities and other outside financing is lessened.

TABLE 10–1. Sources of Funds, Non-farm Non-financial Corporations, 1965–1973 (billions of dollars)

	1965	1966	1967	1968	1969	1970	1971	1972	1973
Internal sources:									
Retained profits	$23.1	$24.7	$21.1	$19.9	$16.0	$10.6	$15.2	$22.7	$34.7
Depreciation and depletion	35.2	38.2	41.5	45.1	49.8	53.6	57.7	63.0	67.5
Inventory valuation	−1.7	−1.8	−1.1	−3.3	−5.1	−4.8	−4.9	−7.0	−17.6
	$56.6	$61.2	$61.5	$61.7	$60.7	$59.4	$68.0	$78.7	$84.6
External sources:									
Bonds	$ 5.4	$10.2	$14.7	$12.9	$12.0	$19.8	$18.8	$12.2	$ 9.2
Bank term loans (est.)	4.3	2.6	2.8	4.4	5.8	2.0	2.0	6.4	7.5
Mortgages	3.9	4.2	4.5	5.8	4.6	5.2	11.4	15.6	16.1
Stocks	—	1.2	2.3	−0.8	2.9	4.8	11.7	10.4	7.4
Bank and other debt (mainly short-term)	13.8	13.9	6.0	15.4	10.5	4.3	5.3	10.7	31.8
	$27.4	$32.1	$30.3	$37.7	$35.8	$36.1	$49.2	$55.3	$72.0
Total sources	$84.0	$93.3	$91.8	$99.4	$96.5	$95.5	$117.2	$134.0	$152.6
Total sources adjusted for price increases (1965 = 100 CPI)	$84.0	$90.7	$86.7	$90.1	$83.0	$77.6	$91.3	$101.0	$108.3
Internal sources adjusted for price increases (1965 = 100 CPI)	$56.6	$59.5	$58.1	$55.9	$52.2	$48.3	$53.0	$59.3	$60.1

Sources: *Survey of Current Business; Federal Reserve Bulletin* (Flow of Funds); term loan data from Bankers Trust Company, *Credit and Capital Markets* (annual).

165

Although the rise from $56.6 billion in total internal sources in 1965 to $84.6 billion in 1973 appears substantial, it barely kept pace with the rise in inflation. If internal sources are adjusted for price changes using the consumer price index, an entirely different picture of the true, real sources (in 1965 dollars) is revealed. The data at the bottom of Table 10–1 show that from 1965 through 1973 total real internal sources changed very little during this period. If a construction index were used, rather than the CPI, to more closely reflect the probable cost of plant and equipment expenditures, a significant decline in real internal sources would have occurred.

The net result was that most corporations were starved for capital during this period and had to seek substantial external funds, which placed an added burden on the capital markets. Most of the external funds, however, have come from borrowing rather than from equity markets. The large growth in external funds is evident from the data, as sources about doubled in the four-year period ended in 1973 for a compounded growth rate of about 18 percent.

Faced with declining profits, yet a desire to keep a stable dividend, retained earnings dropped sharply to a low of $10.6 billion in 1970 before recovering to $34.7 billion in 1973. This, along with a need to finance plant and equipment and other asset expenditures in an inflated economy, forced firms to seek funds from almost any available source. Thus, in addition to issuing bonds and current debt firms tapped other infrequent sources, such as mortgages and common stocks (Table 10–1).

The stock figure, although up sharply in 1971 and 1972, is somewhat illusory in that about 50 percent of this total financing was accounted for by utilities, which by law have to maintain a representative balance between debt and equity. Nevertheless, the rising market in 1971 and 1972 afforded corporations an opportunity to sell stock and retire loans made in 1969. The sharp stock market decline in 1973 and 1974 virtually precluded additional equity financing for most firms.

Bank loans of all types continued to be important sources of funds. In some cases, the rise in mortgages was more a result of lenders "reaching for security" than business corporations revealing a preference for this type of financing (see Chapter 12).

Outstanding Long-Term Corporate Debt

The high level of bond issues (a high of $19.8 billion in 1970) in the early 1970s reflected the pace of economic growth in the postwar period, the rise in prices, and the growing willingness of corporations to borrow to save on income taxes. The sharp drop in this form of financing and the corresponding sharp increase in bank borrowing in

1973 indicated that firms were borrowing short-term in hopes of refinancing in the long-term market when yields declined. In addition, fluctuations reflect variations in the pattern of corporate expenditures, mainly for fixed assets, as well as capital cost conditions in the competitive capital markets. The dominance of bond financing relative to stock financing is somewhat overstated in that convertible bonds are counted as debt when first issued; nevertheless, the total debt of nonfinancial corporations totaled $207.5 at the end of 1973, more than double the amount outstanding in 1965 (see Table 10–2). Financial corporations, including banks, showed a similar growth pattern in corporate bond liabilities outstanding.

TABLE 10–2. Corporate Bonds Outstanding at Year End, 1955–1973 (billions of dollars)

	1955	1960	1965	1970	1973
Nonfinancial corporations	$ 53.3	$ 75.3	$ 97.8	$167.3	$207.5
Financial corporations and banks	5.4	9.9	17.7	25.9	39.9
Total	$ 58.7	$ 85.2	$115.5	$193.2	$247.4

Sources: *Federal Reserve Bulletin*, flow-of-funds tables.

Public Distribution of Bonds in the Primary Market

Public issues of corporate bonds are distributed through investment banking houses. These merchants investigate and buy (underwrite) bond issues for resale to institutions and individual investors. The investment banker provides the issuer with advice on the form, timing, and pricing of bond financing and with continuing counsel after the issue is floated. The banker's check on the financial condition of the issuer, the form and terms of the financing, and the maintenance of a continuous market, and his general investment information and advice are valuable to the investor. By screening issues and influencing their timing and yields, the investment banker plays a major role in the primary bond market.

Formerly called "bond houses," the larger investment banking firms engage in a variety of ancillary activities. Some serve as securities brokers and dealers and as underwriters of stock issues. In the flotation of new issues, some investment bankers are wholesalers, doing the original underwriting and then selling to retail dealers for wider distribution. Others serve also as distributors to the general investment public. Some are national in their operations; others are local. About fifty firms originate and manage the major issues of securities; many hundreds of others are involved in the final sale of the larger flotations.

Investment banking firms acquire new corporate bond issues by either negotiated or competitive bidding. Direct negotiation between issuer and underwriter (acting alone or as the manager of a syndicate) ends in a purchase contract whereby the banker, or a purchase syndicate in the case of larger flotations, acquires the issue at a net price and yield determined by bargaining. Such underwriting is largely confined to industrial and financial offerings. Competitive bidding, in which the issuer invites sealed bids of price or yield or both on an issue whose terms are already determined, is ordinarily required by federal or state statute in the case of public utility and railroad issues. Regardless of the process of acquisition, the final purchase takes the form of a firm commitment.

Two other arrangements sometimes used do not involve total underwriting: (1) "best efforts," or agency selling, whereby the underwriter(s) agrees simply to merchandise the securities at the issuer's risk; this arrangement is used primarily in common stock rather than in bond offerings; (2) "standby" underwriting of convertible bonds; this method involves the guarantee of funds to the issuer from an offering of such bonds by the corporation by privileged subscription to existing stockholders; here the underwriter agrees to take up only the securities not bought through the exercise of rights.

The public offering of corporate bonds in interstate commerce or through the mails is subject to the registration and prospectus requirements of the Securities Act of 1933, save for railroad issues, which are controlled by the Interstate Commerce Commission. State "blue sky" laws apply to intrastate offerings.

The costs of flotation of fully underwritten public issues consist of the banker's gross spread or commission and the expenses of preparation and registration. The former component varies with the size and quality of the issues and the methods of distribution, and ranges between 0.5 and 8 percent.

Direct, or Private, Placement of Bonds

A notable development in the postwar period has been the substantial growth of private placement of bonds with institutions, mostly life insurance companies (see Chapter 5) but also some commercial banks, pension funds, and investment companies. Industrial bonds predominate in such direct sales because railroad and many utility bonds must be sold through competitive bidding. Direct placements avoid the investment banking machinery save for those cases in which investment bankers act as finders or agents at a modest fee (0.25–2 percent). Corporate bond offerings for cash (for both new money and refinancing) from 1955 through 1973 were as shown in Table 10–3. Private placements have experienced a relative decline in recent years as a percentage of total offerings reaching a low of only 16 percent in 1970. From there they rose to 39 percent of total offerings in 1973, only to drop back sharply in 1974 as utility financing increased measurably. The major cause of this general decline from the early 1960s has been the large amounts of publicly-offered securities by utilities and rails who normally use competitive bids and account for almost 50 percent of the new debt financing. Also, life insurance companies, which provide the chief demand for corporate debt placed in this way, have been looking more to the higher yields available on mortgages in recent years and have also seen an increasing share of their investable funds tied up in policy loans and common stocks (as we saw in Chapter 5). In addition, high interest rates and nonrefunding or postponed call provisions substantially encouraged public versus private sales. Furthermore, private placements suffered from the shrinkage in life insurance company funds available for use in the capital market.

TABLE 10–3.　Publicly and Privately Offered Corporate Bonds, 1955–1973 (billions of dollars)

	Publicly Offered	Privately Placed	Total	Privately Placed (Percentage)
1955	$ 4.1	$ 3.3	$ 7.4	45%
1960	4.8	3.3	8.1	41
1961	4.7	4.7	9.4	50
1962	4.5	4.5	9.0	50
1963	4.7	6.2	10.9	57
1964	3.6	7.2	10.8	67
1965	5.6	8.1	13.7	60
1966	8.0	7.5	15.5	48
1967	15.0	7.0	22.0	32
1968	10.7	6.7	17.4	38
1969	12.7	5.6	18.3	31
1970	25.4	4.9	30.3	16
1971	24.8	7.3	32.1	21
1972	19.4	9.5	28.9	33
1973	13.6	8.7	22.3	39

Sources: Securities and Exchange Commission, *Annual Reports; Federal Reserve Bulletin.*

Private placements offer several advantages to the corporation. They reduce the risks of delay involved in registered public offerings, save on costs of flotation (except for any finder's fee), make the funds available sooner, and permit the tailoring of each loan indenture to the particular situation. Smaller corporations find such financing a substitute for bond issues they would have difficulty selling in the open market.

It is also interesting to note the general decline in bond financing in 1973 and 1974 as, again, rates remained at historically high levels, and the deteriorating business climate raised questions among investors as to the ability of some firms to effectively amortize substantial amounts of debt.

Acquisitions of Corporate Bonds

The *net* change in outstanding corporate bonds is shown in Table 10–4. Annual variations in demand for bonds by investors reflect conditions and policies discussed in Chapters 3 through 7. Briefly, life insurance companies, state and local government retirement funds, and individuals have been heavy purchasers of corporate bonds as interest rates on these latter securities made them favored investments.

Ownership of Corporate Bonds

The holdings of corporate bonds at the end of 1973 are shown in Table 10–5. The same institutions and individuals that have been heavy acquisitors of bonds in recent years are, likewise, large holders of these instruments. As noted earlier, in Chapter 5, life insurance holdings dominate all others—they find bonds with their definite yield and long-term maturities attractive investments as their chief investment obligation from the standpoint of income, is to earn at least the assumed rate at which reserves are compounded. Corporate pension fund investment in bonds remains significant, although these instruments have constituted a steadily declining proportion of their total assets because of the greater relative emphasis on common stocks (Chapter 6).

Secondary market activity in corporate bonds, especially high grade corporate bonds, is somewhat limited due to the large institutional ownership that tends to hold these bonds to maturity. The recent fluctuating interest rates that cause sharp drops or rises in bond prices, however, may result in a more active market in the future.

Most trading occurs in the over-the-counter market. The New York Stock Exchange constitutes virtually the entire listed market, with 2,188 issues listed at the end of 1973. The market value of domestic corporate bonds listed on the Big Board was $90.0 billion; bonds of foreign companies amounted to $689 million, and governments of all types added another $29.9 billion.[1] Corporate bonds with market value of approximately $173 billion were traded over the counter.

Of the thousands of unlisted corporate bond issues, probably fewer than 500 are traded on the over-the-counter market in a typical day.

---

[1] New York Stock Exchange, *Fact Book*, 1974.

	1965	1966	1967	1968	1969	1970	1971	1972	1973
Commercial banks	$-0.1	$ 0.1	$ 0.8	$ 0.3	$-0.1	$ 0.2	$ 1.3	$ 1.7	$ 0.4
Mutual savings banks	-0.1	0.3	1.8	1.0	—	1.2	3.3	2.2	-1.0
Life insurance companies	2.4	2.2	3.7	3.6	1.5	1.2	5.4	6.8	5.6
Property and liability insurance companies	0.6	0.7	0.6	1.2	0.8	1.5	0.3	0.8	-1.5
Private, noninsured pension funds	1.7	2.1	1.6	1.7	0.8	2.1	-0.6	-0.8	2.2
State and local government retirement funds	2.1	2.5	3.7	2.6	3.1	4.2	4.8	5.3	5.9
Investment companies (mutual)	0.4	0.4	0.1	0.4	0.2	0.7	0.7	1.7	-0.9
Foreign investors	0.3	—	-0.4	—	0.2	0.3	0.2	0.1	0.1
Individuals and others	0.8	2.8	4.1	3.2	7.3	11.4	8.3	1.9	3.8
Total	$ 8.1	$11.1	$16.0	$14.0	$13.8	$ 22.8	$ 23.7	$ 19.7	$14.6

Sources: See citations in schedules, Chapters 3–7; *Federal Reserve Bulletin*; Bankers Trust Company, *Credit and Capital Markets* (annual); Securities and Exchange Commission, *Statistical Bulletin*. (Some columns do not add to totals due to rounding.)

TABLE 10–5. Ownership of Corporate Bonds, 1973 (billions of dollars)

	Amount	Percentage
Commercial banks	$ 5.8	2.3%
Mutual savings banks	13.1	5.3
Life insurance companies	91.8	37.1
Property and liability insurance companies	7.7	2.9
Private noninsured pension funds	27.0	11.0
State and local government retirement funds	49.0	19.8
Mutual investment companies	4.2	1.7
Individuals and other	48.8	19.8
Total	$247.4	100 %

Sources: *Federal Reserve Bulletin* (Flow-of-Funds tables) and data on institutional investments, Chapters 3–8.

The majority are only occasionally transferred. Even so, about 80 percent of corporate bond resales take place in the "off board" rather than on the organized exchanges. The transactions are handled by broker dealers, mainly the members of the National Association of Securities Dealers. A high concentration of the actual resales are in New York. Only a handful of houses make continuous markets, but the narrow spread between the bid and asked prices of high-grade unlisted issues suggests that buyers and sellers do not suffer from a thin market.

At the end of 1973, 1,964 bond issues of American corporations were listed on the New York Stock Exchange. Of this total, fewer than 100 were actively traded. The sales of listed bonds in 1973 totaled $4.4 billion, or over 80 percent of all listed trading in such securities.[2]

Data on changes in corporate bonds outstanding, listings on exchanges, and trading are increasingly influenced by the growing volume of convertible bonds. These securities, though bonds in name, are convertible into common shares at predetermined ratios and are, in effect, calls on common stock at a fixed price. The volume issued and traded is in part a function of the course of the stock market. In 1973, 31 of the 50 most actively traded bonds on the New York Stock Exchange were convertibles.[3]

Yields

The factors determining interest rates in the capital markets and the interrelations among rates on different instruments are discussed in greater detail in Chapter 13. We comment here on the historical pattern of corporate bond yields.

---

[2] Securities and Exchange Commission, *Statistical Bulletin.*
[3] New York Stock Exchange, *Fact Book,* 1974.

Bond yields, as one important long-term rate, change through time as long-term interest rates in general rise and fall. The spread between yields on straight corporate bonds and on Treasury bonds of like maturities represents the margin required by investors to compensate for the risk of default. It also reflects the relatively poor marketability of corporate bonds.

Figure 10–1 graphs the average annual yields of long-term Treasury bonds, and *Aaa* and *Baa* corporate bonds. The data reveal that the three series rose and fell together, but not to the same degree. The differential between *Aaa and Baa* bond yields and between *Aaa* corporate and long-term Treasury bond yields was by no means uniform through time, reflecting the differences in demand for and supply of securities of different quality.

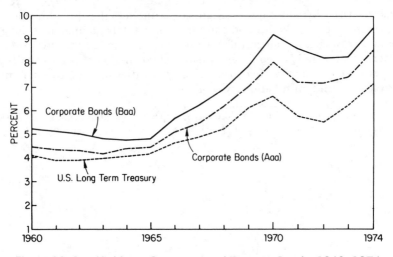

Figure 10–1. Yields on Corporate and Treasury Bonds, 1960–1974
(average yearly yield)

Sources: *Federal Reserve Bulletin; Moody's Bond Survey.* For data, see Appendix, Table A–3.

As yields in general rise, the premium for risk and poorer liquidity tends to increase, although this relationship has been by no means uniform. Also, the risk premium tends to vary with the economy. When the economy is booming, yield spreads tend to narrow—and increase when the opposite obtains.

A most significant development in recent years has been the large spread between the yields on long-term Treasury bonds and *Aaa* corporate bonds. This has been as low as 25 basis points in 1964 and as high as 165 basis points in 1971.[4] This was attributable in part to the heavy debt financing by large corporations—causing corporate bond rates to rise—and to the emphasis by the Treasury on sales of short-term securities, thereby reducing the supply of long-term Treasury bonds—which led to a drop in rates on these issues.

In years of recession, such as 1958, 1960, and 1961, investors require higher compensation for lesser quality, as indicated by the larger spreads among the Treasury, *Aaa*, and *Baa* groups. In 1962 through 1964, declining spreads reflected an opposite tendency. In years of sharply rising interest rates, such as 1966 through 1969, it is normal for the lower quality bonds to suffer most from the credit squeeze and spreads therefore widen. This general rule does not always hold, however, as witnessed by the yield spreads in the 1970 to 1974 period. Yield spreads in 1971 and 1972 were among the greatest for any period, yet these years were years of relative monetary ease. In 1974, a year characterized by very high rates and tight money, the spread dropped between corporate bonds and rose only moderately compared to long term Treasuries. Although difficult to measure, some of the rise in *Aaa* interest rates in 1974 could be attributed to the operating difficulties experienced by many *Aaa* firms—mostly utilities—caused by high interest rates and an inflationary economy.

---

[4] A basis point is one-one hundredth of a percentage point. Thus, 100 basis points are one percent, and a rise of 165 basis points is 1.65 percent.

```
1111111111111111111111111111111111111111111111111111111111111111111111111111111111
1111111111111111111111111111111111111111111111111111111111111111111111111111111111
111111111111111111111111111111111  11111   111   111111111111111111111111111111111
11111111111111111111111111111111  111  1111   111111111111111111111111111111111
111111111111111111111111111111111111  1  11111   111111111111111111111111111111111
11111111111111111111111111111111111111   111111   111111111111111111111111111111111
1111111111111111111111111111111111111   111111   111111111111111111111111111111111
1111111111111111111111111111111111111   111111   111111111111111111111111111111111
11111111111111111111111111111111111  1  11111   111111111111111111111111111111111
11111111111111111111111111111111  111  1111   111111111111111111111111111111111
111111111111111111111111111111111  11111   111   111111111111111111111111111111111
1111111111111111111111111111111111111111111111111111111111111111111111111111111111
1111111111111111111111111111111111111111111111111111111111111111111111111111111111
```

The Corporate Stock Market

Definitions and Concepts

No attempt is made in this book to describe all the legal and financial characteristics of stocks or their role in corporate financial policy. Our concern is with the nature and scope of their primary and secondary markets. A few reminders of their basic features are, however, appropriate.

Corporate stock in the form of transferable certificates represents the equity interest in the company. Each share constitutes a percentage of the total net worth. The owners of the certificates enjoy the basic rights of proprietorship, some of which are, however, delegated to directors and officers or are limited by the corporate charter.

As the residual equity in the company, common stock participates in net assets in liquidation and in net earnings (when declared in dividends) after all claims of creditors and the preferences of any preferred stock have been met. The net assets and earnings, and so the prices of common stocks, are volatile, but the possibility of very high earnings gives these instruments unusual investment and speculative appeal.

Preferred stock ranks above the common in preference to assets and dividends. Participation in assets in liquidation is generally limited to par or a stated preference value; dividends are usually set in the charter at a maximum rate that must be paid before any dividends go to the common. Such dividends are ordinarily cumulative, that is, all past preferred dividends must be paid before any can be paid to the common. Because of their preferences and limitations, preferred stocks possess some of the attributes of bonds. Indeed, the very strongest preferreds rival bonds in strength and yield. Weak preferreds are akin to common stocks in that their dividend prospects are contingent on uncertain earnings and dividends.

Convertible preferred stocks (or bonds) have a dual appeal. They offer the owner the option of exchange into common stock at a predetermined ratio, and so their prices and yields reflect the prospects of the common itself. The conversion feature has little or no value if the market value of the preferred is well above that of the common shares into which it is convertible. The preferred then sells close to its "straight" value. When the market price of the common approaches or exceeds the conversion price, the value of the preferred equals (or exceeds) that of the number of shares of common for which it may be exchanged.

The market value of common stock is mainly a function of its prospective earnings and dividends. Its asset (book) value may have some influence, as will its marketability, that is, access to a good volume of trading. The price-earnings multiplier reflects opinion on the future stability and growth of earnings and dividends. The dividend yields of common stocks are a function of their present and estimated future dividend rates.

Common and preferred stock do not normally have maturity dates. Principal can ordinarily be recovered only through resale. However, two standard provisions of preferred stock give it some of the maturity features of bonds: (1) the right of the issuer to call in the stock at a value set by the charter—the call price forms a plateau or peg through which the market price is unlikely to break unless the stock is convertible or unless call is very unlikely; (2) many preferreds, especially of industrial companies, have a sinking fund or repurchase clause that requires the issuer regularly to retire shares at either a fixed rate or one contingent on earnings. Steady retirement for sinking fund has a supporting influence on market price.

Outstanding Corporate Stock

The year-end market value of all corporate stock of different categories in the United States (Table 11–1) is estimated by the Securities and Exchange Commission. To the total traded stock is added that of closely-held companies. The value of total publicly-held domestic stock is then found by deducting the value of investment company shares (to eliminate double counting), shares of foreign companies, and inter-

TABLE 11–1. Estimated Value of Traded and Closely-held Domestic Corporate Stocks, 1965–1973 (billions of dollars)

	1965	1966	1967	1968	1969	1970	1971	1972	1973
Listed stocks	$573	$514	$ 653	$ 760	$ 683	$ 681	$ 796	$ 933	$ 764
Traded over the counter	181	167	202	248	208	203	241	263	196
Closely-held	130	118	148	174	154	153	179	207	166
	$884	$799	$1,003	$1,182	$1,045	$1,037	$1,216	$1,403	$1,126
Less stock of investment and foreign companies	81	81	98	115	112	114	131	140	127
	$803	$718	$ 905	$1,067	$ 933	$ 923	$1,085	$1,263	$ 999
Less intercorporate holdings	94	75	85	99	80	77	103	109	86
Net domestic stock	$709	$643	$ 820	$ 968	$ 853	$ 846	$ 982	$1,154	$ 913

Source: Securities and Exchange Commission, *Statistical Bulletin.*

corporate holdings. The data reveal both the volatility and the secular rise in common stock values. Although corporate stock values have not fared well since 1968, the chief factor causing the long-term growth has been appreciation in price rather than increases in the number of issues traded.

The Primary Market for New Stock Issues

New corporate stocks are sold to investors both directly by the issuers and indirectly through investment bankers and dealers. Direct selling may be employed by new, weak, and speculative concerns that cannot obtain or afford the services of an investment banker. Sale of securities to employees and executives in connection with savings, stock purchase, and stock option incentives is also direct. Few stock issues are privately placed with institutional buyers; these are chiefly higher-grade preferred stocks of public utility companies.

The chief means of direct sale of common stocks is through the issuance of rights to existing stockholders entitling them to buy new shares (and convertible bonds and preferreds) in proportion to existing holdings. Such "privileged subscriptions" are offered at a discount from current market price; the value of the right itself is determined by the difference between market and subscription price, adjusted for the increase in the number of shares. In some states, the "preemptive right" is required, in others it is optional. In the latter states the corporate charter may require it. Where optional, management assesses the advantages of this method of financing in comparison with either public offering of stock or some other means of financing.

Successful sale of common stock (and of convertible bonds and preferreds) through rights is easiest when the existing stock is already widely held and traded, when the stockholders are enthusiastic and wish to add to their holdings, when the general stock market outlook is favorable, and when the discount below market price is substantial.

The investment banker often participates in the offering of stock through rights by entering into a standby agreement by which, for a fee, he (or a syndicate) agrees to take up any shares not subscribed by stockholders.

A rough approximation of the amount of securities sold by privileged subscription, for the twelve months ending June 30, 1973, regardless of whether the sale was accompanied by standby underwriting, is indicated by the size of the "to securityholders" figure (Table 11–2) within the total of securities offered for immediate cash sale and registered with the Securities and Exchange Commission. The data exclude private placements, categories such as railroad securities that need not be registered, and exempt small issues. A very small percentage of bond and preferred stock total was sold directly to securityholders. About 10 percent of the new common stock was offered through privileged subscription.

TABLE 11–2. Registered Corporate Securities Offered for Immediate Cash Sale, Year Ended June 30, 1973 (millions of dollars)

	Bonds	Preferred	Common	Total
To the general public	$13,852	$2,574	$ 8,894	$25,320
To securityholders	10	2	1,126	1,137
Total	$13,862	$2,575	$10,019	$26,456

Some figures do not add to totals due to rounding.
Source: Securities and Exchange Commission, *39th Annual Report* (1974), p. 165.

Where stock is sold to the public, the use of investment bankers and syndicates depends on the size and quality of the issue and on the range of services needed by the issuers and for which they are willing to pay. It is convenient at this point to summarize the various methods of sale of new bond and stock issues:

(1) Direct sale without investment banker assistance:
    (a) Small, new, and weaker issues (bonds and stocks)
    (b) Employee and executive purchase plans (stocks)
    (c) Privileged subscriptions without standby underwriting (convertible bonds and preferred stock, common stock)
(2) Direct sale with some investment banking services:
    (a) Privileged subscriptions with standby underwriting
    (b) Private sale to institutions, the banker acting as finder (bonds, preferred stock)
(3) Sale through investment bankers:
    (a) On an agency or best-efforts basis (mainly stocks)
    (b) Full commitment underwriting (all types of securities)

Volume and Buyers of New Common Stock Issues

The use of common and preferred stocks in business financing and their importance relative to bonds is indicated by the data in Table 11–3, which covers the gross proceeds of all new corporate securities sold for cash in the United States for both new money and refinancing from 1965 through 1973. The figures include all public and private sales including registered and unregistered issues.

The volume of bond financing has far outstripped that of stock financing over the last two decades. Common stock financing has increased sharply since 1968, however, as large funds have been needed from all sources for corporate expansion. Even preferred stock—often convertible preferred issues—expanded significantly. As discussed in

TABLE 11–3.   Types of New Securities Sold for Cash, 1965–1973
(billions of dollars)

	1965	1969	1970	1971	1972	1973
Bonds, notes, and debentures	$13.7	$18.3	$30.3	$31.8	$26.3	$21.7
Preferred stock	0.7	0.7	1.4	3.7	3.4	3.4
Common stock	1.6	7.7	7.2	10.5	9.9	7.8
Total	$16.0	$26.7	$38.9	$46.0	$39.6	$32.9

Sources: Securities and Exchange Commission, *Annual Reports* and *Statistical Bulletin.*

the previous chapter, the declining corporate profitability and high inflation rate combined in recent years to compound the need for external funds.

The bond figures for the various years are somewhat illusory in that almost 20 percent of the total bond volume consisted of convertible bonds. These latter issues have their greatest appeal when stock markets are rising as in 1971 and 1972. Convertible issues have expanded recently because of their usefulness in merger financing and as a method of reducing the coupon payment during high interest rate periods. Typically, new issue convertible bonds have coupon yields that are from 1½ percent to 3 percent lower than straight debt issues.

The drop in external financing in 1973 compared to 1971 and 1972 was a result of improved corporate profitability and liquidity along with a declining stock market that made stock financing less attractive. The sharp jump in common stock financing in 1971 and 1972 occurred for the opposite reasons—a rising stock market, the need for greater corporate liquidity, and the desire to convert short-term bank loans to long-term securities.

Data in the previous chapter show that the major sources of corporate funds have been internal—retained profits and depreciation allowances. The small volume of new common stock financing relative to the amount of total stock outstanding attests to the minor importance of the primary stock market as a source of funds. The $7.8 billion of new corporate stock issued in 1973 amounted to less than 1 percent of total stock outstanding. This contrasted with bond financing of $21.7 billion in 1973, which represented 10 percent of total corporate bonds outstanding. This difference was accentuated in 1974 as close to 85 percent of new corporate offerings were corporate bonds. The declining stock market caused most firms to shun common stock financing in 1974.

Public utility and communication companies with their tremendous need for capital have been the chief issuers of corporate bonds and stocks. In recent years they have accounted for between 45 and 60 percent of total yearly issues of corporate security issues.

Acquisitions of Corporate Stock

Table 11–4 shows the annual net acquisitions of corporate stock for 1965 through 1973. To avoid double counting, the figures exclude issues of investment companies. The "individuals and others" group includes bank-administered trust funds, foundations and other non-profit organizations, and minor institutions. The data represent only the net increases in stock outstanding after deducting issues sold for refinancing and those retired from earnings. Hence they do not show the full activity of the various institutions in the primary market for stocks.

The growing importance of an institutional market for new stock issues is revealed by the data.

The fact that in 1965 through 1973 institutional holdings of stocks grew more than the net increase in total outstanding stocks means that most of their acquisitions were in the open market. Individuals and others acquired many of the new issues, but were net sellers on balance. Pension funds and insurance companies together absorbed more than the total amount of all new financing. These increased holdings provided very important support to the market for stocks, both new and old, and especially the higher-grade stocks, and contributed to a shift in ownership of the better stocks into institutional hands resulting in the "two tier" stock market.

"Individuals and others" have been large net sellers of stocks throughout the 1960s and 1970s. A number of reasons have been advanced for this selling activity. First of all, individuals have been withdrawing from direct participation in the market in favor of indirect participation through institutions like pension funds and insurance companies. This parallels the general intermediation of funds by individuals noted earlier. Second, individuals, especially in recent years, have been disappointed in the general stock market performance. Third, the high rates of interest on alternative securities have drawn funds from the stock market. Fourth, individuals have not been encouraged to participate directly in the market due to higher commissions charged by brokers, generally high margin requirements, and minimum account balances. Nevertheless, it should be remembered that individuals are still the largest owners of corporate stocks, holding more than $700 billion in market value at the end of 1973. Consequently, in perspective, the net sales of around $7 billion per year could easily reflect the individual's preferences in securing a more favorable and balanced portfolio position among all types of securities.

The minus figure for total new stock acquisitions in 1968 shows that corporations as a whole retired more stock for treasury than they issued. That is, the dollar amount of stock outstanding actually de-

TABLE 11–4.   Annual Net Acquisitions of Corporate Stock, 1965–1973 (billions of dollars)

	1965	1966	1967	1968	1969	1970	1971	1972	1973
Mutual savings banks	$ 0.2	$ —	$ 0.2	$ 0.3	$ 0.2	$ 0.3	$ 0.5	$ 0.6	$ 0.4
Life insurance companies	0.7	0.3	1.0	1.4	1.7	2.0	3.6	3.5	3.6
Property and liability insurance companies	-0.1	0.2	0.9	0.6	0.7	1.1	2.5	2.5	-1.2
Private, noninsured pension funds	3.1	3.7	4.6	4.7	5.4	4.6	9.3	7.1	5.8
State and local government retirement funds	0.4	0.5	0.7	1.3	1.8	2.1	3.2	3.5	3.9
Investment companies (mutual)	1.2	1.0	1.6	1.6	2.4	1.1	0.4	-1.5	-2.3
Foreign investors	-0.4	-0.3	0.8	2.3	1.5	0.6	0.7	2.1	2.8
Individuals and others (residual)	-5.1	-4.2	-7.4	-12.9	-9.4	-5.0	-6.9	-4.3	-5.2
Total	$ —	$ 1.2	$ 2.4	$-0.7	$ 4.3	$ 6.8	$13.3	$13.5	$ 7.8

Sources: Securities and Exchange Commission, *Annual Reports* and *Statistical Bulletin*; Bankers Trust Company, *Credit and Capital Markets* (annual); *Federal Reserve Bulletin* (flow of funds). See also references, Chapters 3–7. (Certain columns do not add to totals because of rounding.)

182

clined. Much of the decline was caused by conglomerates buying up other firms by issuing debt or paying cash and retiring the stock. Companies also retired their own shares through stock tender offers for cash or an exchange of senior securities.

As indicated in Table 10–1, companies have increasingly relied on internal sources of funds rather than on new stock financing, and as noted previously, this was especially true in 1974 when low stock prices, reflected in sharply lower price-earnings ratios, virtually stopped the issuance of new equity securities.

The Secondary Market for Stocks

Securities markets aid in the mobilization of capital and in the transfer of savings by providing facilities for orderly trading. On the organized exchanges, listed securities are bought and sold on an auction basis through brokers. In the over-the-counter market, prices are determined mainly by negotiations between buyers and sellers through dealers acting as principals.

The organized exchanges provide a continuous market for the exchange of outstanding issues that meet the listing requirements. But mere listing does not automatically guarantee good marketability. Large orders are often difficult to fill without a substantial price movement from the previous trade.

The New York Stock Exchange has the strictest listing requirements and serves as a prototype for the other exchanges. At the end of 1973, 2,058 stock issues of 1,560 different companies were listed on the exchange. The market value of these stocks totaled $721 billion and the value of trades during the year amounted to $146 billion, or a turnover ratio of about 20 percent. The increase in the turnover rate from the early 1960s which was approximately 14 percent, was caused in part by the expanding role of institutions in the stock market.

The American Stock Exchange (ASE), also located in New York, generally lists the securities of smaller, more unseasoned companies than those that qualify for the "Big Board." Activity on the ASE has increased in the last decade and amounted to nearly 13 percent of the total number of trades on organized exchanges in 1973. As the ASE tends to list small firms, however, they accounted for less than 6 percent of the total market value of shares traded on the exchanges in 1973.

The eleven regional exchanges provide trading facilities for stocks with a local interest, but the bulk of their activity is in "Big Board" issues that are also listed on the regionals ("multiple listing").

The great increase in share ownership by the institutions has precipitated a number of new arrangements for buying and selling large blocks of stock. These new arrangements have resulted in an active market in listed securities "off the board" and in the over-the-counter market.

In response to this competition as well as to pressure from the SEC, commissions are now negotiated on large trades and will be expanded to all trades by 1975. This has not been accomplished without a great deal of turmoil among brokerage houses as several went bankrupt or were forced to seek a merger partner. Although these failures and other problems cannot be blamed entirely on negotiated commissions, it is true that the intense competition for institutional business resulting in lower commission charges has reduced brokerage revenues. The demise of some brokerage houses and the consolidation of others has not seriously affected the marketability of stocks.

A much larger number of securities are traded in the over-the-counter (or unlisted) market. This has been estimated at about 50,000 securities in all with about 14,000 stocks and 3,500 bonds being actively traded. The total value and volume of bonds traded is much larger in the over-the-counter market than on listed exchanges; however, the opposite holds for trades in common stocks.

Transactions in federal securities are off-board, as are those of all but a few state and municipal bonds. Most corporate bonds are unlisted, as are all but a few bank, insurance, and mutual fund shares and a large number of industrial and utility shares. At the end of 1973, the value of stocks actively traded over the counter was estimated at $196 billion, about 25 percent of the aggregate of the market value traded on organized exchanges.

As noted earlier, trading on the over-the-counter market is not confined to unlisted securities. A number of listed securities are bought and sold in the "third market," which consists of dealers with an inventory of listed stocks. The volume of "third market" trading in stocks listed on the New York Stock Exchange was $10.2 billion (1973), or 7 percent of the volume on the exchange.[1]

The "fourth market," where institutions interested in selling or buying securities deal directly with each other without the services of a broker or dealer has not grown in importance. The methods and procedures already developed for handling large institutional orders efficiently and economically—including negotiated commissions— through brokers and dealers have been the main reasons for this lack of growth in the fourth market.

Also, the Securities and Exchange Commission, charged with the responsibility of regulating the exchanges and securities markets, has placed increased emphasis on stock market efficiency in an effort to reduce transaction costs while improving the operations of security brokers and dealers.

---

[1] Securities and Exchange Commission, *Statistical Bulletin* (March 27, 1973), p. 364.

Ownership of Corporate Stock

At the end of 1973, over 30 million individuals, or 12 percent of the United States population, owned stock of publicly-held corporations.[2] This represents a drop from the 1972 high of about 32 million as many investors indicated their dissatisfaction with stocks and their preference for the higher current yields available on bonds and savings deposits.

Table 11–5 shows the institutional ownership of corporate stocks held by institutions from 1960 through 1973.[3] In addition to the institutions we have studied, the table also includes closed end investment companies, foundations, and educational endowments. At the end of 1973, all institutions together held 24 percent of the value of stocks outstanding. If holdings of personal and common trust funds (generally under control of banks) are added, the percentage rises to 32 percent.

Private noninsured pension funds continue to be the largest institutional holder of common stocks. At the end of 1973, their holdings constituted more than 38 percent of the holdings of all institutions. Investment companies, normally heavy purchasers of stocks, were slowed in 1972 and 1973 due to the large number of redemptions. The drop in the holdings of these two largest institutions in 1973 over 1972 also reflects the sharp market drop in 1973.

Perhaps the most significant fact revealed in the table is the substantial funds committed to corporate stocks by insurance companies—both life and property—in the 1970s. This again reflects the relaxation of laws regarding investment by life companies in stocks and the general stress on performance and capital gains by insurance companies in the portfolio management policies.

---

[2] Sources: *New York Stock Exchange Fact Book* 1974, p. 50.

[3] Data on the distribution of all outstanding stocks, especially institutional holdings, are incomplete or inconsistent. Opinion differs concerning the value of all corporate stocks outstanding—a difficult estimate because of lack of firm information on over-the-counter stocks. The list of institutions holding stocks also differs from source to source. The Securities and Exchange Commission totals for institutional holdings at the end of a given year differ considerably from that calculated in the Federal Reserve flow-of-funds data as the former includes bank personal trust funds, which are nominal but not actual owners of shares.

Assets held by bank trust departments are omitted from the table because these are not owned, but are managed by the banks for the benefit of others. At the end of 1972, common stocks held totaled $277 billion, of which $223 billion were in trust accounts and $54 billion in agency accounts. Deducting the value of stocks on employee benefit funds managed by the banks, so as to avoid duplication with the pension fund figures in the table, produces the still formidable figure of $177 billion in stocks under bank management for personal trusts and estates. (Federal Deposit Insurance Corporation, *Trust Assets of Insured Commercial Banks, 1972, 1973.*)

TABLE 11–5.   Ownership of Corporate Stock by Major Institutions,
1960–1973 (billions of dollars)

	1960	1965	1970	1973
Mutual savings banks				
Preferred	$ 0.3	$ 0.4	$ 0.7	$ 1.2
Common	0.4	1.0	1.8	2.8
Life insurance companies				
Preferred	1.8	2.9	3.5	6.3
Common	3.2	6.2	11.9	19.6
Property and liability insurance companies a				
Preferred	0.8	1.1	1.6	3.3
Common	8.6	14.1	16.0	24.3
Private, noninsured pension funds				
Preferred	0.7	0.8	1.6	1.0
Common	15.8	40.0	65.5	89.5
State and local government retirement funds				
Preferred	—	0.2	0.4	0.5
Common	0.4	1.4	7.6	18.1
Investment companies b				
Preferred	0.7	0.6	1.1	1.3
Common	14.1	30.3	38.5	31.1
Foundations				
Preferred	0.4	0.4	0.4	0.4
Common	13.1	19.1	21.6	24.1
Educational Endowments				
Preferred	0.2	0.1	0.1	—
Common	3.8	6.9	7.7	8.8
Total	$ 64.3	$125.5	$180.0	$232.3
Market value of traded stocks	$388	$753	$844	$960
Percentage held by institutions	17%	17%	21%	24%

a Excludes holdings of stock in insurance companies.
b Includes open-end companies only.
Sources: Securities and Exchange Commission, *Statistical Bulletin*, and sources
cited in Chapters 3–8.

The steady shift in stock ownership (as measured by dollar amount)
to institutions reflects not only the growth of savings held by them,
but also their increasing interest in common stocks as investments in
a growing and inflationary economy. The *relative* decline in individuals' holdings has been accelerated by the big breaks in stock prices
and the general market sluggishness since 1965 especially 1973 and
1974. As before, however, the net holdings of corporate stocks by
individuals have continued to rise over the long run with the secular
rise in stock prices.

The percentage of stocks held by the institutions we have studied
(Table 11–5) was 24 percent at the end of 1973. Although the totals
and percentages exclude bank-administered trusts, closed-end invest-

ment companies, nonprofit corporations, and minor institutions, the increase in institutional ownership is apparent.

Stock Trading and Institutional Activity

The market value of stocks (preferred and common) traded on all registered exchanges decreased from $204 billion in 1968 to $178 billion in 1973, and the total number of shares traded declined from $6.3 billion to $5.7 billion.

According to the Securities and Exchange Commission, purchases and sales of four institutional groups—private noninsured pension funds, open-end investment companies, life insurance companies, and property-casualty companies—reached all-time record levels, totaling $99.7 billion in 1972 but declined to $85.9 billion in 1973. The 1973 total was equal to nearly 50 percent of the volume of trading on all registered exchanges.[4]

The New York Stock Exchange has measured the role played by institutions in stock market activity for several short test periods. The broad list covers all major and minor institutions including nonmember broker-dealers. In the last test period (first half of 1971) institutions accounted for 52.4 percent of all trading activity on the "Big Board." [5]

Combining the ownership of securities with the trading activity produces the portfolio turnover ratio for institutions.[6] The turnover rate has increased steadily in recent years for all institutions and reached 45 percent for mutual funds alone in 1972 declining to 39 percent in 1973. The rate for private pension funds in 1973 was 16.5 percent, life insurance companies 33 percent, and property-casualty insurance companies 20.3 percent, in contrast to the rate for all New York Stock Exchange stocks of 22 percent.[7] The turnover rate for pension funds and insurance companies should be relatively low due to their long-term commitments on their liabilities and assets.

Yields and Rates of Return on Stocks

Preferred Stock

The yields on preferred stocks as a whole rise and fall with the general level of interest rates. The return on individual issues reflects the market estimate of their quality and marketability and any special features such as convertibility.

---

[4] Securities and Exchange Commission, *Statistical Bulletin* (March 20, 1974 and April 3, 1974). Not all trades were in listed stocks.

[5] New York Stock Exchange, *Fact Book*, 1973, p. 53.

[6] The activity rate is the average of purchases and sales divided by the average value of stock portfolio for the period.

[7] Securities and Exchange Commission, *Statistical Bulletin* (April 3, 1974), p. 401.

Dividends on preferred stocks are a distribution of profits and are contingent upon earnings and declaration of the dividend. Preferred dividends may not be paid in a given year even though earnings are sufficient to cover them. On other occasions, preferred dividends have been paid when the firm is operating at a loss. As most investors tend to view a preferred dividend as an implied contractual agreement, failure by the firm to declare and pay preferred dividends, when due, generally implies the firm is in grave financial condition.

The yields on high-grade bonds and preferred stocks are shown in Figure 11–1. As revealed by the data, the yields on long-term bonds have exceeded those on preferred stocks since 1963. Preferred rates have risen since the 1960s to more or less match the higher interest rates. The negative spreads reflect the shortage of new preferred issues,

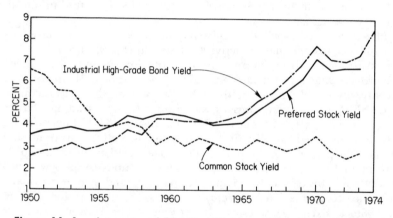

Figure 11–1.   Interest and Dividend Yields on High-Grade Industrial Bonds, Preferred Stocks, and Common Stocks, 1950–1974

Sources: *Moody's Bond Survey, Stock Survey,* and *Moody's Industrials.* For data, see Appendix, Table A–4.

the increase in the safety of preferreds, the conversion feature on several preferred issues, and, most important, the special demand by institutional investors subject to income taxation who enjoy an exemption of 85 percent of the dividend received. Other things equal, the after-tax return on the dividend received by a corporation is greater than the same interest received on a high grade taxable bond. In fact, some high-grade preferred stocks have yields lower than the yields on the bonds of the same company. In this case, it would not be advisable for an individual to hold the preferred stock rather than the bond unless the preferred has a conversion feature, or the probabilities of calling the preferred at a substantial premium are high.

The figure shows the stability in yields and interest rates from 1955 through 1965. Since then, through 1974, rates have generally risen to historic levels with preferred and corporate bonds yielding above 8 and 9 percent respectively during some months of 1974.

Common Stock

The returns on common stocks are different from contractual-type securities like bonds and preferreds in that their return is theoretically unlimited. The common shareholder receives not only the dividend declared from residual earnings, if any, but also enjoys potential capital appreciation in the value of the stock as a result of favorable reinvestment funds that were obtained either from borrowed sources or from retained earnings. As common stock ownership is riskier than bonds or preferred stocks, its expected and realized return, including dividend plus capital appreciation, should be higher than senior security instruments offering a more certain return.

Historically, total rates of return on common stocks have been around 9 to 10 percent per year with about 60 percent representing dividend yield and 40 percent coming from capital appreciation. The famous study by Lorie and Fisher, for instance, showed that ignoring taxes and assuming dividend reinvestment, the average rate of return on all stocks listed on the NYSE from January 1926 through December 1965, was 9.3 percent compounded annually.[8] Other evidence has corroborated the long-run average return on common stocks of about 9 percent annually.[9] Moreover, since stock price levels have risen little or in some cases have declined from 1965 through 1974, long-term rates calculated including these years would be considerably less than the 9.3 percent noted above. Thus, it is not surprising that, with little capital appreciation, the investor is demanding a higher dividend return which comes with declining prices and increasing dividend, as in 1974.

The return on corporate stocks for any given year, however, can be large and highly variable. Yearly increases in average stock prices exceeding 20 percent are not uncommon when stocks are on the rebound from previous lows; a drop of 15 to 20 percent in a bear market is also quite possible. Nevertheless, as stocks should be considered long-term investments, it is the overall long-term rate that is of prime interest here.

Lorie also noted that longer-term rates (10 to 15 years) were abnormally high after World War II when the average rate of return on

---

[8] J. Lorie and L. Fisher, "Rates of Return on Common Stocks," *Journal of Business*, January 1964.

[9] J. Lorie and M. Hamilton, *The Stock Market: Theories and Evidence* (Homewood, Ill.: Richard D. Irwin, Inc. 1973), p. 31.

stocks was 12.6 percent.[10] The abnormally high yield in the postwar period was achieved at a time when many foreign countries lacked productive capacity, inflation was low, raw materials were plentiful, and domestic demand was strong—a combination of factors not often duplicated. In any event, rates of return on common stock over long periods have been around 9 percent annually and a return of over 12 percent for an extended time period would be abnormally high.

Conversely, the average rate of return on common stocks including both dividend and price appreciation (which was nonexistent) since the early 1960s has been less than 4 percent per year. By any standard of comparison with past performance, this return has to be considered abnormally low.

Just how devastating the stock price performance has been is revealed in Figure 11–2. The *percentage* decline from December, 1964, through October, 1974, is shown for the Dow Jones average of 30 industrial stocks, the (weighted) Standard & Poor's composite index of 500 stocks, and the Indicator Digest (unweighted) average of all stocks listed on the New York Stock Exchange.[9] The ending prices compared to the opening price (at 100 percent) were 76 percent, 72 percent, and 47 percent, respectively. The larger decline in the Indicator Digest index is attributable to the fact that it is a simple average of all stock prices not weighted by the number of shares outstanding, and therefore is not influenced by the size of the constituent companies.

If the "normal" appreciation in stock prices of about 4 percent per year had continued through 1974, assuming 1965 to be normal, the Dow Jones Industrial average would have been close to 1400 instead of the actual 590 (December, 1974).

Furthermore, the cataclysmic drop in stock prices in 1973–1974 was highly unusual in light of improved corporate earnings. Stocks sold at their lowest price-earnings ratios in 20 years—many as low as 3- or 4-to 1. Amid rampant inflation, common stocks had lost their value as an inflation hedge, except possibly over the very long run.

Reasons for the great weakness in stock prices, especially in 1974, include the shock of Watergate, the oil-energy crisis, the high yields available on competing fixed-income investments, and the expectations of declining corporate earnings, particularly during the economic recession that continued into 1975.

The data in Figure 11–2 show that the current dividend yield on

---

10 *Ibid.*, p. 36.

9 It is important to note that Figure 11–2 shows the percentage change rather than the actual change in prices. The beginning and ending actual prices were: Dow Jones Industrials, 874.13 and 665.52; Standard & Poor's 500, 84.75 and 73.90; Indicator Digest, 50.54 and 23.65.

The authors are indebted to MacKay-Shields Financial Corporation, New York, for preparing the chart.

Figure 11–2.   The Ten-Year Stock Market Record

Prepared by MacKay-Shields Financial Corporation, New York.

common stocks was more than 4 percentage points below the yields on high grade bonds in late 1973. This inverse gap implied that the expected capital appreciation on the average common stock had to be considerably above 4 percent per year to make common stock investment preferred over bonds for the average investor. Since the average spread between the total return on common stock and high-grade bonds has been on the order of about 5 percentage points, that is, dividend yield plus price appreciation amounting to about 9.3 percent annually has exceeded long-term, high-grade bond yields of around 4.3 percent, and with high-grade bonds yielding (1974) 9 percent, stocks should be expected to yield near 13 percent for historic differentials to hold—an abnormally high return for common stocks. Dividend yields rose in 1974 to about 5 percent, as prices declined, reducing the size of the inverse yield gap to less than 4 percent.

The conclusion follows that, if the historical differential (at 5 percent) in total return on common stocks over bonds is to be maintained at present levels of interest, stocks should show abnormally high returns which include either substantial capital appreciation or a high dividend yield. Otherwise, investors should prefer high-yielding bonds and other investments. In the period 1965 through 1972, there was no secular capital appreciation in common stock prices, and in 1973–1974, the drop created an intermediate-term declining trend. It follows that if common stocks are to equal the yield on high-grade bonds plus an additional increment to offset inflation, under the conditions prevailing toward the middle 1970's they must offer unusually high dividend yields. Many stocks of good quality were yielding 7 to 10 percent or more in 1974.

The low prices, low price-earnings ratios, high earnings yields, and high required dividend yields in 1973–1974 resulted in such high costs of equity capital as to virtually preclude corporations from financing with common stock, and they wer⸴ forced to meet their capital market needs with high-cost debt financing and/or retained earnings.

```
1212121212121212121212121212121212121212121212121212121212121212121212121212
1212121212121212121212121212121212121212121212121212121212121212121212121212
12121212121212121212121212121    12121    121    121    1212121212121212121212121212
121212121212121212121212121212    212    2121    121    1212121212121212121212121212
12121212121212121212121212121212121    1    12121    121    1212121212121212121212121212
1212121212121212121212121212121212    212121    121    1212121212121212121212121212
12121212121212121212121212121212121    1212121    121    1212121212121212121212121212
1212121212121212121212121212121212    212121    121    1212121212121212121212121212
12121212121212121212121212121212121    1    12121    121    1212121212121212121212121212
121212121212121212121212121212121212    212    2121    121    1212121212121212121212121212
12121212121212121212121212121212121    12121    121    121    1212121212121212121212121212
1212121212121212121212121212121212121212121212121212121212121212121212121212
1212121212121212121212121212121212121212121212121212121212121212121212121212
```

The Mortgage Market

Basic Characteristics

A mortgage is a lien on real property to secure a loan. The mortgage and the actual note are different instruments, but we shall use the term *mortgage* to represent the combination. Corporate bonds secured by pledge of fixed assets and chattel mortgages secured by personal property and business equipment are excluded from our discussion. Some secured business loans are included in the commercial mortgage category. Mortgages are almost exclusively capital-market instruments in that their maturity may run five to forty years. Consistent with the hedging principle, proceeds obtained from mortgage commitments are normally used to finance long-term capital assets.

Mortgages appeal to investors because the tangible assets pledged can be inspected and valued and are property of substantial importance to the borrower. Furthermore, yields on mortgages are frequently higher than those on other fixed-income securities of similar maturity. This reflects the specialized nature of mortgages, their lesser marketability compared with that of bonds and stocks, and the delays involved in foreclosure and final settlement in the event of failure.

Most modern mortgages require the borrower to amortize the principal by remitting a periodic sum covering principal, interest, and usually property taxes and insurance. The shift to amortized loans stemmed from the adoption by the Home Owners' Loan Corporation and by savings and loan associations after the shortcomings of single-principal-payment loans became apparent in the depression of the 1930s. Amortization was also required by the Federal Housing Administration for insured loans (1934) and by the Veterans Administration for guaranteed loans (1944).

Other characteristics of the modern mortgage are lower downpayments, higher loan-to-value ratios, and lengthening of final maturity to as long as forty years on some liens. Periodic repayment (often monthly) provides a turnover of investors' funds and a steady growth in the owner's equity, reducing some of the risk from this combination of features. The modern mortgage has had a tremendous impact on the real estate market, especially on home ownership, and has been at least partly responsible for the diversion of a flood of savings into real estate financing through the expansion of institutions investing in such credits.

Types

In addition to differences in size, risk, geographical origin, and other factors, mortgages can be classified in a number of ways, of which the following categories are useful for our purposes.

(1) By type of property pledged:
Farms
1–4-family residences
Multifamily dwellings (apartments)
Commercial and industrial property
(2) By level of lien:
First mortgages
Junior mortgages (second, third)
(3) By type of lien:
Conventional
Government-supported: FHA-insured, VA-guaranteed
(4) By use of property:
Owner-occupied: residential, commercial
Rental: Residential, commercial
(5) By type of borrower:
Consumers
Corporations
Small businesses
Farmers
(6) By purpose:
New construction
Acquisition of existing property
General financing

(7) By type of lender:
    Financial institutions
    Governmental agencies
    Individuals

Size and Growth

Table 1–2 showed that, of all debt instruments, mortgages have had the greatest expansion in the postwar period. Since 1970, the net annual increase in the amount outstanding—the flow of funds into mortgages—has averaged about $50 billion a year and at the end of 1973 was running at the rate of about $75 billion yearly. Mortgages outstanding at the end of 1973 totaled $635 billion. With about 8 percent of total mortgage debt retired yearly, this means that the amount of new mortgage debt written was over $100 billion annual rate at the end of 1973.

Table 12–1 shows the mortgage debt outstanding at the end of

TABLE 12–1.   Mortgage Debt Outstanding, at Year End, 1960–1973
(billions of dollars)

	1960	1965	1970	1973
Farm	$ 12.8	$ 21.2	$ 31.2	$ 39.4
Residential:				
1–4-family	141.3	212.9	280.2	386.4
Multifamily	20.3	37.2	58.0	85.4
	$161.6	$250.1	$338.2	$471.8
Commercial and industrial	32.4	54.5	82.3	123.9
Total	$206.8	$325.8	$451.7	$635.1
Conventional	$144.5	$244.6	$342.5	$500.1
FHA-insured	32.6	50.1	71.9	85.0
VA-guaranteed	29.7	31.1	37.3	50.0
Total	$206.8	$325.8	$451.7	$635.1

Sources: *Federal Reserve Bulletin;* National Association of Mutual Savings Banks, *National Fact Book* of Mutual Savings Banking, (New York, annual).

selected years in the postwar period, classified by major types of property pledged and by major types of liens.

Farm Mortgages

Farm mortgage debt has grown somewhat less than total mortgages in the 1970s. This can be explained by (1) large amounts of personal property financing by farmers on equipment purchases in lieu of mortgage financing, (2) a tendency for farms to sell less often than single-family homes, (3) the general decline in farm population, (4) less developed financial markets in rural areas, and (5) substantial down-payments by farmers on large purchases.

Farm mortgage debt is typically first mortgage debt financed by conventional means. Only a small portion is FHA- or VA-supported; it is, however, often guaranteed by other special agencies. This debt is incurred mainly for financing property, although the proceeds are sometimes used for general purposes.

Commercial banks and life insurance companies historically have been the largest suppliers of farm mortgages; however, in recent years, there has been a steady drift toward financing by governmental agencies such as the Federal Land Banks, which make long-term loans through National Farm Loan Associations, and the Farmers Home Administration, which makes one- to five-year operating loans and farm-ownership loans (see Table 12–5). At the end of 1973, commercial banks and life insurance companies together held $11.5 billion, or 29 percent of all outstanding farm mortgages, down from 35 percent in 1968. Federally-sponsored credit agencies and Federal budget agencies together held $11.7 billion, or 30 percent, in 1973, which was up from 18 percent of the amount outstanding in 1968. Individuals and others including real estate trusts held about $16.1 billion, or 40 percent of the total. Much of the holdings by individuals were a result of second contracts on sale of properties when the seller carried back some of the financing for the purchaser.

Home Loans

Home mortgages (on one- to four-family homes) constitute the largest single category of mortgages. Loans secured by one-to-four family dwellings amounted to 60 percent of total mortgages outstanding at the end of 1973, down from about 70 percent in 1960. The relative decline for home mortgages has been a result of sharply increased financing of multifamily and commercial properties as well as the increased difficulty individuals have experienced in securing mortgages at interest rates they are willing to pay and in sufficient amounts that they can qualify for the loan, meet the downpayment requirements, and make the sharply increased monthly payments.

Nevertheless, net home mortgage financing (new financing less repayments) has increased every year since World War II and now runs about $40 billion a year although the latter amount is highly variable from year to year.[1] This substantial growth reflects both the demand for housing and the availability of mortgage financing from institu-

---

[1] To show farm mortgage debt as separate from residential debt is not quite accurate, as the total of the former in Table 12–1 includes some mortgages incurred for home purposes.

tions and the federal government. Population, consumer incomes, and construction costs all rose during the postwar period, as did the supply of funds available to savings associations and other financial institutions. The result has been a tremendous overall increase in home construction and financing in the postwar period, even though the amount of construction often varies sharply from year to year.

Housing Starts

Annual private residential housing starts reached 1,908,000 units in 1950. Housing starts were low at only 1,165,000 units in 1966 as high interest rates cut demand for new housing and disintermediation at savings associations caused a lack of available funds. Housing starts rose to an all-time high in 1972 to 2,345,000 units as interest rates declined from previous highs in 1970 and 1971 and mortgage funds were plentiful. As mortgage funds became more restricted in 1973 and 1974, however, along with sharply higher interest rates, housing starts fell abruptly to less than 1,650,000 units in 1974.

TABLE 12–2.   Housing Starts and Residential Construction Activity, 1955–1973

	1955	1960	1965	1970	1973
Housing starts (000's)					
Private	1,626	1,252	1,473	1,434	2,045
Public	20	44	37	35	12
Total	1,646	1,296	1,510	1,569	2,057
Number of family units (000's)					
1-family	a	1,009	965	815	1,132
2-family and more	a	287	545	654	925
Total		1,296	1,510	1,469	2,051
Mobile home shipments (000's)	a	103	216	401	580
Private residential construction activity, excluding mobile homes (in billions of dollars)	$18.7	$22.5	$27.9	$31.9	$58.1

a Not available.
Sources: *Federal Reserve Bulletin;* United States League of Savings Associations, *Savings and Loan Fact Book* (Chicago, annual); U.S. Department of Commerce, Bureau of the Census, *Construction Reports,* Series C20, C30.

The wide fluctuations in housing starts from year to year are caused by the double-barreled effect of monetary policy. When money is tight and interest rates are high, individuals resist paying the higher rates and cut demand. At the same time, savings associations are generally discouraging any new loans as they are experiencing or at least fearful of disintermediation. Consequently, people are not buying homes and savings associations are not encouraging them to do so. The opposite result obtains in periods of easy money.

The data in Table 12–2 reveal the dominance of single-family homes in residential construction, the variability in total starts from year to year, and the total dollar value of private residential construction activity.

Two or more family units, although still accounting for a minority of total private housing starts, have recorded relative increases in recent years. This has been caused by (1) sharply higher land costs making high density housing more economically feasible, (2) demographic and life-style changes revealing a preference for smaller families, and recreation-type apartment living, (3) higher costs of home construction causing postponement of home buying, (4) readily available mortgage financing on multifamily properties due to the growth of real estate investment trusts, and (5) liberal tax advantages on multifamily units that stimulate investor interest.

The figures for housing starts do not include mobile home shipments as they are frequently considered personal property rather than real estate. If mobile home shipments are included, then total units started (or shipped) would amount to 2,625,000 for 1973 with mobile homes accounting for 580,000 units or 22 percent of the total.

Types of Mortgage Liens

The three nonfarm basic home mortgage loans are conventional loans with or without insurance or guarantee, those insured by the Federal Housing Administration, and those guaranteed by the Veterans Administration. Table 12–1 shows the amounts of each type *outstanding* at the end of selected years.

Conventional loans have consistently been the most important category, approximately 75 percent of total outstanding in recent years. This is up from 70 percent only a few years earlier as the influx of abundant private funds into the mortgage market coupled with the general disenchantment with the loan procedures and time delays of FHA and VA loans pushed conventional mortgages to record levels.

Although representing only about 13 percent of the total mortgage debt financing, FHA-insured mortgage loans have increased steadily in the postwar period at a growth rate comparable to that of conventional financing. At the end of 1973 outstanding FHA mortgages totaled $85 billion, a $52 billion increase since 1960 and an annual compound growth rate of 7¾ percent. This compares favorably with the 8 percent annual growth rate in conventional mortgages during the same period.

The programs under FHA auspices have not all grown at this rate, however. For instance, FHA financing of single-family homes has increased only modestly (about 5 percent per year) while multifamily financing has increased better than 30 percent per year since 1969. The growth in multifamily financing has been a result of a shift in emphasis in federal housing in the early 1970s toward low cost housing and, particularly, low cost multifamily housing, as well as a preference by several large institutional investors for government-insured mortgages.

There are numerous housing programs established under the National Housing Act administered by the FHA. Six programs (sections in the act) deserve brief mention here because of their size and activity: (1) Section 203, (2) Section 207, (3) Section 220, (4) Section 221, (5) Section 235, and (6) Section 236.

Section 203 of the act provides insurance of mortgages on loans to finance new and existing dwellings if they are first-mortgage amortized loans bearing a maximum nominal interest rate of 9.5 percent (August 1974) with the mortgagor paying an additional 0.5 percent to the FHA mutual insurance fund as an insurance premium. Maximum maturities range for as long as 35 years, with maximum loan-value ratios as high as 97 percent. Section 203 has been the standard financing arrangement for the one-to-four-family program that accounts for the bulk of FHA financing.

Section 207 provides for mortgage insurance for the construction and/or rehabilitation of multifamily units as well as for mobile home parks. Section 220 provides mortgage insurance on construction or repair of single- or multifamily projects in urban renewal areas. Section 221 [especially 221 (d)(4)] insures mortgages of multifamily projects designed for low-to-moderate income families. The above programs are considered nonsubsidized in that the interest rate paid can be up to the maximum rate listed above and no special payments are otherwise made to tenants or owners.

There are also several subsidized housing programs established by the National Housing Act. Some of them include such benefits as rent supplement payments, interest-free loans to nonprofit corporations and below market interest rates (BMIR) for construction of multifamily housing projects. Two presently active programs are established under sections 235 and 236. Section 235 provides for an FHA interest subsidy to low income families that essentially reduces the monthly payments of the mortgagor on a single-family home. Section 236 is the multifamily counterpart to section 235 and provides interest subsidy to the owner or investor who rents to low income families at a reduced rate.

Historically, the FHA has set maximum rates that may be charged by lenders on nonsubsidized loans insured by the FHA. Typically, the maximum rate is below the going market rate but it is raised occasionally, or lowered, depending upon the competitive position with respect to yields on conventional mortgages and long-term bonds (Table 12–6). In recent years, FHA-insured loans have been heavily discounted to reflect the going market rates. Thus, the homeowner, while receiving a lower interest rate through FHA financing, found that the lender was charging him a higher loan fee than on a conventional loan to make up the difference. The FHA has worked to eliminate these discount "points" by taking a more flexible position on interest rate ceilings. Accordingly, recent legislation was introduced to remove all interest rate ceilings on FHA and VA loans and let these rates move with market levels.

The nominal rate on FHA/VA loans was raised to a maximum of 9½ percent in 1974 reflecting the record level of prevailing interest rates. But even then the rate failed to match market yields, which were 9½ to 10 percent and higher at that time on multifamily properties, excluding loan discounts.

Until 1969, FHA-insured loans could be purchased by qualified institutions only. Individual investors became eligible in that year, but their demand has not been substantial. The chief market for FHA-insured loans is still the Federal National Mortgage Association (FNMA) and, more recently, the Federal Home Loan Mortgage Corporation (FHLMC). In 1973, the association committed funds to their purchase at the annual rate of $8.9 billion, while the FHLMC committed $1.6 billion.

With their controlled appraisals, stated credit standards, and amortized terms, FHA loans have had an immense effect toward standardization of lending practices. They have been chiefly responsible for the acceptance of high loan-to-value ratios and longer-term loans of up to forty years in some cases.

The Serviceman's Readjustment Act of 1944, commonly called the "GI Bill of Rights," as amended, provides for the guarantee by the Veterans Administration of institutional loans for the financing of veterans' homes, farms, and businesses. The maximum maturity of home loans is thirty years except for farm home loans, for which it is forty years.

Yield rate on VA loans approximates that on FHA loans and, therefore, has suffered the same consequences. VA loan rates were often unattractive to lenders relative to those on other mortgages and bonds, and consequently, they sold at substantial discounts. Similarly, the rate was listed as 9.5 percent late in 1974, but legislation was also introduced to remove rate ceilings entirely. Although VA loans with their 100 percent loan-to-value ratio and guarantee by the Veterans Administration (to $17,500 or 60 percent of the amount of the loan, whichever is less) are attractive, the value of new recordings (Table 12–1) and the total amount of outstanding VA mortgages has leveled out and will probably decline in the future as the number of eligible veterans diminishes and loan repayments exceed new recordings.

Junior Mortgages

Much obscurity surrounds the amount and use of second mortgages, primarily because they are held by individuals rather than by reporting institutional investors. As of 1960, the Bureau of the Census estimated the residential dollar volume at $3.8 billions, or 2.4 percent of residential debt outstanding.[2] The amount is probably over $20 billion today. Their revival is an interesting feature of the modern mortgage market and reflects the great postwar demand for housing that has required many buyers to present and sellers to accept a junior lien to bridge the gap between the conventional first mortgage plus available equity and the selling price of the property. Junior mortgages fill a substantial need in financing houses above the middle-income bracket that are not eligible for sufficient FHA or VA financing. This in turn stems from the restricted loan-to-value ratios required by institutional lenders.

The use of junior mortgage financing has increased in recent years as purchasers assume existing mortgages to minimize closing costs and receive a lower interest rate than the current market level. Some mortgages written with an institution, however, contain a provision that any loan assumption must receive prior approval from the lender. At time of sale, the lender may raise the interest rate to the market level.

Second mortgage financing, called "gap" financing, has grown in importance especially in multifamily and commercial properties. When the downpayment on the purchase of an apartment or other similar property is insufficient to clear the seller's equity—the difference between the sales price and the existing total mortgage balance—a "gap" exists. Some lenders specialize in providing this special second mortgage type financing to fill the gap. This financing might take the form of a straight second mortgage or a "wrap around" mortgage, in which an institution writes a new loan for the entire amount of outstanding debt, including the first mortgage, with the institution making payment on the first mortgage. In any event the marginal interest rate on the gap financing is customarily around 14 to 18 percent or higher.

The modern second mortgage often requires rapid amortization of principal or matures over a period seldom longer than five years. Steady repayment of principal, along with that of the senior mortgage, builds an increasing equity. However, subordination to the first lien often requires a high yield ranging from 11 to 16 percent.

The seller who is willing to accept a second lien can retain it or, in some cases, sell it to a permanent holder through local mortgage brokers and dealers, who discount the principal balance from about 20 to 40 percent. Such loans are likely to be used most frequently in

---

[2] U.S. Department of Commerce, Bureau of the Census, "Residential Finance," *Census of Housing*, V (1960), Part 2, p. xxiii.

periods of tight money (such as 1966, 1969, and 1974) when adequate senior financing is limited. They are also often used for general fundraising purposes when the property already supports a first lien.

Because most large institutions are, in the main, prohibited from holding junior mortgages, individuals and specialized real estate firms are the chief investors in such loans.

Multifamily (Apartment) Loans

Loans secured by multifamily dwellings have grown substantially in recent years and accounted for 18 percent of all residential loans outstanding in 1973. The rise in land value, the shift back to metropolitan living, and higher interest rates on these loans enabling a plentiful supply of available funds for multiunits have encouraged greater construction of apartments. Regulations governing such loans have been relaxed and greater government participation in this sector has also been a contributing factor.

The number of private nonfarm housing starts other than one-family residences increased from 582,000 in 1968 to 1,069,000 in 1972 as abundant funds and FHA programs fueled the rapid expansion. Dips in the rising secular trend occurred in 1966, 1969, and 1973 (to 925,000) recession conditions, and in 1974 as tight money and disintermediation restricted the flow of funds to mortgages.

In recent years, builders have been able to get high loan-to-value ratios on new apartment construction loans as funds were available but at rates considerably in excess of single-family homes. In addition, lenders often demanded equity participation or a share of the income from the project. This availability of apartment financing has not always been the case; the social pressure for mass home-ownership and easy financing that characterizes the single-dwelling market is lacking, except in the case of FHA-insured loans, on multifamily dwellings.

Large apartment loans are in demand by mutual savings banks, real estate investment trusts, and by life insurance companies (Table 12–5). Many are obtained in the national market either by direct representatives of the investors or through the efforts of local mortgage correspondents. As in the case of commercial and industrial loans, institutional investors, especially life insurance companies and REITs, have developed a preference for large mortgages on income properties and those that provide some equity participation.

Commercial and Industrial Mortgages

Loans secured by business property (other than apartments) are highly specialized instruments, mainly in amortized conventional form, with final maturities ranging from ten to thirty years. Such mortgages constituted 19 percent of total mortgage debt outstanding at the end of 1973. They are incurred by builders and developers for construction purposes and by business firms for general financing. This latter category of commercial loans has been a prime factor in the rapid growth of commercial mortgages as firms have sought financing from all sources in a relatively tight money market coupled with high interest rates. In addition, many commercial mortgage loans are classed as term loans by banks and insurance companies and are excluded from the regular mortgage category, as are mortgage bond issues issued by corporations.

Industrial mortgages to finance the construction and acquisition of manufacturing properties are frequently amortized within a period as short as ten years because of their special risks. Recent years have seen longer amortization periods in order to reduce payments caused by increased interest rates.

Loans on retail shopping centers, department stores, and warehouses are often secured by property leased to large national tenants. Such mortgages are in effect two-name paper. Yields on the best of these approximate the yields on good-grade corporate bonds. Many residential construction loans that will eventually be refinanced on a permanent basis are classed as commercial until taken out by the original or ultimate investor. Thus, this category is not completely distinguishable from that of residential liens.

The Primary Mortgage Market

In Chapters 3 through 7, the role of the major institutions in supplying funds to the primary mortgage market was discussed. The demand for mortgage financing follows the housing cycle, which, in the postwar period, appears to have a longer swing than the general business cycle. When peaks and valleys do coincide either with the general cycle or with ease and tightness of capital (such as in 1969 and 1974), marked variations appear in housing starts, construction volume, and mortgage financing. A greater variation might have taken place except for the large use of long-term federally supported programs and loans, which are often used in a countercyclical fashion.

The data in Table 12–3 show the annual changes in the major categories of outstanding mortgage loans from 1965 through 1973. As noted previously, the volatility of the net flow of funds into mortgages results from variation in the amount of construction and capital-market conditions. The late 1960s were characterized by smaller increases in farm mortgages and by the gradual growth in nonfarm residential and commercial mortgages. The early 1970s witnessed continuing moderate farm mortgage financing, but sharply higher mortgage financing in nonfarm and commercial properties that was almost double the average net additions in the 1965 to 1969 period. Again, the plentiful funds from all institutions, federal programs, a large number of new household formations, and tax benefits from real estate ownership all contributed to the rapid growth in the 1970s.

TABLE 12–3.   Annual Changes in Mortgages, 1965–1973
(billions of dollars)

	1965	1966	1967	1968	1969	1970	1971	1972	1973
Farm	$ 2.2	$ 1.8	$ 2.3	$ 2.2	$ 1.9	$ 1.8	$ 2.0	$ 2.6	$ 4.0
1–4-family	15.4	10.7	12.4	15.2	15.6	13.4	28.0	40.7	41.0
Multifamily and commercial	8.0	8.8	8.3	10.0	10.3	11.3	18.9	25.5	24.9
Total	$25.6	$21.6	$23.0	$27.4	$27.8	$26.4	$48.9	$68.8	$69.9

Sources: *Federal Reserve Bulletin.* See that source for primary sources.

Annual Changes in Owners' Shares

Table 12–4 shows the annual amounts of funds supplied to the market by the major investors from 1965 through 1973. The factors influencing the annual flows were discussed in Chapters 3 through 7, and are briefly summarized here.

The large increases in funds placed in mortgages in 1971 to 1973 by commercial banks, mutual savings banks, and savings and loan associations were a direct result of the large savings inflows experienced by these institutions during the same period. The total flow of funds into these institutions, largely into savings accounts, is an important determinant in the availability of mortgage funds. Hence, during tight money as in 1966, 1969, 1973, and 1974, net mortgage loans are likely to diminish or only modestly increase as higher rates on competing investments are favored investments.

Although mortgages represent the primary investments for mutual savings banks and savings and loan associations, they are not nearly so important to commercial banks. Furthermore, commercial banks have added to mortgage holdings as additional security for commercial type loans, and to secure construction loans that have permanent financing elsewhere. Thus, rather than an overt search for mortgages, much of it has been "reaching for security." The fact that many banks fostered the growth of real estate investments trusts was also a contributing factor to the revived interest in mortgages.

The generally steady increase in mortgage acquisitions by savings associations was interrupted by the drying up of their fund flows in 1966, 1969, and 1970. However, record inflows in 1971 and 1972 caused the net increase in mortgages in those years to reach all-time highs and total more than the previous seven years combined. Multifamily mort-

TABLE 12–4. Annual Acquisitions of Mortgages, 1965–1973
(billions of dollars)

	1965	1966	1967	1968	1969	1970	1971	1972	1973
Commercial banks	$ 5.6	$ 4.7	$ 4.6	$ 6.7	$ 5.4	$ 2.3	$ 9.8	$16.8	$19.7
Mutual savings banks	4.1	2.7	3.2	2.8	2.7	1.9	4.2	5.6	5.7
Savings and loan associations	9.0	3.8	7.5	9.3	9.5	10.2	23.9	31.9	25.9
Life insurance companies	4.9	4.6	2.9	2.5	2.0	2.3	1.1	1.8	3.8
Private (noninsured) pension funds	0.6	0.5	0.2	—	0.2	0.1	−0.6	−0.6	−0.2
State and local government retirement funds	0.7	0.8	0.5	0.4	0.6	0.8	0.3	−0.3	−0.1
Federally-sponsored credit agencies	1.1	2.6	1.8	2.1	4.5	5.5	3.5	4.1	7.1
Real estate investment trusts	—	—	—	0.2	0.8	2.1	2.5	4.9	4.5
Individuals and others	−0.4	1.9	2.3	3.4	2.1	1.2	4.2	4.6	0.7
Total	$25.6	$21.6	$23.0	$27.4	$27.8	$26.4	$48.9	$68.8	$69.9

Sources: See citations in schedules, Chapters 3 through 7; Bankers Trust Company, *Credit and Capital Markets* (New York, annual).

gages accounted for a substantial part of this expansion in the 1970s (Table 4–9). The sharp rise in interest rates in 1974 accompanying disintermediation again caused mortgage additions to decrease such that mortgage loans made were less than one-half that of 1973 for the comparable period.

Mutual savings banks' mortgage experience has been similar to that of savings and loan associations as the two are closely allied. As noted in Chapter 4, however, mutual savings banks have added much more to their holdings of bonds due to the favorable returns on these securities compared to mortgages. In 1974 mutual savings banks likewise experienced deposit withdrawals with the result that net additions to mortgages increased only moderately in that year.

Two major institutions—federal agencies (of all types) and real estate investment trusts—have grown in importance in the mortgage market in the 1970s. The role of federal credit agencies has expanded considerably as the Federal National Mortgage Association, the Government National Mortgage Association, and the Federal Home Loan Mortgage Corporation all added significantly to their holdings of mortgages. These latter institutions deal primarily in the secondary market for mortgages (discussed later) and supply liquidity to the mortgage market in general.

Real estate investment trusts are the newest significant institution in the mortgage market. As noted in Chapter 7, their dramatic growth in the 1970 to 1973 period was a result of investor acceptance of REITs as a suitable investment, the demand for multifamily housing, and favorable tax benefits available in real estate investments that encouraged borrowing from REITs. Unfortunately, many of the operations of REITs turned out to be ill-conceived and poorly managed such that bankruptcy or sharply curtailed operations resulted. Consequently, investor confidence has waned and REITs will be fortunate to match their mortgage acquisitions and growth in the future with that in the early seventies.

Other institutions have contributed minor amounts to mortgages in recent years. Life insurance investment shows the volatility discussed in Chapter 5; in very recent years, high-yielding and more marketable corporate bonds have been attractive, and, as a result, home loans have lost their appeal. Pension fund investment in mortgages increased substantially until 1967 when they placed even more emphasis on purchase of common stocks. The acquisitions of individuals and minor institutions continue to show little relation to the variations in the annual net increases of total mortgages.

Ownership of Mortgages: 1973

Table 12–5 summarizes the ownership pattern of outstanding mortgage debt of all types at the end of 1973. Savings and loan associations held 36 percent of the total, reflecting their increasing share of single-family residential financing and their growing interest in multifamily instruments. Their preference for conventional loans is very evident. The "Individuals and others" category held 12 percent of the total debt, predominantly of the conventional type. Along with federal credit agencies, they form the chief market for farm loans.

The table shows a degree of specialization on certain types of mortgages for each institution. Life insurance companies, for instance, tend to invest in commercial and multifamily properties rather than single-family homes. This reflects their need to place very large amounts of funds with a minimum of paper work. The opposite holds for mutual savings banks and savings and loan associations which have shown a preference in the past for single-family homes. Commercial banks take more of an intermediate position and have relatively large holdings in both single-family and commercial mortgages.

Federal credit agencies, mutual savings banks, individuals, and others tend to have relatively large holdings of federally-underwritten—FHA and VA—loans.

If the shrinkage in net savings of institutions continues, together with the "disintermediation" or diversion of savings to open-market

TABLE 12–5. Ownership of Mortgage Debt, December 31, 1973 (billions of dollars)

	Commercial Banks	Mutual Savings Banks	Savings and Loan Associations	Life Insurance Companies	Federal Agencies (All types)	Individuals and Others	Total
Farm	$ 5.4	$ 0.1	—	$ 6.1	$ 11.7	$ 16.1	$ 39.4
Residential:							
1–4-family	$ 68.0	$ 44.2	$188.1	$ 22.0	$ 35.5	$ 28.6	$386.4
Multifamily	6.9	16.8	22.5	18.4	8.5	12.3	85.4
	$ 74.9	$ 61.0	$210.6	$ 40.4	$ 44.0	$ 40.9	$471.8
Commercial and industrial	38.8	12.1	21.5	34.9	—	16.6	$123.9
	$119.1	$ 73.2	$232.1	$ 81.4	$ 55.7	$ 73.6	$635.1
Conventional	$107.6	$ 44.5	$202.4	$ 67.8	} $ 55.7	} $ 73.6	$500.1
FHA-insured	8.2	15.8	29.7	9.2			85.0
VA-guaranteed	3.3	12.9		4.4			50.0
	$119.1	$ 73.2	$232.1	$ 81.4	$ 55.7	$ 73.6	$635.1

Sources: *Federal Reserve Bulletin*; *Federal Home Loan Bank Board Journal.* See also sources cited for institutions, Chapters 3 through 7.

investments that was evident in 1974, a shift in the ownership of mortgages will likely continue toward more government agency or direct
government holdings and away from private financial institutions.

Mortgage Companies

We have previously referred to the special role of mortgage companies as correspondents in originating and servicing loans for institutional investors. They deserve special mention in a discussion of the
primary market for mortgages.

Nature and Functions

The modern mortgage company is typically a closely held, private corporation whose principal activity is originating and servicing residential
mortgage loans for institutional investors. It is subject to a minimum
degree of federal or state supervision, has a comparatively small capital
investment relative to its volume of business, and relies largely on commercial bank credit to finance its operations and mortgage inventory.
Such inventory is usually held only for a short interim between closing
mortgage loans and their delivery to ultimate investors.[3]

Although mortgage companies may hold permanent mortgages in
their own name, they are primarily merchants of residential mortgages. They seek out loans, secure interim bank financing, resell the
loans to institutions, and thereafter service the loans for the final
owner.[4] They are not to be confused with mortgage brokers, who
serve solely as intermediaries and maintain no continuous relationship with borrower or investor.[5]

Mortgage companies are similar to investment banking concerns
in that they are involved mainly in the distribution of new instruments. They originate mortgages and collect an origination fee of
from 1 to 2.5 percent from borrowers or, as is often the case for conventional loans, from the investor in the form of a premium of about
0.5 percent above par. However, in contrast to the investment banking
firm, the mortgage company operates primarily on the basis of prior
and continuing relationships with the institutions it serves as "correspondent." Typically, it derives at least one-half of its income from the
administration or servicing fee charged for collecting and remitting
interest and principal of monthly amortized loans and from otherwise

---

[3] B. Klaman, *The Postwar Rise of Mortgage Companies,* Occasional Paper 60
(New York: National Bureau of Economic Research, Inc., 1959), p. 1.

[4] Other activities include making construction loans, serving as mortgage dealers,
and writing property insurance.

[5] Mortgage companies, as defined herein, are often known as "mortgage bankers."
The latter term, however, may be appropriately applied to all institutions that engage in mortgage financing.

representing the investor throughout the life of the mortgage. Other income is derived from interest on mortgages held in inventory and from insurance and other ancilliary activities.[6]

By originating mortgage loans in areas needing financing and by placing them with institutions in areas enjoying surplus funds, the mortgage company has been very instrumental in the development of a national mortgage market. Its contribution was greatly accelerated by the advent of FHA-insured and VA-guaranteed loans in 1934 and 1944, respectively.

> These federal programs, providing for the underwriting of mortgages on very liberal terms to borrowers, were basic to the accelerated post-war demand for home mortgage loans, to the flow of funds from institutional investors across state borders, and to the growth of large-scale home builders and mass merchandising programs.[7]

Mortgage companies are in all states, with a concentration in the South and West, where local funds are insufficient to meet the demand for mortgage loans. The correspondent system brings in funds from the eastern capital market.

Size and Volume of Services

S. B. Klaman estimated that in 1955 there were 865 mortgage companies with combined assets of $1.8 billion and with average assets of $2.1 million.[8] By 1970, the number had grown to over 2000 with assets of over $4\frac{1}{2}$ billion. Assets and net worth are not, however, the best measures of operations because outside funds, chiefly bank loans, support mortgages held in inventory. The volume of mortgages serviced is the best indicator.[9] They serviced $82 billion in mortgages in 1970 or 17 percent of the outstanding total. Their emphasis was on loans on residential properties.

---

[6] The traditional annual servicing fee has been 0.5 percent of the outstanding principal balance of small residential loans, although lower rates have appeared recently. Fees on apartment and commercial property loans are considerably smaller because these are easier to service.

[7] Klaman, *Postwar Rise*, p. 5.

[8] Klaman, *Postwar Rise*, p. 19. As of December 31, 1968, 242 companies, representing 40 percent of the mortgage company members of the association, had assets totaling $2.4 billion. Mortgage Bankers Association of America, *Mortgage Banking 1968: Trends, Financial Statements and Operating Ratios*, Research Committee Trends Report No. 7 (Washington, 1969), Table 6a.

[9] As Colean points out, "a company that made loans only on commitment from an investing institution would show less assets than one that inventoried loans by the use of bank credit for uncommitted future sale, even though the volume of business done might be the same in both cases." M. L. Colean, *Mortgage Companies: Their Place in the Financial Structure*, a monograph prepared for the Commission on Money and Credit (Englewood Cliffs, N.J.: Prentice-Hall, Inc., 1962), p. 8.

Role in the Mortgage Market

Mortgage companies perform their role of originators and servicers of mortgages through their relationships with three institutional investors. In 1968, 45 percent of their servicing volume was for life insurance companies; 22 percent, for mutual savings banks; and 12 percent, for the Federal National Mortgage Association.[10] They do relatively little business with savings and loan associations, which typically originate and service their own credits, and service a modest amount for commercial banks. Mortgage companies are also the principal users of the FNMA as a secondary market.

In 1968 and 1969, mortgage companies lost much of their traditional role of originators of home mortgages as institutions diverted funds to other investments. Mortgage companies had to develop more loans on income properties and offer incentives such as variable yields, equity participations and other "kickers" to attract funds, especially from life insurance companies.

Large institutional investors are originating more of their own loans than before, and commercial banks are entering the servicing field, so that mortgage companies are broadening their activities to include holding more permanent inventories of mortgages, selling more to individual investors and to pension funds, and expanding related lines of business such as real estate brokerage and insurance. Such an expanded role will require further growth in the size and resources of the typical company.

Bank loans are used to carry two types of mortgages: (1) those for which investors have made advance commitments but which will be delivered later, and (2) those accumulated for later placement when the opportunity arises. An extensive "warehousing" operation requires a sufficient spread between the rate on bank loans and the mortgage rates. The operations of the mortgage company are therefore directly affected by changes in general credit policy.

As of the end of 1971, a sample of mortgage company members of the Mortgage Bankers Association of America showed bank notes payable representing 63 percent of total assets, compared with 11 percent representing net worth.[11]

Uses of Funds

In 1971, for all mortgage companies combined, it was estimated that the mortgage loan inventory constituted about 60 percent and construction loans 30 percent of total assets.[12] It is not surprising that

---

[10] Mortgage Bankers Association of America, *Mortgage Banking, 1970* (Washington, 1972).

[11] *Ibid. 1971* (Washington, 1973), p. 22.

[12] *Ibid.*

FHA-insured and VA-guaranteed loans on one-to-four-family houses predominated. The FHA mortgage (and later the VA-guaranteed mortgage) avoided state restrictions on loan-to-value ratios, overcame the diverse foreclosure requirements in the various states, and with its uniform property requirements and appraised procedures became "outwardly a negotiable instrument of general acceptability." [13] The conditions making for the development of a national market led to a broad geographical distribution in which the mortgage company played the leading role.

The Secondary Mortgage Market

Three basic transactions take place in the total mortgage market: (1) originating and holding of mortgages by investors; (2) origination of mortgages by institutions and mortgage companies as agents with prior commitments to deliver them to other investors, who are in effect the principals and the ultimate permanent investor; and (3) transfer of outstanding mortgages from old owners to new owners. Secondary market activity involves the third operation.

The secondary market was primarily local in scope until the advent of FHA-insured and VA-guaranteed loans in 1934 and 1944, respectively. As we have seen, the uniformity of standards and terms and the new features of government support gave these instruments homogeneity and thus made them readily transferable, and facilitated the flow of mortgage funds across geographical barriers. In recent years, conventional loans have been taking on common characteristics, but each one still represents a separate credit risk.[14]

Nevertheless, the secondary mortgage market did not become well developed until the last half of the 1960s with the rapid development of the "second tier" of mortgage lenders.

Individual and institutional investors use the secondary market to acquire and sell mortgages—chiefly residential—either directly through their own contacts or through mortgage brokers.[15] Most of the latter are local concerns, although a few large firms in big cities operate on a national scale. Investors sell mortgages through brokers to switch funds into other assets or to acquire them for immediate delivery to round out portfolio requirements that have not been fulfilled by advance commitments. The brokers' commissions on secondary transfers run from 0.25 percent to 0.5 percent, depending mainly on the size of the loan.

---

[13] Colean, *Mortgage Companies*, p. 23.

[14] In recent years, about a dozen privately owned companies have been established to insure conventional mortgages. Examples are Continental Mortgage Insurance, Inc., a subsidiary of CMI Investment Corporation, and Mortgage Guarantee Insurance Corporation, a subsidiary of MGIC Investment Corporation.

[15] These should not be confused with the mortgage banking companies described previously.

Commercial banks make construction loans for later retention or resale. They "warehouse" loans as inventory that can be liquidated or held and transact transfers among families. Savings banks only recently have made use of the secondary market. Insurance companies occasionally make construction loans but prefer to acquire permanent loans from others and seldom resell in the secondary market. Savings and loan associations originate virtually all of their mortgage holdings. Some of their construction loans may be transferred to others. They have turned more to the secondary market to satisfy their overall portfolio needs since 1970. As we have seen, mortgage companies are engaged mainly in originating loans for resale to others. Their activities in the secondary market are modest. Individuals and federal agencies deal primarily in the secondary market. The secondary market emphasis by the FNMA, GNMA, and Federal Home Loan Mortgage Corporation (FHLMC) deserves separate discussion.

Federal Credit Agencies in the Secondary Market

Federal credit agencies participate in the secondary market by buying and selling mortgages. They also make loans to the primary lenders they support. FNMA, GNMA, and the FHLMC have no direct contact with the public but instead offer their securities through brokers, commercial banks, savings associations, and others.

When deposit flows are strong as in 1971 and 1972, federal (sponsored and other) agencies tend to reduce their support in the mortgage market and restrict their secondary operations. When opposite conditions hold, they increase their mortgage support.

The original purpose of the FNMA in 1938 was to provide a secondary market for FHA-insured residential mortgages. In 1948, FNMA operations were expanded to include VA-guaranteed mortgages. In 1954, its basic functions were redefined into three main areas of support: (1) management and liquidation of mortgages acquired from a variety of other government agencies, (2) special assistance programs for subsidized housing and other government home programs, and (3) secondary market operations in which FHA and VA mortgages were to be acquired from mortgage companies and institutions.

In 1968, under Title VIII of the Housing and Urban Redevelopment Act, the management and liquidation and the special assistance functions of the FNMA were transferred to a new agency, the Government National Mortgage Association (GNMA). (See later discussion of GNMA operations). After the retirement of its preferred stock, FNMA became a separate and private corporation and its stock was listed on the New York Stock Exchange. Its secondary market operations, under which purchases had been determined by the volume of government-supported mortgages attracted at market yields, were shifted to a "free market" system. FNMA does not originate mortgages; it makes commitments for existing mortgages only.

Institutions, such as commercial banks and mutual savings banks, that have been approved as "sellers" enter into a selling agreement with FNMA that provides for the institution to be qualified to service the mortgage offered for sale and to own stock in FNMA.

In 1968, the Free Market System (FMS) was introduced and greatly facilitated the secondary market in mortgages. Previously, the FNMA unilaterally established the price it was willing to pay for FHA and VA mortgages on a take-it-or-leave-it basis. Under the FMS, FNMA holds preannounced purchase auctions, usually biweekly, and each week the association indicates the total volume of forward commitments it will make to purchase eligible mortgages within 3 months, 6 months—up to a maximum of 18 months. The mortgages must be delivered to FNMA during the commitment period and must meet FNMA quality standards.

In 1970, FNMA was authorized to operate in the secondary market for conventional loans to provide an expanded mortgage portfolio and add depth to the conventional mortgage market. Since 1970, mortgage loans almost doubled from $15½ billion at that time to over $28 billion in August 1974.

In August 1974, FNMA-held mortgages consisted of $26.2 billion in FHA/VA loans and $1.8 billion in conventional loans. The latter holdings are expected to increase substantially over the next few years due to the relative decline of FHA/VA financing and FNMAs purchase plans for conventional mortgages.

The Government National Mortgage Association (GNMA) was established in 1968 to take over the former FNMA operations (see above) that were left with the Department of Housing and Urban Development when FNMA became a private corporation. In addition to the special assistance function and the management and liquidations function, a third function, the mortgage-backed security program—called Ginnie Mae "pass throughs"—was inaugurated. Under this last function, GNMA issues its own securities guaranteeing monthly principal and interest payments. These securities are backed by pools of mortgages guaranteed by the FHA, VA, or Farmers Home Administration. Hence, the Ginnie Mae securities are backed by the full faith and credit of the federal government and are riskless securities.

As of September 1974, GNMA mortgage holdings totaled $4.1 billion with FHA-issued mortgages constituting better than 90 percent of the total and VA loans the balance.

In order to facilitate the operations of savings and loan associations in particular and the secondary mortgage market in general, the

Federal Home Loan Mortgage Corporation, called "Freddy Mac," was created in 1970. The corporation's stock, $100 million, is held by the twelve regional Federal Home Loan Banks and is under the supervision of FHLB officials. Additional financing has come from issuing bonds and advances from the FHLB System.

Their operations in the secondary market are accomplished by purchasing mortgages originated by others. When money is tight, they provide liquidity by purchasing mortgages originated by others. When money is tight, they provide liquidity by purchasing mortgages from institutions and reverse the process when mortgage funds are plentiful.

Since 1970, FHLMC holdings have risen sharply and amounted to $3.5 billion at the end of August 1974. More than half of this total were FHA or VA mortgages ($1.9 billion) with the remaining amount in conventional mortgages ($1.6 billion).

As seen by the data above, most of the mortgage activity by FNMA, GNMA, or FHLMC has been in FHA and VA Loans. Although all three are allowed to purchase conventional loans, this preference for government-backed mortgages reflects their safety, national scope, uniformity of provisions, terms, and, consequently, better marketability than is available on conventional loans.

The secondary market for conventional loans, however, should continue to develop much more on a national scale as the relatively low risk in single-family mortgages and the high, long-term interest rate on newer mortgages make these securities appealing to institutional investors.

Mortgage Yields

The data in Table 12–6 and Figure 12–1 provide mortgage yield information from 1955 through 1974; the figures compare the averages of conventional and FHA mortgages and the yields on long-term corporate bonds. The data reveal both the geographical and annual variations in mortgage yields as conditions in the capital market have changed. Tight money conditions in 1966, 1969, 1973, and 1974 show up in all the mortgage series and in the bond rate. Yields on FHA mortgages (for puchases of new homes) were less variable than those on conventionals because of standardization and the influence of the fixed nominal rate. The first column in the table illustrates the recent change in allowing for more flexibility in the fixed contract rate. Using annual averages, comparison with the second column reveals that FHA mortgages have sold at a discount in the secondary market. Before declining, their average market yield reached nearly 10 percent in October 1974 against a nominal yield of 9 percent.

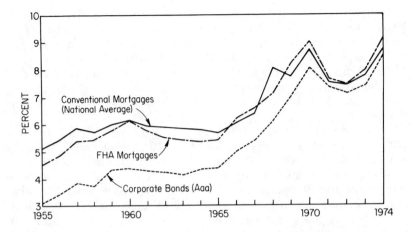

Figure 12–1.   Average Yields on FHA and Conventional Mortgages and
Corporate Bonds, 1955–1974

Source: *Federal Reserve Bulletin; Federal Home Loan Bank Board, Journal;*
U.S. Department of Commerce, *Construction Review.* Aaa corporate bonds are
Moody's series.

TABLE 12–6.   Yields on Mortgages and Bonds, 1955–1974

	FHA Mortgages (New Homes)		Conventional Home (New Homes) Mortgages		Aaa
	Contract Rate, Percentage	Market Yield, Percentage	National Average, Percentage	Western Average, Percentage	Corporate Bonds, Percentage
1955	4.5	4.6	5.2	5.4	3.06
1960	5.75	6.2	6.2	6.7	4.41
1961	5.75–5.25	5.7	6.0	6.5	4.35
1962	5.25	5.6	5.9	6.3	4.33
1963	5.25	5.5	5.8	6.4	4.26
1964	5.25	5.4	5.8	6.3	4.40
1965	5.25	5.5	5.7	6.4	4.49
1966	5.25–6.00	6.3	6.1	6.5	5.13
1967	6.00	6.6	6.3	6.8	5.51
1968	6.00–6.75	7.2	6.8	7.5	6.18
1969	6.75–7.50	8.3	7.7	8.5	7.03
1970	7.50–8.50	9.0	8.3	9.0	8.04
1971	8.00–7.00	7.7	7.6	8.3	7.39
1972	7.00	7.5	7.5	8.0	7.21
1973	7.00–8.50	8.0	7.8	8.3	7.44
1974 (10 mon.)	8.25–9.50	9.5	8.7	9.0	8.50

Sources: *Federal Reserve Bulletin;* Federal Home Loan Bank Board, *Journal;*
U.S. Department of Commerce, *Construction Review;* Aaa corporate bonds are
Moody's series; The Mortgage Banker (yellow section).

Conventional yields on new homes were consistently above the FHA rate until 1966. Since then, conventional loan rates (with higher risk) have been below FHA market rates. This inconsistency can be explained in part by the relatively low default risk on conventional homes, the buyers market that has existed in FHA/VA loans, and the propensity of lenders to prefer conventional loans—causing lower rates—over FHA loans with the extra paper work and time delays.

In September 1974, mortgage yields reached all-time highs. In areas particularly short of capital, yields above 10 percent on single-family homes, and 11 percent on commercial and multifamily units, were common. This compared with the prime rate of 12 percent on short-term loans and 9¼ percent on long-term high-grade bonds. In addition, a peculiar difficulty faced some would-be borrowers: where market yields on mortgages equaled or exceeded the usury ceilings in some states, new mortgage financing had to await changes in legislation.

In comparing the open-market rate on high-grade corporate bonds and on conventional mortgages, a lag in the rate of change in the latter due to the lack of a fully national flow of funds is apparent. Changes in mortgage yields appear somewhat more volatile in recent years. The spread between the annual average high-grade bond yield and the mortgage yields widens as mortgage yields rise. Although the FHA yields are now more flexible, there is aversion on the part of institutional investors to paying a price substantially different from par. Even during periods of rising effective yields, many investors are unwilling to move funds into mortgages when yields on other investments are also rising.

Typically, yields on mortgages exceed those on *Aaa* corporate bonds; however, the pattern was reversed in late 1974 as the average corporate bond (*Aaa*) yielded 9.2 percent versus 9.0 for the average new conventional mortgage (Figure 12–1). This was partially a result of government programs designed to aid the mortgage market.

In spite of some development of the national mortgage market, geographical differences in mortgage rates exist. Yield spreads exist in the capital-surplus areas in the East and Middle Atlantic regions and in the capital-seeking West and Southwest. The spread narrows to as low as 0.25 percent during periods of credit ease and widens to as much as 0.50 to 0.75 percent during tight money periods. (The data in Table 12–6 do not reveal these extremes, as the national average is higher than the eastern average.) In late 1974, when the national average yield of conventional loans on new single-family homes stood at 9.0 percent, the western rate ranged between 9 and 10 percent.

```
13131313131313131313131313131313131313131313131313131313131313131313131313131313
13131313131313131313131313131313131313131313131313131313131313131313131313131313
1313131313131313131313131313    31313    313    313    313    31313131313131313131313131313
13131313131313131313131313131    131    1313    313    313    31313131313131313131313131313
131313131313131313131313131313    3    31313    313    313    31313131313131313131313131313
1313131313131313131313131313131        131313    313    313    51313131313131313131313131313
131313131313131313131313131313131313    3131313    313    313    31313131313131313131313131313
131313131313131313131313131313131    131313    313    313    31313131313131313131313131313
1313131313131313131313131313131313    3    31313    313    313    31313131313131313131313131313
13131313131313131313131313131313131    131    1313    313    313    31313131313131313131313131313
1313131313131313131313131313131313    31313    313    313    313    31313131313131313131313131313
13131313131313131313131313131313131313131313131313131313131313131313131313131313
13131313131313131313131313131313131313131313131313131313131313131313131313131313
```

Summary: Sources and Uses, and the Yield Pattern

Total Sources and Uses of Funds, 1965 through 1973

In Chapters 3 through 7, the sources of funds for capital-market use were itemized for each major institution, together with their disposition in the various categories of instruments. In Chapters 8 through 12, the demand for intermediate- and long-term funds on the part of major users was presented. In this chapter, the over-all sources and uses are collated. Four categories of sources are included that were not given separate treatment, save for the flow of their funds into various instruments: business corporations, state and local governments proper, foreign investors, and the residual—individuals and others. This last category includes bank-administered trust funds and minor institutions. Two additional uses are included in the master schedule: bank term loans to business and foreign securities acquired mainly by institutions.

Explanation of two procedures is again pertinent. First, it was noted that except for those of commercial banks, most institutional funds flow into intermediate- or long-term use. To determine commercial bank sources, data on the actual application of these funds to capital-market use were employed. Second, all maturities of federal and federal agency securities were considered. This procedure was based on two factors: (1) the constant transfer and arbitraging among the various maturities of these instruments, making distinction by maturity somewhat unrealistic; and (2) the lack of reliable data on the maturity composition of the investments of several institutions.

Table 13–1 combines the totals of the detailed data presented in Chapters 3 through 12 into a master array of net flows of capital-market funds for 1965 through 1973. Details on the variations of the components of the total sources and uses of capital-market funds were presented in previous chapters.

After rising moderately from 1965 through 1969, the total flow of funds into the capital market burgeoned in the early 1970s with the total for 1973 almost tripling the amount for 1965.

In 1966, a year of great credit strain, major institutions sharply reduced their rate of acquisition of capital-market instruments, as the traditional flow of savings fell off substantially. That the total sources for that year equaled those of 1965 is attributable in part to the continued growth of pension and retirement funds and of investment companies. But the major factor was the sharply increased contribution of noninstitutional suppliers of funds—federal agencies, government and foreign investors, and individuals. Their direct investments, in large part, replaced the shrinking contributions of savings institutions.

The year 1967 saw a sharp rebound in funds accumulated in institutions of all types, which continued well into 1968. But credit strain eventually build up and cumulated in another credit crunch in 1969, reflected in the highest yields on record in the capital market up to that time. This led to only a $2.7 billion increase in capital market flows in 1969 over 1968.

The data from 1970 through 1972 reveal a strong upward trend that was not always reflected in the individual institutional flows. In particular, 1972 had more than double the 1969 level of capital market flows, an increase of $72.2 billion. Prime contributors to the dramatic rise in capital flows during this period were commercial banks, savings and loan associations, and foreign investors. Contributing significant amounts, but to a lesser degree, were life insurance companies and mutual savings banks. The trend did not continue in 1973, however, as fund flows declined by 8½ billion.

The capital market benefitted greatly from the increased competition in savings deposits, which increased substantially due to a higher rate of personal savings and a relaxed monetary policy. Interest rates, however, still remained relatively high during this period as the threat of inflation and continued strong loan demand prevailed. The worldwide threat of inflation coupled with the more stable political and economic (especially currency) atmosphere in the U.S., encouraged foreign investors to place funds in the capital market in record amounts. The $27.2 billion invested by foreigners in 1971 was almost three times as much as any previous year. Although dropping sharply in 1972, foreign investment of $10.7 billion was still the fourth largest amount invested by any group in the capital market. Another sharp drop in foreign investment in 1973 resulted from increasing domestic and international uncertainities.

As can be seen in the lower panel of Table 13–1, the primary beneficiaries of the rapid advancement in capital market funds in the 1970s were mortgages, corporate bonds, and government securities, in that order. Of the large suppliers, noted earlier, foreigners tended to place most of their funds in U.S. government securities; commercial banks and savings associations favored mortgages.

The data on inflow also show a marked instability in institutional contributions and, especially, a sharply varying commercial bank investment policy.

As for uses of funds, the chief factors of instability have been the fluctuating net additions to outstanding federal securities and mortgages. Net changes in outstanding federal agency securities have followed a contracyclical pattern at the agencies step up their financing in periods of pressure. As we have seen, net additions to municipal bonds fluctuate because of very special influences. Variations in net additions to corporate bonds reflect the pattern of their yields and, more importantly, the changing reliance by corporations on internal sources and new stock issues.

Capital Flows and Market Yields

The annual yield averages in Table 13–2 conceal the magnitude of interim variations. They are, however, useful in showing the relationship between the flow of funds into and out of the capital markets and the prevailing rates. First of all, the general upward drift in interest rates through 1970, the moderate decline in 1971 and 1972, and the resumption of the upward drift in 1973 and 1974 are apparent for all security issues including common stocks, which are affected more by special conditions than by the general supply of and demand for long-term funds. The large spread between bond and stock yields did, however, contribute substantially to the stock market weakness in 1969, 1970, and especially in 1974 as investors sought higher current yield investments. The large increase in dividend yield in 1974 to over 5 percent was a result of a declining stock market coupled with some increased dividends.

As expected, the greatest volatility was found in shorter-term securities, particularly bills and notes, and, as shown in the table, U.S. Treasury bonds with three to five year maturities. Corporate bond and mortgage yields exhibited a strong upward trend declining only slightly in the early seventies and late 1974. Though the rise in rates on corporate bonds and mortgages paralleled the increases in other securities, they rose relatively more as the demand for these

TABLE 13–1. Sources and Uses of Capital-Market Funds, 1965–1973 (billions of dollars)

	1965	1966	1967	1968	1969	1970	1971	1972	1973
Sources:									
Commercial banks	$12.7	$6.8	$26.5	$23.3	$ 0.9	$26.0	$ 32.7	$ 38.4	$ 32.2
Federal Reserve banks	3.8	3.5	4.8	3.8	4.2	5.0	8.5	0.3	9.3
Mutual savings banks	3.7	2.5	5.2	4.3	2.8	3.7	8.8	9.7	4.5
Savings and loan associations	9.6	4.2	9.2	10.1	9.8	11.4	29.2	36.3	25.9
Life insurance companies	7.7	6.6	7.5	7.8	5.3	6.0	10.2	12.5	13.3
Property-liability insurance companies	1.2	2.2	2.2	2.5	2.3	4.0	6.2	6.2	2.5
Private pension funds	5.2	5.9	5.9	6.9	6.2	7.1	7.8	6.8	8.8
State and local government retirement funds	3.2	3.7	3.9	4.5	5.1	6.4	6.9	7.8	9.3
Investment companies (open-end)	1.6	2.0	1.2	2.1	2.1	2.0	0.8	0.3	-2.7
Real estate investment trusts	—	—	—	0.2	0.8	2.1	2.5	4.9	4.5
Federally sponsored agencies	1.3	3.7	1.9	2.1	4.2	8.1	5.1	4.1	11.5
Business corporations	-0.5	-2.4	-2.8	0.8	-3.3	-0.7	3.1	-1.4	-1.9
State and local governments	2.1	1.3	0.6	1.6	2.8	-0.1	-1.0	4.0	1.6
Foreign investors	-0.1	-2.3	1.8	0.9	-0.9	10.4	27.2	10.7	3.2
Individuals and others	-2.4	11.7	-7.3	-2.3	28.8	0.8	-10.2	7.5	19.3
Total sources	$49.0	$49.1	$60.3	$68.6	$71.3	$91.7	$134.8	$148.1	$138.6

TABLE 13–1 (continued)

	1965	1966	1967	1968	1969	1970	1971	1972	1973
Uses:									
U.S. government securities	1.7	0.9	8.2	9.8	-1.0	12.9	25.9	19.0	7.9
Federally-sponsored agency bonds	2.0	5.0	-0.6	3.2	9.1	8.4	3.8	6.2	19.6
State and local government bonds	6.8	6.3	7.9	9.8	10.7	11.4	17.0	13.5	10.5
Corporate bonds	8.1	11.1	16.0	14.0	13.8	22.8	23.7	19.7	14.6
Corporate stocks	—	1.2	2.4	-0.7	4.3	6.8	13.3	13.5	7.8
Mortgages	25.6	21.6	23.0	27.4	27.8	26.4	48.9	68.8	69.9
Bank term loans	4.4	2.7	2.9	4.5	5.9	2.3	2.0	6.7	7.8
Agency term loans	0.1	0.1	0.1	0.1	0.1	0.3	—	0.3	0.3
Foreign Securities	0.3	0.2	0.4	0.5	0.6	0.4	0.2	0.4	0.2
Total uses	$ 49.0	$ 49.1	$ 60.3	$ 68.6	$ 71.3	$ 91.7	$134.8	$148.1	$138.6

For sources of data, see detailed schedules in Chapters 3 through 12. Corporate bonds include term loans of life insurance companies. Some columns of sources do not add to totals because of rounding.

221

TABLE 13–2.   Yields of Selected Capital-Market Instruments, 1965–1974

	1965	1966	1967	1968	1969	1970	1971	1972	1973	1974 (11 mo.)
U.S. Treasury, 3–5 years	4.2	5.2	5.1	5.6	6.9	7.4	5.8	5.9	6.9	7.9
U.S. Treasury long-term	4.2	4.7	4.6	5.3	6.1	6.6	5.7	5.6	6.3	7.0
Aaa state and local bonds	3.2	3.7	3.7	4.2	5.5	6.1	5.2	5.0	5.0	5.6
Aaa corporate bonds	4.5	5.1	5.5	6.2	7.0	8.0	7.4	7.2	7.4	8.5
125 industrial common stocks	3.0	3.4	3.1	2.9	3.1	3.6	3.0	2.6	2.9	4.4
Conventional home mortgages	5.7	6.1	6.3	6.8	7.7	8.3	7.6	7.5	7.8	8.6

Source: *Federal Reserve Bulletin; Moody's Investors Service.* Bond and stock yields are Moody's series. Mortgage yields are from Chapter 12.

loans outstripped the supply. The high rates on short-term instruments contributed to this temporary imbalance. Aside from money market instruments, the greatest volatility was found in the intermediate-term federal rate. Mortgage yields showed the least variation reflecting the lack of a truly national competitive market and strong resistence of borrowers to sharply higher rates.

Tight money conditions are revealed by the very high rates in 1969, 1970, and 1974 and by the substantial excess of intermediate-term yields over long-term yields on federal government securities in those years.

Annual changes in the bond and mortgage yields series show only an approximate relationship with the change in total supply of, and demand for, long-term funds as shown in Table 13–1. This is partially explained by the fact that the yields in Table 13–2 are yearly averages and hence tend to obscure sharp changes occurring within the year. Second, demand and supply changes tend to be dominated by other factors such as monetary policy and the rate on personal savings. Third, it is the interrelationship between total demand and supply that determines ultimate interest rate levels.

In general, when the total sources of funds does not exhibit good growth (around 5 percent or more) over the previous year, tight money conditions are indicated. This, of course, is only a rough approximation as tight money does not follow a yearly schedule. Nevertheless, the tight money periods of 1966, 1969, and 1973 to 1974 were characterized by minimal growth in total sources of funds.

The differential effects of interest rates on the uses of funds, as applied to each of the representative securities, is revealed in the tables. Given the transitivity and arbitrage process between interest rates, when money is tight, short-term rates tend to rise relatively more than long-term rates and funds tend to flow to the short-term instruments.

Consequently, long-term bonds and mortgages are likely to suffer from a lack of available funds and total amounts committed to these securities will tend to moderate, all other things equal. In 1966, 1970, and 1974, tight money periods, total funds flowing to mortgages declined compared to previous years. Funds flowed to mortgages in 1971 and 1972 as interest rates declined, but again the flow fell off in late 1973 and in 1974 due to high costs of mortgage money and disintermediation from savings banks and associations.

The flow of funds to corporate bonds is a little more difficult to explain. Amounts committed to corporate bonds actually increased in each of the tight money periods, 1966, 1970, and 1973–1974. This reflected, however, the need for funds by businesses and the declining stock market, which made the sale of stock undesirable and left borrowing as the only acceptable alternative for most firms. In this respect, the need for funds by users dominated the preference for short-term securities by suppliers of funds and, as a result, substantial long-term loans were made to businesses at high interest rates.

Rates on municipal bonds showed more volatility and a less dramatic longer-term increase through 1973, but they tended to follow the general market conditions of "over-demand" and "under-supply" of funds in 1966, 1969, and 1974. The effects of the enormous financing needs in all segments of the market in the latter years were discussed in previous chapters.

Are changes in long-term yields a result or a cause of changes in the supply of and the demand for capital-market funds? In general, our previous discussion of the individual markets would suggest that both possibilities are true. The question could be handled more explicitly if we were to examine, in addition to the data on long-term sources and uses of funds, the changing liquidity requirements of institutional and individual suppliers and uses of funds as well as changes in personal savings habits. We have equated capital-market sources and uses, but we have not discussed the changes in liquid funds nor the impact of *total* funds devoted to both short- and long-term employment. Also, we have not studied the shifting demand *between* short- and long-term uses. Unfortunately our short discussion does not permit such an analysis and the reader should keep in mind the caution suggested in Chapter 1, namely, that a somewhat arbitrary segregation of the flow of long-term funds within the total investment market fails to present the total picture.

A Concluding Statement

Our study has revealed the institutionalization of savings, the expanding role of institutions in funnelling savings into the various capital markets and the impact of their investment policies on both the primary and secondary markets for longer-term instruments. We have also shown the demands made upon the markets by individuals, businesses, and governments seeking longer-term funds for a wide variety of purposes. We have measured the combined influence of supply and demand forces on prices and yields, with special attention to the dramatic developments in the late 1960s and early 1970s.

The contribution of the capital markets to economic growth and the free flow of funds has increased greatly in the postwar period. The efficiency of the market structure has been enhanced by the expansion of investment banking activity, the broadening geographical range of institutional investment, the development of correspondent systems, and the improvement of secondary markets. But there are still important barriers to a really free flow of funds. Efficient capital markets require market agencies and organizations that function on a national scale, a minimum of restraints on investment policy, minimum government regulation of prices and yields, and widespread information concerning prevailing market conditions and prices so that yields can reflect the full play of supply and demand. Much progress has been made toward these goals. However, when drastic pressure for funds in the face of limited supply produces the conditions that prevailed in 1969–1971 and 1973–1974, the virtues of even more efficient markets, in which prices and yields reflect full national flow of and demand for funds, may conflict with national policy. Reduction in defense spending, implementation of domestic programs of great importance, and putting a brake on the inflationary spiral may require business, monetary, and fiscal controls antagonistic to unrestrained markets.

Appendix

TABLE A–1. Yields on U.S. Government Securities, Selected Dates, 1961–1974

	May 1961	Sept. 1966	June 1967	Jan. 1970	Mar. 1971	July 1971	July 1972	Aug. 1974	Dec. 1974
3-month bills	2.29	5.36	3.53	7.87	5.38	5.39	3.98	8.96	7.15
6-month bills	2.44	5.79	3.88	7.78	3.50	5.62	4.50	9.11	7.10[a]
9–12 month issues	2.72	5.80	4.40	8.82	3.66	5.73	4.90	8.88	6.78[a]
3–5 year issues	3.28	5.62	4.96	8.14	4.74	6.77	5.85	8.64	7.22
Long-term issues	3.73	4.79	4.86	6.86	5.71	5.91	5.57	7.33	6.78

[a] Estimated.
Source: *Federal Reserve Bulletin*.

TABLE A–2.   U.S. Government and Municipal Bond Yields, 1955–1974

	Long-Term Treasury (1)	State and Local Government (2)	(3)	Spread (1) over (2)	Spread (3) over (2)
		Aaa	Baa		
1955	2.84	2.18	3.14	0.66	0.96
1960	4.01	3.26	4.22	0.75	0.96
1965	4.21	3.16	3.57	1.05	0.41
1966	4.66	3.67	4.21	0.99	0.54
1967	4.85	3.74	4.30	1.11	0.56
1968	5.26	4.20	4.88	1.06	0.68
1969	6.10	5.45	6.07	0.65	0.62
1970	6.59	6.12	6.75	0.47	0.63
1971	5.74	5.22	5.89	0.52	0.67
1972	5.63	5.04	5.60	0.59	0.56
1973	6.30	4.99	5.49	1.31	0.50
1974 a	7.07	5.82	6.44	1.25	0.62

a Eleven months.
Sources: *Federal Reserve Bulletin; Moody's Bond Survey.*

TABLE A–3.   Yields on Corporate and Treasury Bonds, 1960–1974

	Corporate Baa (1)	Aaa (2)	Spread (1) over (2)	U.S. Treasury Long Term (3)	Spread (2) over (3)
1955	3.53	3.06	0.47	2.84	0.22
1960	5.19	4.41	0.78	4.01	0.40
1965	4.87	4.49	0.38	4.21	0.28
1966	5.67	5.13	0.54	4.66	0.47
1967	6.23	5.51	0.72	4.85	0.66
1968	6.94	6.18	0.76	5.25	0.93
1969	7.81	7.03	0.78	6.10	0.93
1970	9.11	8.04	1.07	6.59	1.45
1971	8.56	7.39	1.17	5.74	1.65
1972	8.16	7.21	0.95	5.63	1.58
1973	8.24	7.44	0.80	6.30	1.14
1974 a	9.24	8.54	0.70	7.07	1.47

a Eleven months.
Sources: *Federal Reserve Bulletin; Moody's Bond Survey.*

TABLE A–4.   Yields on High-Grade Bonds, Preferred Stocks,
and Common Stocks, 1950–1974

	Aaa Industrial Bonds (1)	10 High-Grade Industrial Preferreds (2)	125 Industrial Common Stocks (3)	Spread (2) over (1)	Spread (3) over (1)
1955	3.00	3.69	3.93	0.69	0.93
1960	4.28	4.48	3.48	0.20	−0.80
1965	4.45	4.07	2.98	−0.38	−1.47
1966	5.12	4.67	3.44	−0.45	−1.68
1967	5.49	5.13	3.11	−0.36	−2.38
1968	6.12	5.62	2.93	−0.50	−3.19
1969	6.93	6.15	3.14	−0.78	−3.79
1970	7.77	7.03	3.60	−0.74	−4.17
1971	7.05	6.55	2.98	−0.50	−4.07
1972	6.97	6.66	2.65	−0.31	−4.32
1973	7.29	6.67	2.94	−0.62	−4.35
1974 [a]	8.36	7.45 [b]	4.40	−0.91	−3.96

[a] Eleven months.
[b] Estimated.
Sources: *Moody's Bond Survey, Stock Survey,* and *Moody's Industrials.*

References

Statistical sources are cited throughout the book. The following list is restricted to recent major works and articles. The reader will also find most useful the May 1964 supplement to the *Journal of Finance*, which contains an inventory of research, both books and articles, prepared by the Exploratory Committee on Research in the Capital Markets of the National Bureau of Economic Research.

Allen, J. B., "Factors Determining the Volume of Certificates of Deposit Outstanding: A Case Study of the Drain-Off in 1969." *American Economist,* Fall 1971, pp. 32–38.

American Bankers Association, *The Commercial Banking Industry.* Englewood Cliffs, N.J.: Prentice-Hall, Inc., 1962. A monograph prepared for the Commission on Money and Credit.

American Institute of Banking, *Savings and Time Deposit Banking.* New York, 1968.

American Mutual Insurance Alliance, et al., *Property and Casualty Insurance Companies: Their Role as Financial Intermediaries.* Englewood Cliffs, N.J.: Prentice-Hall, Inc., 1962. A monograph prepared for the Commission on Money and Credit.

Atkinson, T. R., *Trends in Corporate Bond Quality.* National Bureau of Economic Research, New York, 1967.

Bartel, H. R., Jr., and E. T. Simpson, *Pension Funds of Multiemployer Industrial Groups, Unions, and Nonprofit Organizations.* New York: National Bureau of Economic Research, 1968.

Benston, G. S., "Savings Banking and the Public Interest." *Journal of Money, Credit and Banking*, February 1972, pp. 133–226.

Black, R. P., and D. E. Harless, *Nonbank Financial Institutions*. Richmond, Va.: Federal Reserve Bank of Richmond, 1969.

Board of Governors of the Federal Reserve System, *Flow of Funds Accounts, 1965–1973 (1974 Supplement)*. Washington, D.C., 1974.

————, *Federal Reserve System: Purposes and Functions*. Washington, D.C., 1963.

Brady, E.A., "A Sectoral Econometric Study of the Postwar Residential Housing Market." *Journal of Political Economy*, April 1967, pp. 147–58.

Break, G. F., et al., *Federal Credit Agencies*. Englewood Cliffs, N.J.: Prentice-Hall, Inc., 1963. Research studies prepared for the Commission on Money and Credit.

Brimmer, A. F., *Life Insurance Companies in the Capital Market*. East Lansing, Mich.: Bureau of Business and Economic Research, Graduate School of Business Administration, Michigan State University, 1962.

Calvert, G. L., ed., *Fundamentals of Municipal Bonds*, 9th ed. Washington, D.C.: Securities Industry Association, 1972.

Colean, M. L., *Mortgage Companies: Their Place in the Financial Structure*. Englewood Cliffs, N.J.: Prentice-Hall, Inc., 1962. A monograph prepared for the Commission on Money and Credit.

Commission on Financial Structure and Regulation, *Report* (popularly called the Hunt Commission Report). Washington, D.C., 1971.

Comparative Regulations of Financial Institutions. Subcommittee on Domestic Finance, House Banking and Currency Committee, U.S. Congress, 1963.

Council of Economic Advisers, *Report of the Committee on Financial Institutions to the President of the United States*. Washington, D.C.: Government Printing Office, 1963.

Cox, E. G., *Trends in the Distribution of Stock Ownership*. Philadelphia: University of Pennsylvania Press, 1963.

Davis, R. G., and L. Banks, "Interregional Interest Rate Differentials." *Monthly Review*, Federal Reserve Bank of New York, August 1965, pp. 165–74.

Dawson, J. C., *A Flow-of-Funds Analysis of Savings-Investment Fluctuations in the United States*. Princeton, N.J.: Princeton University Press, 1965.

De Leeuw, Frank, and Nkanta F. Ekanem, "The Supply of Rental Housing." *American Economic Review*, December 1971, pp. 806–17.

Fair, R. C., "Disequilibrium in Housing Models." *Journal of Finance*, May 1972, pp. 207–21.

Federal Home Loan Bank Board, *Study of the Savings and Loan Industry*. Washington, D.C., 1970 (four volumes).

Federal National Mortgage Association, *Background and History of the Federal National Mortgage Association*. Washington, D.C., 1969.

Federal Savings Institutions. House Committee on Banking and Currency, Report No. 1642, 90th Cong., 1st sess. Washington, D.C.: Superintendent of Documents, 1967.

Fellner, William, et al., *Fiscal and Debt Management Policies*. Englewood Cliffs, N.J.: Prentice-Hall, Inc., 1963. A series of research studies prepared for the Commission on Money and Credit.

The First Boston Corporation, *Handbook of Securities of the U.S. Government and Federal Agencies.* 26th ed. New York: The First Boston Corporation, 1974.

Fisher, L., and J. H. Lorie, "Rates of Return on Investments in Common Stock: The Year-by-Year Record, 1926–1965." *Journal of Business,* July 1968, pp. 291–316.

Fraser, D. R. and P. S. Rose, "Bank Entry and Bank Performance." *Journal of Finance,* March 1972, pp. 65–78.

Friend, I., *Investment Banking and the New Issues Market.* Cleveland: World Publishing Company, 1967.

Friend, I., et al., *Private Capital Markets.* Englewood Cliffs, N.J.: Prentice-Hall, Inc., 1964. Research studies prepared for the Commission on Money and Credit.

Friend, I., M. Blume, and J. Crockett, *Mutual Funds and Other Institutional Investors: A New Perspective.* New York: McGraw-Hill, 1970.

Gaines, T. C., *Techniques of Treasury Debt Management.* New York: The Free Press, 1962.

Goldfeld, S. M., "Savings and Loan Associations and the Market for Savings: Aspects of Allocational Efficiency." *Study of the Savings and Loan Industry.* Vol. II. Washington, D.C.: Federal Home Loan Bank Board, 1969.

Goldsmith, R. W., *A Study of Saving in the United States* (three volumes). Princeton, N.J.: Princeton University Press, 1955–1956.

———, *Financial Intermediaries in the American Economy since 1900.* Princeton University Press, 1958.

———, *The Flow of Capital Funds in the Postwar Economy.* New York: Columbia University Press, 1965.

———, *Financial Institutions.* New York: Random House, Inc., 1968.

Gramlich, E. N., "State and Local Governments and Their Budget Constraint." *International Economic Review,* June 1969, pp. 163–82.

Grebler, L., *The Future of Thrift Institutions.* Danville, Ill.; Joint Savings and Mutual Savings Banks Exchange Groups, 1969.

Greenbaum, S. I., and Mukhtar M. Ali, "Entry, Control and the Market for Bank Charters." *Journal of Finance,* May 1974, pp. 527–35.

Gurley, J. G., and E. S. Shaw, *Money in a Theory of Finance.* Washington, D.C.: Brookings Institution, 1960.

Guttentag, J.M., and M. Beck, *New Series on Home Mortgage Yields since 1951.* New York: Columbia University Press, 1970.

Hamburger, M. J., "Household Demand for Financial Assets." *Econometrica,* January 1968, pp. 97–118.

Harris, D. G., "Some Evidence on Differential Lending Practices at Commercial Banks." *Journal of Finance,* December 1973, pp. 1303–11.

Hawk, W. A., *The United States Government Securities Market.* Chicago: Harris Trust and Savings Bank, 1973.

Henning, C. N. et al., *Financial Markets and the Economy.* Englewood Cliffs, N.J.: Prentice-Hall, Inc., 1974.

Hirshleifer, J., *Investment, Interest and Capital.* Englewood Cliffs, N.J.: Prentice-Hall, Inc., 1969.

Homer, S., *A History of Interest Rates.* New Brunswick, N.J.: Rutgers University Press, 1963.

Institutional Investor Study Report of the Securities and Exchange Commission. 92nd Congress, 1st Session, House Document No. 92–64. Washington: U.S. Govt. Printing Office, 1971.

Investment Company Institute, *Management Investment Companies.* Englewood Cliffs, N.J.: Prentice-Hall, Inc., 1962. A monograph prepared for the Commission on Money and Credit.

Jacobs, D. P., *et al., Financial Institutions,* 5th ed. Homewood, Ill.: Richard D. Irwin, Inc., 1971.

Jeffers, J. R., and J. Kevon, "A Portfolio for Government Securities." *Journal of Finance,* December 1969, pp. 905–19.

Jones, L. D., *Investment Policies of Life Insurance Companies.* Boston: Division of Research, Graduate School of Business, Harvard University, 1968.

Jones, O., "Private Secondary (Mortgage) Market Facilities." *Journal of Finance,* May 1968, pp. 359–66.

Kendall, L. T., *The Savings and Loan Business: Its Purposes, Functions, and Economic Justification.* Englewood Cliffs, N.J.: Prentice-Hall, Inc., 1962. A monograph prepared for the Commission on Money and Credit.

Kessel, R. A., *The Cyclical Behavior of the Term Structure of Interest Rates.* New York: National Bureau of Economic Research, 1965.

Klaman, S. B., *The Postwar Rise of Mortgage Companies.* Occasional Paper No. 60. New York: National Bureau of Economic Research, Inc., 1959.

———, *The Postwar Residential Mortgage Market.* Princeton, N.J.: Princeton University Press, 1961.

Klein, M. A., "On the Causes and Consequences of Savings and Loan Deposit Rate Inflexibility." *Journal of Finance,* March 1972, pp. 79–87.

Kroos, H. E., and M. R. Blyn, *A History of Financial Institutions.* New York: Random House, 1971.

Kuznets, Simon, *Capital in the American Economy: Its Formation and Financing.* Princeton, N.J.: Princeton University Press, 1961.

Life Insurance Association of America, *Life Insurance Companies as Financial Institutions.* Englewood Cliffs, N.J.: Prentice-Hall, Inc., 1962. A monograph prepared for the Commission on Money and Credit.

Lindow, Wesley, *Inside the Money Market.* New York: Random House, 1972.

Ludtke, J., *The American Financial System: Markets and Institutions.* 2nd ed. Boston: Allyn and Bacon, 1967.

Lutz, F. A., *The Theory of Interest.* Chicago: Aldine Press, 1968.

Malkiel, B. G., *The Term Structure of Interest Rates.* Princeton, N.J.: Princeton University Press, 1966.

Mayne, L. S., "Supervisory Influence on Bank Capital." *Journal of Finance,* June 1972, pp. 637–51.

Meiselman, D., *The Term Structure of Interest Rates.* Englewood Cliffs, N.J.: Prentice-Hall, Inc., 1962.

Meltzer, A. H., "Credit Availability and Economic Decisions: Some Evidence from the Mortgage and Housing Markets." *Journal of Finance,* June 1974, pp. 763–77.

Michaelman, J. B., *The Term Structure of Interest Rates: Financial Intermediaries and Debt Management.* New York: Intext Educational Publishers, 1973.

Money Market Instruments. 2nd ed. Cleveland: Federal Reserve Bank of Cleveland, 1965.

Morrissey, T. F., "The Demand for Mortgage Loans and the Concomitant Demand for Home Loan Bank Advances by Savings and Loan Associations." *Journal of Finance,* June 1971, pp. 687–98.

Murray, R. F., *Economic Aspects of Pensions: A Summary Report.* New York: National Bureau of Economic Research, 1968.

National Association of Mutual Savings Banks, *Mutual Savings Banks: Basic Characteristics and Role in the National Economy.* Englewood Cliffs, N.J.: Prentice-Hall, Inc., 1962. A monograph prepared for the Commission on Money and Credit.

Nelson, R. L., *The Investment Policies of Foundations.* New York: Russell Sage Foundation, 1967.

Norgaard, R. L., "An Examination of the Yields of Corporate Bonds and Stocks,." *Journal of Finance,* September 1974, pp. 1275–86.

Pease, R. H., and L. O. Kerwood, eds., *Mortgage Banking.* 2nd ed. New York: McGraw-Hill Book Company, 1965.

Pesanto, J. E., "The Interest Sensitivity of the Flow of Funds through Life Insurance Companies: An Econometric Analysis." *Journal of Finance,* September 1974, pp. 1105–21.

Peterson, J. E., "Response of State and Local Governments to Varying Credit Conditions." *Federal Reserve Bulletin,* March 1971, pp. 209–32.

Piper, T. R., and S. Weiss, "The Profitability of Multibank Holding Company Acquisitions." *Journal of Finance,* March 1974, pp. 163–74.

Polakoff, H. E. et al., *Financial Institutions and Markets.* Boston: Houghton Mifflin, 1970.

Pyle, D. H., "On the Theory of Financial Intermediation." *Journal of Finance,* June 1971, pp. 737–47.

Rabinowitz, Alan, *Municipal Bond Finance and Administration.* New York: John Wiley & Sons, Inc., 1969.

Report of the Securities and Exchange Commission of the Public Policy Implications of Investment Company Growth. Report of the Committee on Interstate and Foreign Commerce, House Report No. 2337, 89th Cong., 2d sess., December 2, 1966. Washington, D.C.: Government Printing Office, 1966.

Report of the Special Study of the Security Markets of the Securities and Exchange Commission (five parts). House Document No. 95, 88th Cong., 1st sess., Washington, D.C.: Government Printing Office, 1963.

Robbins, S., *The Securities Markets: Operations and Issues.* New York: The Free Press, 1966.

Robinson, R. I., *Postwar Market for State and Local Government Securities.* Princeton, N.J.: Princeton University Press, 1960.

———, The Management of Bank Funds, 2nd ed. New York: McGraw-Hill Book Co., 1962.

———, "The Hunt Commission Report: A Search for Politically Feasible Solutions to the Problems of Financial Structure." *Journal of Finance,* September 1972, pp. 765–78.

Robinson, R. I., and D. Wrightsman, *Financial Markets: The Accumulation and Allocation of Wealth.* New York: McGraw-Hill Book Co., 1974.

Schaaf, A. H., "Regional Differences in Mortgage Financing Costs." *Journal of Finance,* March 1966, pp. 85–94.

Schneiderman, P., "Planned and Actual Long-Term Borrowing by State and Local Governments." *Federal Reserve Bulletin,* December 1971, pp. 977–87.

Schott, F. H., "Disintermediation Through Policy Loans at Life Insurance Companies." *Journal of Finance,* June 1971, pp. 719–29.

Secondary Market Facilities for Conventional Mortgages. Hearings before a Subcommittee of the Committee on Banking and Currency, U.S. Senate, 88th Cong., 1st sess., September 1963.

Sharpe, W. F., *Portfolio Theory and Capital Markets.* New York: McGraw-Hill Book Co., 1970.

Sloane, P. E., "Determinants of Bond Yield Differentials, 1954–1959." *Financial Markets and Economic Activity,* New York: Wiley, 1967.

Smith, H. C., "Institutional Aspects of Interregional Mortgage Investment." *Journal of Finance,* May 1968, pp. 348–58.

Smith, P. F., *Economics of Financial Institutions and Markets.* Homewood, Ill.: Richard D. Irwin, Inc., 1971.

Sparks, G., "An Econometric Analysis of the Role of Financial Intermediaries in Postwar Residential Building Cycles." *Determinants of Investment Behavior,* New York: National Bureau of Economic Research, 1967.

Stigler, G. J., "Imperfections in the Capital Market." *Journal of Political Economy,* June 1967, pp. 287–92.

A Study of Federal Credit Programs. Subcommittee on Domestic Finance, Committee on Banking and Currency, House of Representatives, 88th Cong., 2d sess. Washington, D.C.: Government Printing Office, 1964.

A Study of Mortgage Credit. Subcommittee on Housing and Urban Affairs of the U.S. Senate Committee on Banking and Currency, 90th Cong., 1st sess., May 22, 1967. Washington, D.C.: Government Printing Office, 1967.

A Study of Mutual Funds. Prepared for the Securities and Exchange Commission by the Wharton School of Finance and Commerce, August, 1962. Report of the Committee on Interstate and Foreign Commerce, 87th Cong., 2d sess. Washington, D.C.: Government Printing Office, 1962.

Van Fenslermaker, J., ed., *Readings in Financial Markets and Institutions.* Englewood Cliffs, N.J.: Prentice-Hall, Inc., 1969.

Van Horne, J.C. *Function and Analysis of Capital Market Rates.* Englewood Cliffs, N.J.,: Prentice-Hall, Inc., 1970.

Welfing, Weldon, *Mutual Savings Banks: The Evolution of a Financial Intermediary.* Cleveland: Press of Case Western Reserve University, 1968.

West, R. R., "Bond Ratings, Bond Yields and Financial Regulation: Some Findings." *The Journal of Law and Economics,* April 1973, pp. 159–68.

Wolf, C. R., "Bank Preferences and Government Security Yields." *Quarterly Journal of Economics,* May 1971, pp. 283–303.

Wrightsman, D., "Pension Funds and Economic Concentration." *Quarterly Review of Economics and Business,* Winter 1967, pp. 29–36.

Index